Receptive Methods in Music Therapy

of related interest

Improvisation
Methods and Techniques for Music Therapy Clinicians, Educators, and Students
Tony Wigram
Foreword by Professor Kenneth Bruscia
ISBN-13: 978 1 84310 048 5   ISBN-10: 1 84310 048 7

Songwriting
Methods, Techniques and Clinical Applications for Music Therapy Clinicians, Educators and Students
Edited by Felicity Baker and Tony Wigram
Foreword by Even Ruud
ISBN-13: 978 1 84310 356 1   ISBN-10: 1 84310 356 7

Microanalyses in Music Therapy
Methods, Techniques and Applications for Clinicians, Researchers, Educators and Students
Edited by Thomas Wosch and Tony Wigram
ISBN-13: 978 1 84310 469 8   ISBN-10: 1 84310 469 5

A Comprehensive Guide to Music Therapy
Theory, Clinical Practice, Research and Training
Tony Wigram, Inge Nygaard Pedersen and Lars Ole Bonde
ISBN-13: 978 1 84310 083 6   ISBN-10: 1 84310 083 5

Clinical Applications of Music Therapy in Developmental Disability, Paediatrics and Neurology
Edited by Tony Wigram and Jos De Backer
Foreword by Colwyn Trevarthen
ISBN-13: 978 1 85302 734 5   ISBN-10: 1 85302 734 0

Clinical Applications of Music Therapy in Psychiatry
Edited by Tony Wigram and Jos De Backer
Foreword by Jan Peuskens
ISBN-13: 978 1 85302 733 8   ISBN-10: 1 85302 733 2

Music Therapy in Health and Education
Edited by Margaret Heal and Tony Wigram
Foreword by Anthony Storr
ISBN-13: 978 1 85302 175 6   ISBN-10: 1 85302 175 X

Music Therapy Methods in Neurorehabilitation
A Clinician's Manual
Felicity Baker and Jeanette Tamplin
With a contribution by Jeanette Kennelly
Foreword by Barbara L. Wheeler
ISBN-13: 978 184310 412 4   ISBN-10: 1 84310 412 1

Receptive Methods in Music Therapy
Techniques and Clinical Applications for Music Therapy Clinicians, Educators and Students

Denise Grocke and Tony Wigram

Foreword by Professor Cheryl Dileo

Jessica Kingsley Publishers
London and Philadelphia

First published in 2007
by Jessica Kingsley Publishers
116 Pentonville Road
London N1 9JB, UK
and
400 Market Street, Suite 400
Philadelphia, PA 19106, USA

www.jkp.com

Library of Congress Cataloging in Publication Data
A CIP catalog record for this book is available from the Library of Congress

British Library Cataloguing in Publication Data
A CIP catalogue record for this book is available from the British Library

ISBN-13: 978 1 84310 413 1
ISBN-10: 1 84310 413 X

Printed and bound in Great Britain by
Athenaeum Press, Gateshead, Tyne and Wear

This book is dedicated to three generations of my family: my parents, who nurtured my musical development, my two children, Aylin and David, who have supported me over many years, and to the newest generation – to Harry and Sam who represent joy and hope for the future.

Denise Grocke

I dedicate this book to Juliette Alvin, a sometimes forgotten pioneer of music therapy who inspired me and many hundreds of others with her incredible vision of the therapeutic power of music, and to my wife and three boys – musicians all, who in their own way use their talents to give people their music.

Tony Wigram

Acknowledgements

The authors wish to thank many people who have made contributions to this book. During sabbatical leave the first author (DG) was attached to the Royal Children's Hospital, Melbourne, and the Calvary Health Care Bethlehem Hospital in Melbourne. Music therapists of those hospitals trialled some of the ideas in this book, and contributed clinical vignettes describing methods and approaches. The authors wish to thank Beth Dun, Helen Shoemark and Clare Kildea (music therapists at the Royal Children's Hospital, Melbourne); Bridgit Hogan, Matt Holmes, Karen Hamlett and Melina Roberts (music therapists at Calvary Health Care, Bethlehem Hospital). Music therapists working in various facilities also contributed clinical vignettes, including Katrina McFerran (Very Special Kids), Katrina Stathis (Monash Medical Centre, Melbourne), Emily Shanahan (St Paul's School, Melbourne), Susan Bray Wesley (Arcadia Hospital, Bangor, Maine, USA), John Hedigan (Odyssey House, Melbourne), Rachel Nendick (Melbourne), Rachael Martin (Melbourne), Karin Schou (Aalborg, Denmark) and Joanna Booth (Auckland, New Zealand). Thanks also to music therapy students in 2005 at the University of Melbourne, particularly Tania de Brincat, Margaret Gilbert, Joyce Lim and Jason Kenner. Lyn Weekes (Physiotherapy Advisor UK Rett Syndrome Association) was involved in the original work on music and movement and vibroacoustics in the 1980s. David Wigram and Lisa Tomkins contributed expertise in the design and musical examples, and Jo Ryan provided essential secretarial support.

Contents

List of Figures

List of Tables

List of Plates

Foreword

Receptive Methods in Music Therapy is the third book in a series aimed at providing practitioners with knowledge and skill in the three main categories of music therapy (MT) intervention: improvisation, song composition and listening. Although last in this series, I consider this book to be the most important and far-reaching for several reasons.

The phenomenon of music requires a sound source and a recipient. Thus, no matter how the music is produced in MT, e.g. through improvisation, composition, live or pre-recorded music, it is ultimately received or heard by the client. Furthermore, hearing the music, however produced, is at the heart of the therapeutic process and its most essential component. Because of this, the significance of this book cannot be underestimated, as it examines in great detail the many factors that contribute to successful therapeutic listening experiences. These factors are thus relevant to all music therapy methods.

Receptive MT methods, as a category, are perhaps the most diverse in terms of the types of music employed. As a rule, music is selected or created based upon the preferences of the client. Music may be pre-composed, specially composed or improvised, based on the client's need, and vocal and/or instrumental music representing the gamut of styles within and across clients' cultures may be employed. Music may be presented to the client through live performance or improvisation by the therapist, via CD player, computer or vibroacoustic device. Overall, the music selected is limited only by the broadest definition possible of what one considers 'music'.

Likewise, the clinical goals that may be addressed in receptive MT are broad and diverse. Because listening to music influences all aspects of the person simultaneously, therapists structure music listening experiences to stimulate reactions and effect changes in clients' physical, psychological, cognitive, social, developmental, aesthetic and/or spiritual domains. Thus, for example, music listening may be used to: promote psychological insight, enhance relaxation, evoke imagery, structure movement, alter mood, summon memories, assist learning, facilitate transcendence, reduce heart rate and blood pressure, and foster creativity.

When compared to other MT methods, receptive approaches are the most versatile with respect to the range and characteristics of the clinical populations with whom they may be used. Although it is clear that certain receptive methods may be contraindicated for some client groups, receptive methods in general can be adapted to clients across all levels of physical and psychological functioning and of all age ranges, i.e. from babies in utero to persons in their last moments of life. As hearing is the most enduring and pervasive of the senses, even clients who are not conscious may benefit from MT. Further, clients who have impairments in hearing may also 'feel' the vibrations created by music.

The power and transformative potential of receptive methods cannot be understated, and I use my own work with medical and hospice patients to emphasize this point. It is impossible to describe in words the difference a song, a familiar musical selection or therapist-improvised music has made during the most critical moments of human existence. And it is both the privilege and overarching responsibility of the music therapist to provide competent skill and presence during these final life encounters.

Their importance and clinical significance notwithstanding, receptive methods of MT are at once the easiest to understand intuitively but perhaps the most difficult to explain in terms of their differentiation from other practices. Over the years, when I have been asked to explain my discipline to a non-professional, I have often had remarks such as: 'Oh yes, I understand music therapy. I listen to music all the time when I'm sad (angry, tense, etc.) and it helps me a lot.' Although many people understand the therapeutic effects of music from a self-help perspective, it is very difficult to explain why a music therapist is needed for this benefit to occur!

Similarly, I often see confusion among medical professionals who may well understand the therapeutic effects of taped music programs in medical units (music medicine approaches), but who fail to comprehend the need for the specialist skills of a music therapist in delivering such intervention and taking clinical responsibility for it. Thus, music therapists who use receptive methods, and especially those who use pre-recorded music in such settings, must be prepared to define their role as therapist and its significance. Research must continue to document the comparative efficacy of MT vs. music medicine approaches.

Thankfully, the authors of this book have provided a massive amount of information concerning the role of the music therapist, the requisite clinical skills and ethical precautions surrounding the implementation of these methods. They emphasize the significance of the therapist's presence and the need for competent verbal skills to process clients' reactions to receptive methods. Needless to say, the skill required to use such wide-ranging receptive methods with such diverse clinical groups is nothing but substantial and, to this end, the authors have succeeded in providing a text that is both comprehensive and practical. They include a wealth of extremely useful 'how to' information: for MT educators, who have in this single compendium the breadth of materials necessary to teach these methods in the most efficient way possible; for MT students, who can rely on this text for guidance in acquiring both basic and more advanced skills; and for MT professionals who can refine their existing skills and also acquire skills in new areas. Of special significance in this book are the details provided on the 'specifics' of the methods: the detailed scripts for inductions, the clinical examples and protocols of various clinicians. These details serve as clear and instructive guidelines for clinical competence. This book will make us all more effective practitioners of receptive MT methods.

The information in this text is offered with compelling authority. The authors are internationally known experts in MT, both widely regarded advanced clinical specialists, educators and researchers in different receptive methods. The amalgamation of their respective expertise (representing more years of experience than this writer can politely state), has resulted in a unique blend of perspectives within a text that is instructionally sound, clinically competent and based on the best research information available in the field.

I am indeed honored to have been asked by the authors, both highly esteemed and beloved colleagues, to write the foreword for this book – a most significant contribution to the MT literature. Its impact on the discipline will be both immediate and enduring. Most importantly, its impact will continue to be felt by our clients, who will, in our more competent hands, reap the powerful and transformative benefits of music listening.

Cheryl Dileo
Professor of Music Therapy, Temple University

Introduction

Since ancient times, music has been recognised as a catalyst for stimulating the emotions and inducing rest and relaxation, and the Greek philosophers of the fifth century BC were quite prescriptive about the type of music that was to be played to people who had afflictions. The mode in which the music was written was thought to have specific health benefits, for example, Plato (428 BC–348 BC) declared the Dorian mode fitting for steadfast endurance, whereas the Phrygian mode on the other hand was considered fitting for acts of peace and acquiescence (*The Republic*, III, 399a–b). Music (and the arts in general) were highly regarded as important elements of the moral fibre of the society, and the following words are attributed to Plato:

> Music is a moral law. It gives a soul to the universe, wings to the mind, flight to the imagination, a charm to sadness, and life to everything. It is the essence of order, and leads to all that is good, just and beautiful, of which it is the invisible, but nevertheless dazzling, passionate, and eternal form. (*Wordsworth Dictionary of Musical Quotations* 1991, p.45)

Over the intervening centuries poets, playwrights and authors have written about the power of music to alter moods and to excite the senses. 'If music be the food of love, play on' wrote Shakespeare (*Twelfth Night*, I.i.1), and 'Music hath charms to soothe a savage breast, to soften rocks, or bend a knotted oak' (Congreve *The Mourning Bride*, I.i.1) is also a testament to the effect of music on human emotion. In the nineteenth century, physicians began to measure the effect of music on physiological functions of the body, the earliest study measuring the effect on heart rate and respiration (Dogiel 1880, cited in Radocy and Boyle 1988). A key element of such research was the playing of recorded music. In fact recorded music was preferred as an independent variable since it could be controlled.

Research in the 1940s and 1950s tended to use the same pieces of music to represent stimulative and sedative music (Lundin 1967), for example Souza marches were chosen as stimulative, while Sibelius' 'The Swan of Tuonela' was often chosen as the sedative music choice. As more became known about the effect of music on the physiology of the body, new research was emerging to indicate that music was effective in opening up the mind, and a new field of Guided Imagery and Music (GIM) emerged (Bonny and Savary 1973).

Music therapists began to explore in more depth the diverse responses of clients to different types of music, and recognised that music that was familiar and in the preferred style was the most effective with patients. Music therapists began to develop individualised music programmes for clients in different contexts – for women in labour (Clark, McCorkle and Williams 1981; Hanser and O'Connell 1983), and patients experiencing stress (Hanser 1985; Scartelli 1989) or anxiety pre-surgery (Spintge and Droh 1982), or in intensive care (Bonny 1983). These receptive uses of music, where the patient benefited by listening and attending to the music, then discussing any feelings or responses with the therapist, became moulded into a group of methods termed 'receptive music therapy' (Bruscia 1998a).

Although receptive music therapy has been studied in research projects, there is usually very little detail about the stimulus itself. Often no recording details are given, nor information about the performers. Sometimes the name of the work is not mentioned, instead a vague description of sedative or stimulative music suffices. Rarely is there mention of how the therapist prepares the patient/client for the listening experience, nor what the therapist does to assist the patient in discussing his or her receptive experience. This gap in the literature is being addressed in the present book, the purpose of which is to provide a text on receptive music therapy methods in which each aspect of providing the receptive experience is explained.

Receptive Methods in Music Therapy is the third book in a series of texts dedicated to clinicians, eductors and students of music therapy. The previous two books have explained the methods and techniques used in improvisation and songwriting in music therapy. In *Improvisation* (2004), Tony Wigram describes therapeutic methods and musical techniques through written procedures, notated illustrations and recorded CD examples that can be learnt and applied in music therapy practice. The text explains improvisation skills for music therapy students who are in training, but also defines more complex and difficult therapy procedures for qualified therapists. It provides a comprehensive range of improvisational skills and techniques that can be practised and rehearsed, and also helps identify the specific music therapy 'techniques' that demonstrate what is causing change and development in the therapeutic intervention.

Baker and Wigram (2005) then produced an edited volume on *Songwriting*, in which the contributors were an international group of music therapists who defined and explained procedures in writing songs with clients. Again, the actual procedures and methods for writing songs, including techniques for developing the lyrics, composing the music and recording and performing the songs, were defined by the contributors in each chapter of the book, and collated at the end in a summary of methods and techniques.

Music therapy clinical practice has three main methods. The first two are described above – namely practical music making through structured or free improvisation (Wigram 2004) illustrated in the first book of the series, and songwriting (Baker and Wigram 2005), described in the second book of the series. The third group of methods is receptive music therapy. It remains, then, for this book to explain this third arm of music therapy method, and to describe the wide variety of ways through which the use of recorded music, and the playing of music to clients, can be applied.

Evidence-based practice in receptive music therapy

It is important to clarify that this series of books on music therapy methods describes techniques for intervention that have been used for many years in clinical practice, and have been found to be effective and useful. This evidence, grounded in clinical practice, is referred to as evidence-based practice. The American Music Therapy Association recognises the importance of evidence-based practice in the current definition of music therapy:

> Music Therapy is the clinical and evidence-based use of music interventions to accomplish individualised goals within a therapeutic relationship by a credentialed professional who has completed an approved music therapy program. (American Music Therapy Association 2006)

The techniques and methods described in this book and in the two previous books are founded on extensive applications in clinical practice by experienced clinicians. Frequently, the means by which the effectiveness of these methods is evaluated is through positive results from consistent applications, case reports presented at clinical case meetings, and peer evaluation in conferences and seminars. Music therapy methods may sometimes be supported by controlled studies, but as in many of the therapy professions, including the more traditional approaches in psychotherapy, physiotherapy, occupational therapy and speech and language therapy, the evidence of effect frequently relies primarily on anecdotal accounts written by therapists in case studies, clinical reports and other publications.

This book therefore does not attempt to provide a comprehensive review of research studies, but rather focuses on descriptions of therapeutic methods and procedures used by many qualified music therapists, supported, where relevant, by case material.

Receptive methods in music therapy

Attitudes to using receptive methods to promote therapeutic change and development vary within countries, and particularly between countries. In the United Kingdom, the definition of music therapy talks about an active relationship in music between client and therapist, typically developed through improvised music making. In the USA and Australia, a more eclectic model is practised, including singing songs, song writing, improvisation and receptive methods.

Receptive music therapy encompasses techniques in which the client is a recipient of the music experience, as distinct from being an active music maker. Most adult clients have listened to music at home and have been moved by music of different genres and styles according to their own preferences. Most people will have experienced the 'chills up the spine' response when listening to a piece of music that is particularly meaningful, or particularly moving. And most people would relate to T.S. Eliot's words 'you are the music while the music lasts' ([1941] 1991, p.197), written no doubt from a perspective of listing to music as distinct from playing it (although the phrase applies to both).

Yet in some areas of music therapy practice, receptive music therapy has not enjoyed wide appeal. Perhaps receptive music therapy has been merged in clinicians' minds with the development and expansion of Guided Imagery and Music, a specific use of receptive music therapy developed by Dr Helen Bonny in the 1970s. Is it that music therapists feel unsure or uncomfortable about using receptive methods unless they have completed training in what is now termed the Bonny Method of Guided Imagery and Music (BMGIM)? While BMGIM is the most internationally known model of receptive music therapy, there are many more widely used methods that involve using recorded music or playing to clients that fall into the category of receptive music therapy, and these are explained in this book.

Definitions of receptive music therapy

In *Defining Music Therapy* (1998a), Bruscia outlines 'Types of Music Experiences' in music therapy (pp.113–125). In this chapter Bruscia provides a thorough overview of the different types of methods used in music therapy clinical practice, including improvisatory experiences, composition experiences and receptive experiences. It is useful at this point, therefore, to review the different types of receptive experiences that will be referred to in this present book and to establish the primary definition for receptive experiences.

Bruscia's definition states:

> In receptive experiences, the client listens to music and responds to the experience silently, verbally or in another modality. The music used may be live or recorded improvisations, performances or compositions by the client or therapist, or commercial recordings of music literature in various styles (e.g. classical, rock, jazz, country, spiritual, new age). The listening experience may be focused on physical, emotional, intellectual, aesthetic or spiritual aspects of the music and the client's responses are designed according to the therapeutic purpose of the experience. (Bruscia 1998a, pp.120–121)

Bruscia describes many variations of receptive experiences, and for each one he provides a clear definition. The following receptive music therapy methods will be found in this present book:

- music relaxation for children and adults in different clinical settings (Chapters 3 and 4)
- imaginal listening – including unguided music imaging, guided music imaging and group music and imagery (Chapter 5)
- song (lyric) discussion – where the song serves as a springboard for discussion of the client's life issues (Chapter 6)
- song reminiscence – the method of using songs to promote discussion and reflection (Chapter 6)
- music listening experiences based on the client's preferred music (Chapter 7)
- music appreciation activities – where the therapist helps a client to understand and appreciate the aesthetic value of music (Chapter 7)

- music collage – Bruscia lists this method under Compositional Experience, however in this book it refers to the presentation of art-work stimulated by listening to music (Chapter 8)

- somatic listening, such as the use of music in vibroacoustic therapy (Chapter 9)

- eurhythmic listening – applied to body exercises, fine and gross motor sequences and other motor behaviours (Chapter 10).

The purpose of this book is to bridge the gap in the music therapy literature by providing a textbook specifically targeted at students, clinicians and educators who want to develop skills in using receptive music therapy methods. The book covers a range of receptive methods and explains in detail what is involved in each method, and what skills need to be developed. The book is also intended for clinicians, both new and established, in order to stimulate interest in receptive methods. The field of music therapy has grown so widely in its 60 years of existence, and it is likely that music therapists have learned many skills during their education and clinical training, and these skills will have been honed through years of clinical practice. However, music therapists, like all professionals, need to be challenged and excited by new areas of practice, or by new approaches to music therapy. It is hoped that this book will stimulate interest in the receptive approaches.

There are some aspects in this book that parallel what is covered in the early stages of training in BMGIM – i.e. at Introductory (level 1) and Intermediate (level 2) training. However the book does not provide comprehensive instruction in BMGIM, and it is not possible to conduct a BMGIM session based on the explanations in this book.

There are also many techniques and methods described in the book that should be used only by a qualified music therapist, as the procedures and techniques assume that anyone applying them will have already completed study in the foundational theoretical, clinical and music skills essential to practise as a music therapist. The ethical guideline at the end of this introduction and at the beginning of the previous two books make that very clear. Therefore music therapists can, and should, be offering receptive experiences for clients, and this book is positioned firmly in this arena.

Overview of the book

The book focuses on receptive techniques to be used in therapy sessions – it is a 'how to do it' book as every chapter provides clear guidance on methods of intervention. It includes work with individuals and groups, and it includes work with children and adults. It includes contraindications for the techniques and methods, and it includes an analysis of appropriate music to use in each type of method.

The book covers a range of commonly used receptive music therapy methods. It does not offer a comprehensive viewpoint, instead the methods that are best known to the authors and their colleagues have been chosen. When working with clients in receptive music therapy, therapists use verbal dialogue skills in order to understand the client's experience. These verbal dialogue skills are also referred to as counselling and psychotherapy skills. How a therapist directs a verbal dialogue can be influenced by values and beliefs that the therapist brings to the therapeutic relationship, and in Chapter 1 these are explored, along with common verbal processing skills. These skills are essential in developing a therapeutic presence that facilitates the therapeutic process with clients of all ages. Chapter 1 also describes how and when the therapist might improvise music in a receptive way, that is, for the client or patient to listen to the improvisation. This is particularly appropriate at the beginning of the session, or in the early development of a therapeutic relationship with the client/patient.

Chapter 2 addresses the significant elements in music that is chosen for receptive methods. Music to enhance relaxation, for example, has elements that differ from music chosen to elicit imagery. These parameters are explained and further examples are provided throughout the book.

Relaxation with children is explained in Chapter 3. Facilitating relaxation with children differs according to their age and their capacity to distinguish fantasy and reality. Relaxation approaches are separated into different age groups as a guideline to therapists, noting of course that there will always be individual differences and that the guidelines are not absolute. Suggestions for music selections are interspersed throughout the chapter.

Relaxation for adults in covered in Chapter 4, and inductions are written out in full so that the beginning therapist can read these verbatim, until the style of giving inductions is developed. Music therapists who work in diverse clinical contexts provide examples from clinical practice, and music suggestions are included throughout the chapter.

Chapter 5 introduces the reader to visualisations and guided or unguided music and imagery with individual clients and in groups. The therapeutic value of imagery is discussed, particularly in relation to working with adults in medical settings, who are coping with anxiety and pain, and also in other contexts where clients are seeking personal growth.

The therapeutic discussion of songs and lyrics is outlined in Chapter 6. This is a method that is particularly effective with adolescent-aged clients who listen to songs, on average, several hours a day. These songs speak to the experience of relationships, identity and world issues, as well as many other themes. Current songs and their potential discussion themes are outlined in this chapter.

Listening to music, and music appreciation, are described in Chapter 7, and results of a study of preferred volume level for clients with intellectual disability are presented.

Music collage is a method first described by Susan Munroe (1984), and is used in palliative care and with people who have dementia or mental illness, or those seeking personal growth. Music collage is explained in Chapter 8, and volunteers have allowed their collages to be reproduced as a means of illustrating this method. Music, drawing and narrative (MDN) is another form of receptive music therapy combined with art media, which is described in Chapter 8.

Vibroacoustic therapy is the focus of Chapter 9, including guidelines for building the equipment and developing the software. Various clinical applications are explained and illustrated.

Chapter 10 discusses movement and music with children who have cerebral palsy, and the exercises outlined in this chapter have been developed in conjunction with a physiotherapist.

Receptive methods in music therapy are used in clinical practice across all age groups, and within this book we have asked experienced music therapists to provide clinical vignettes to illustrate their approach in giving receptive music therapy sessions to clients. These clinical applications cover work with hospitalised children who may be in pain or anxious, or unable to express in language the experience of hospitalisation and surgery. Receptive methods allow children of all ages to use the creativity of imagery to address some of their fears and traumas. In addition, drawings can provide a non-verbal expression of the child's experience of music and imagery.

Music therapists who work in special schools have also contributed material to this book. They explain their creative approaches to relaxation with children who have special needs.

Receptive music therapy approaches are used extensively in helping adult clients, including those with psychiatric or mental illness, residents in aged care facilities, and patients who are hospitalised because of neurological disorders, cancer and other illnesses. Some music therapists use receptive methods first to establish rapport before offering active music therapy, and the music therapists who have contributed material to this book have given details of relaxation inductions, imagery and choice of music. The overarching aim is to provide detailed explanations of the procedures involved in offering receptive music therapy methods to clients and patients.

Appropriate music selections are listed within each chapter, relative to the method that is explained in the chapter. These selections are predominantly from the Western classical tradition as these are the selections that the authors know to be effective from clinical practice and research (Smith and Joyce 2004). Often the patient/client's preferred music genre is the most effective music to use, and therefore jazz, country and western, 'new age', rock, minimalist, trance, meditative and other styles of music are also suitable. In many clinical situations the music therapist can discuss with the client (or client group) what music is preferred, however there are some clinical situations where the therapist must make the decision him- or herself. Readers are encouraged to note styles of music that are effective and to build up an individualised library of appropriate music for receptive music therapy methods.

Ethical guidelines

The therapeutic methods and techniques defined and described in this book are for use by qualified clinical music therapy practitioners and students in training who have completed or are undertaking supervised clinical training.

Chapter 1

Engaging with Clients Verbally and Musically

Bruscia's definition of receptive music therapy (mentioned in the Introduction) states, 'In receptive experiences, the client listens to music and responds to the experience silently, verbally or in another modality' (Bruscia 1998a, p.120). In order for the therapist to understand the client's response, there is often a dialogue between the client and therapist about the experience. The therapist needs skill to facilitate this dialogue, and to maintain a 'therapeutic presence' (Egan 1986, p.78) that facilitates the discussion of the experience. This chapter identifies the skills and attributes of the therapist that lead to the development of an empathic therapeutic presence.

The chapter is structured in three parts. The first section explores the beliefs and values that a therapist brings to music therapy practice which underpin the development of a therapeutic presence. The second section outlines the verbal processing techniques commonly used by therapists to assist in building rapport with clients, to understand their musical experiences, and to help them face difficult moments in therapy. The third section of the chapter addresses skills required when using empathic improvisation with clients who respond silently, because they are either pre-verbal or non-verbal or when the experience is beyond words (supra verbal).

Beliefs and values that impact on interaction with patients

Beliefs and values underpin who we are, and they influence the attitudes we bring to the therapeutic relationship with all clients, irrespective of age, context and the method of music therapy we use – whether improvisation, song singing and song writing, or receptive techniques. Many courses in music therapy throughout the world require students to engage in personal therapy, or group therapy, as a necessary element for training in music therapy. The purpose is to enable the trainee music therapist to understand personal issues and to work through, or begin to work through, any conflict evident in conscious and unconscious emotions and behaviour. These issues may have developed through the beliefs and values that have been demonstrated and reinforced through family, schooling and religious influences.

When a person applies for entry to the music therapy course at the University of Melbourne, he or she must undertake an audition and an interview. The audition tests the level of musicianship on the principal instrument, vocal skill, and ability to accompany simple songs on guitar. During the interview we ask a series of questions about the person's motivation for wanting to study music therapy, and what inspired him or her to want to become a therapist. Most applicants reply that the motivation to study music therapy comes from a desire to share their love of music to help other people. Many applicants also talk about their experience of growing up with a family member who has an illness or disability, and this experience can shape attitudes to illness and disability, and the personal attributes that the person brings to being a therapist.

Other applicants talk about their motivation to study music therapy arising from 'wanting to help others', a belief that can often be traced to a religious upbringing. A fourth response from applicants is that the person has grown up in a family of helpers – for example, doctors, nurses, social workers – and therefore music therapy appeals to him or her because of the family values instilled over many years.

Underpinning all of these motivations is that the applicant is a proficient musician, and at the university audition and interview we assess the ability of the applicant to express him- or herself musically and to engage the listener in a manner that indicates good communication through the music.

Later in the university interview we ask applicants to what areas of music therapy they are drawn and which they would find confronting. We pose a question about how the applicant would manage a clinical situation with a child or adult client who was not responsive in music therapy. This question assesses whether the applicant would feel disappointed or frustrated or that he or she had failed.

Over the years we have seen a pattern in the replies to these questions. Some applicants have been inspired to become a music therapist because someone in their family has a condition or illness that has prompted the person to want to be a therapist. When we ask about the clinical scenario regarding a client who is non-responsive, those with a family history of illness or disability often reply that they would accept that person's non-responsiveness and move on to something else. Others, who come from different backgrounds, often reply to the clinical scenario by stating that in the face of non-responsiveness they would keep trying until the person showed some sort of response.

Neither approach to therapy is inappropriate, however, they are qualitatively and philosophically different, which demonstrates that music therapists bring to the therapeutic context different beliefs and values that influence therapeutic decisions.

Exercise

1. Take a few moments to think about the people who have been important to you in your life, from a young child through to the present day. What

values and beliefs did they demonstrate that are important to you? Have you adopted those same values and beliefs in your life? You might want to take 10–20 minutes to reflect on these questions and write about them.

2. Think about people in your life who have demonstrated values that you oppose. These might be people in your family, from a previous friendship, or figures in public life. Think about the values that they demonstrated and reflect on why these values are abhorrent to you. You might want to write about these.

Having identified beliefs and values that you hold dear, it is easy to see that clients whom you meet in a clinical setting who have similar beliefs to yourself will be easy to relate to. Conversely, clients who hold beliefs that you oppose may be more difficult to relate to in a therapeutic relationship.

The following three examples describe situations from clinical practice in which the beliefs and values of the music therapist have been challenged by the client.

- **Example 1**: A newly qualified music therapist was commencing a group music therapy session, when a client disclosed that he had stolen property (a television) from a motel in which he was staying. The music therapist challenged the client about this behaviour and a long discussion developed, delaying the start of the group music experience. After the group had finished, the music therapist stated that she wanted the client to realise that it was unlawful to steal other people's property (a value that she held strongly).

- **Example 2**: A music therapy student was singing quietly to a young child, who was in coma following a car accident, and who was not expected to live. The child's mother, who had been driving when the accident occurred, sat away from the child, reading a women's magazine and listening to her own music on a Walkman. The student music therapist was upset that the mother was so disengaged from the child, and this affected how 'present' the student was in her singing to the child. The student wanted to say to the mother 'How can you not be close to your child when she is dying?' (The student's belief system was that the mother should be sharing in the child's music, instead of her own.) The student controlled her reaction and suggested to the mother that she join in the singing to the child, but the mother declined and remained isolated from her child. The student finished the session, but then needed to de-brief from the experience, to try and understand the mother's response.

- **Example 3**: A music therapist recalled working with a woman who had been admitted to hospital after using heroin. The woman had two children at home and was eight months pregnant with another child. The woman stated that her goals for therapy were to get out of hospital as soon as possible, so that she could start taking drugs again as this was the only time she felt OK. The therapist recalled wanting to 'shake the woman's shoulders' and suggest she try being more responsible to her children. The therapist didn't take that action, of course, but the feeling was very strong. Instead, the therapist controlled his impulses, and adopted an empathic response to her situation.

In each of the three cases above the therapist was challenged by the clash of his or her own values and those expressed or demonstrated by the client. In each case the therapist responded appropriately by sensing the needs of the client and working with positive regard and empathy. Many other situations can arise, however, when values are tested.

Working with adult clients in individual and group contexts often invites discussion of issues that are potentially contentious, for example, the use of recreational drugs, religious beliefs, politics, family relationships and intimate relationships, to mention a few. The values and beliefs that we bring as therapists can influence the direction the session takes. Unconsciously we may encourage exploration of an issue that is important to us, and ignore other issues.

Factors that influence our attitude to clients

The Codes of Ethical Practice that govern the practice of music therapy throughout the world state that a music therapist shall not discriminate against clients by race or culture, socio-economic status, age, gender, sexual orientation, religious beliefs and practices and political orientation. While no one would question this stance, in practice it is necessary to reflect on attitudes evident in the therapeutic relationship that can be triggered by any of these factors.

Nelson-Jones (2003) outlines ten aspects that may influence our attitude with clients, the most pertinent of which are summarised here:

RACE, CULTURAL AND SOCIAL CLASS INFLUENCES

With the increase in social migration all over the world, therapeutic relationships are significantly influenced by the cultural norms of both client and therapist. Subtle communication cues and personal space are culturally sensitive. For example, some clients may want to stand or sit close to the therapist and engage in physical contact, while others clients may prefer a wider personal space that involves no physical contact. And in many cultures, a person's problems can only be discussed within the family and not with strangers, hence a distrust of therapists. Many cultures are hierarchically structured, and members of the family may defer to the head of the family rather than make independent decisions (Laungani 1999). Clients that have been subjected to racial oppression or abuse in their homeland may hold mistrust of a system that encourages open and honest expression of feelings and beliefs.

Clients who have immigrated from other countries may experience a range of emotions while adapting to the norms of a new country, including anger/intolerance at the host country, social withdrawal, depression and anxiety. A loss of cultural roots may lead to wanting to return home and rejection of the host country. These emotions span a wide spectrum of feelings and behaviours and a sensitive, empathic therapist must be responsive to them. For example, Alladin (1999) compares qualities that are polarised between 'Western' thinking and 'Eastern' thinking. A healthy person from a Western viewpoint is one who is assertive, independent, and freely expresses opinions and feelings. However, from an Eastern perspective, a healthy person is one who is more submissive, dependent, in control of passions and family oriented (Alladin 1999, p.95). Such opposite ideals set up potential for complicated therapeutic relationships unless the differences can be understood and respected.

AGE

A therapeutic relationship where both therapist and client are of similar age may develop a closeness that is similar to a friendship, given that both are at a similar stage of life, and this will influence the quality of the therapeutic relationship. A relationship between a young therapist and an older client may develop child–parent dynamics, or grandchild–grandparent dynamics. Conversely an older therapist working with young clients may feel the desire to parent, or over-protect.

GENDER ISSUES AND SEXUALITY

Therapists need to be comfortable with their views about, and attitudes toward heterosexuality and homosexuality, as these are constantly triggered in therapeutic relationships. In addition, sensitivity to gender issues arises when a male therapist works individually with a female client and vice versa. The concept of personal space applies, and therapists may find themselves sitting further away, or closer to a client of the same or opposite sex, depending on their own sexual orientation.

RELIGION OR PHILOSOPHY

Disagreements about religious beliefs can become heated, particularly when working with adult client groups. Since these beliefs have often been instilled from childhood, and the belief system is complex and may be firmly entrenched, the client can feel very strongly about issues of what is right and wrong. The therapist's role is to remain objective, not to allow his or her own personal beliefs to intervene. For example, a challenging situation arose when supervising a therapist who works with a woman who often speaks 'in tongues' during a Guided Imagery and Music session. To some people 'speaking in tongues' might represent a deeply spiritual experience, to others it might be seen as verging on psychotic behaviour, and for others it might represent a defence mechanism that needs to be handled carefully (a defensive mechanism functions to protect the client from facing challenging issues). All of the above three interpretations are valid, and depending on the belief system of the therapist, could be handled in three quite different ways. The therapist who believes that 'speaking in tongues' is a spiritual experience may choose to affirm the client's experience, allowing the client to experience it more fully. The therapist who considers it possible psychotic behaviour might ask the client direct questions about his or her state of mental health. The therapist who believes that 'speaking in tongues' is a defence mechanism might want to explore what the client was feeling just prior to speaking in tongues to determine what prompted the activation of the defence mechanism. While each of these responses is valid, it is possible that each therapist could hold strong views that their approach was correct! When faced with clinical situations that cause concern and feel unresolved, the therapist should seek professional supervision to address the issues being raised.

Exercise:

Think about some of the clients with whom you are working at the moment, or have worked with recently. Choose a range of ages, different cultural backgrounds and different gender orientations. Take time to think about each person individually, isolating any aspect that may influence your relationship with that person. Reflect on whether your values and beliefs have been evident in how you relate to the person in music therapy.

　　　If you are a student and currently not working with clients, then reflect on people close to you, or in your class.

Verbal processing of client's experiences in music therapy

In principle, music therapists use the medium of music in order to carry out therapy. The experience of creating music, whether sung, or played, or listened to, can be an emotional one and music therapists will need to discuss the experience with the client. To understand the client's experience fully, music therapists may use skills that are normally associated with counselling and psychotherapy. Music therapists do not need to undertake comprehensive training in counselling, however some of the basic counselling skills are important to the music therapist in order to explore and process music experiences with clients. These skills are particularly relevant when working with clients who are articulate and cognitively able to engage in dialogue. In this section of the chapter, verbal skills necessary when working with articulate clients are explored. Later in the chapter we will cover skills necessary when working with clients who are not articulate and cannot express their feelings and experiences clearly.

　　　Nolan (2005) refers to verbal processing as 'an integral part of…music therapy practice' (p.18) and that there are 'volumes yet to be written about the uses of verbal processing in music therapy' (p.19). In fact we rely on verbal processing a great deal during a music therapy session, to:

1.　　discuss with clients how they are feeling on the day, and what has happened since the last music therapy session

2.　　find a focus for the music therapy session

3.   understand responses to a musical experience

4.   gather more information about the client's experience that enables us to 're-enter into the musical experience with new insight and more developed therapeutic alliance' (Nolan 2005, p.18)

5.   give feedback to the client about our own experience (where appropriate)

6.   give interpretations of what the client is doing, or what is happening (where appropriate), and

7.   close a session.

Some music therapists prefer *not* to use words to dialogue with clients after a music experience, mainly because they believe that talking intrudes on the musical experience. Even so, therapists talk with their clients, if for no other reason than to greet them at the start of a session and to get a sense of how the therapy is progressing. And so the verbal component of music therapy is an area needing further exploration and attention. Wheeler, Shultis and Polen (2005) refer to these skills as 'verbal facilitation', and outline skills that help in encouraging communication as well as responses that are not helpful to the progress of therapy (2005, pp.135–146).

In order for music therapy students to gain skill in verbally processing musical experiences, and in light of a paucity of information written in the music therapy literature, the human relations (counselling) literature provides a useful theoretical framework. Fully qualified counsellors base their verbal therapy on discussing issues with their clients and helping them to make changes in their lives. Therefore some counselling skills are not appropriate to music therapy because we direct our client's attention to a musical experience. However some of the basic counselling skills resonate well with what we do in music therapy and these skills are considered below.

Table 1.1 sets out some of the skills that are common to music therapy and to counselling and the point at which the skills are differentiated.

Key proponents in the human relations field have written about certain skills needed to be an effective counsellor (Egan 1998; Nelson-Jones 2003). Some of these theoretical concepts are common to music therapy practice. For example, empathy is recognised as a key element for any therapeutic encounter.

All therapists would agree that one of the principal requirements of a sensitive therapist is the ability to empathise. Empathy is defined by Nelson-Jones (2003) as 'the capacity to identify oneself mentally with [the client] and to comprehend the client's inner world' (p.30). Egan (1986) comments that empathy 'involves understanding the experiences, behaviours and feelings of others as *they* experience them' (1986, p.87), and Rogers explains 'it means entering the private world of the other and becoming thoroughly at home in it...temporarily living in the other's life, moving about in it delicately without making judgments' (Rogers 1980, p.142).

Table 1.1 A comparison of verbal processing in counselling practice and music therapy practice

Common ground

Effective counsellors and music therapists are good listeners. They actively listen to their clients, and they use skills of empathy, reflection, paraphrasing and probes (all defined later in the chapter) to understand the issue/s the client brings.

Counselling practice	Music therapy practice
The counsellor works with the client to determine areas of change in the client's life. Counsellors may use challenging verbal interventions and indicate blocks that the client might have toward change.	Music therapists offer a range of musical experiences to help clients express their life issues in a creative way. This may be through improvisation, through song singing, song writing, or receptive methods.
Counsellors explore options and make connections between the client's patterns of behaviour. Counsellors establish goals with the client for changes in his or her life. They set up strategies to help the client achieve the changes. Counsellors confront resistance and they help clients stay committed to their growth (Egan 1998).	Music therapists use verbal processing skills to find a focus for the therapy session and to facilitate dialogue with the client about how the music therapy session unfolds. But the music therapist facilitates a musical expression of those issues, and later uses discussion/verbal processing to determine what the client's experience of the music session has been and, where appropriate, also the therapist's experience. There is a mix of verbal and music processes, but predominantly the music therapist uses music as the therapeutic modality.
Counsellors rely on verbal language and interchange with their clients, although some counsellors also use creative modalities to augment the verbal therapy.	

Egan (1986) articulates a range of skills that enable the helping professional to be empathetic. First he puts forward an acronym that represents key factors. The acronym SOLER is built on the following points and is discussed here in relation to the music therapy context:

S   Sit 'squarely' in front of the client, not turned away, or slumped in a chair. In music therapy sitting 'squarely' might be difficult if the therapist is playing keyboard, or piano, however in the discussion of the music experience the music therapist needs to be able to make appropriate eye contact with the client, and this involves being 'square-on' to the client. However, sitting 'square-on' may also be contraindicated with clients who find direct eye contact confronting, for example with children who have autism.

O   Maintain an 'open' attitude to the client, shown by being interested in what the client is saying or doing and being focused on the client (not gazing away from the client). In music therapy the 'open' attitude also applies to how we respond to a client's musical expression. The music therapist adopts an 'open' listening in improvisation, or in creating a song, or in attending intently to a person's experience of receptive listening.

L   This is associated with 'leaning toward' the client, not away from him or her. The position a music therapist holds while strumming a guitar, or engaging in shared playing on percussion or Orff instruments, models the 'leaning toward' position very well. It can be more difficult while playing a keyboard or piano, but the point remains that leaning toward shows an interest in the client, and a degree of comfortableness in being engaged with the client.

E   This stands for 'eye contact'. When talking with clients (between music making or listening to music), eye contact is essential. We engage in eye contact to show interest, and to remain focused on what is being said. However, sustained eye contact or intense eye contact can be uncomfortable for a client, therefore the therapist intuitively monitors the degree of direct eye contact with the client. Essentially the client has less eye contact with the therapist, than the therapist with the client (Egan 1998). The client is more likely to avoid eye contact with the therapist, however the therapist needs to sustain a 'soft' eye contact so that when the client does look back to the therapist, the client sees that the therapist is still focused on him or her.

R   This stands for a 'relaxed' posture or position. A stiffly held posture may convey that the therapist is anxious or not fully present to the experience that is unfolding. If the therapist has his or her arms folded across the body, this might suggest a barrier is being put up.

Exercise:

Use the SOLER approach next time you are talking in depth with someone (client or family member or housemate). Notice the quality of the interaction when you are fully attending to the person who is speaking to you. Adopting the SOLER posture encourages others to tell their stories. They pick up on the body language as being empathic to their situation.

Apart from the fundamental SOLER attitudes, music therapists also need verbal processing skills to encourage the client to explore feelings, emotions and thoughts after a music therapy experience. Egan (1986, 1998) identifies these skills as:

1.   active listening

2.   reflecting

3.   paraphrasing

4. open questions

5. probes (to elicit more information), and

6. focused questions.

Other skills that we also apply in music therapy include:

7. providing choice

8. being comfortable with silence

9. establishing, developing and maintaining a therapeutic presence, and

10. closing a session.

1. ACTIVE LISTENING

As the term suggests, 'active' listening requires active attention of the therapist. Active listening implies that the therapist listens and attends to what is being said and is wholly present to the client while he or she is speaking. In normal conversation the discussion moves equally between two people, but in the therapeutic context the relationship is not equal. The client is encouraged to express his or her feelings and to uncover aspects of his or her life that need to be explored, and the role of the therapist is to support the person doing that. The therapist does not engage in the same type of self-reflection of his or her life with a client, therefore the relationship is not equal.

One of the fundamental requirements of 'active' listening is to attend to what is being said. This may sound both simplistic and obvious, but one of the biggest mistakes new therapists make is that they sometimes only half listen to what is being said, then mentally start to compose a reply. Often clients only need a non-committal 'uh-huh' to help them continue what they need to say. The skill in 'active' listening then is to stay focused on what the client is saying in order to respond in a sensitive manner, relating to all the content of what the client has been saying, rather than 'filtering' only part of it.

Table 1.2 sets out the important features of effective listening skills, and also compares these to ineffective or poor listening skills.

It is important to remember that 'active' listening requires effort from the therapist to stay focused on the client and not be drawn into distracting thoughts or actions. Egan summarises this well: 'Think: what can I hear, NOT, what can I say' (Egan 1998).

By active listening we get a sense of what the client is experiencing, and how he or she might be feeling. By staying 'with the client' rather than trying to move ahead, we demonstrate a capacity to 'be there' emotionally, and therefore are more likely to respond in an authentic and empathic way (Egan 1986, p.87).

Many clients need help in exploring what they want to express, and so active listening is coupled with reflecting techniques and paraphrasing. We will look at each of these in more detail.

Table 1.2 A comparison of effective and poor listening skills	
Effective listening skills	**Poor listening skills**
Maintaining appropriate eye contact while the client is speaking	Looking or turning away from the client, or looking 'past' him or her, or rapid shift in eye movement
Allowing the person to complete what he or she is saying	Interrupting the flow of language, or trying to guess what the client is saying
Giving the person time to speak	Looking at a watch or the clock and commenting on how much time is left (although this might be appropriate if it is the very end of a session and the therapist needs to close the session)
Staying relaxed while listening to the client	Fidgeting, changing body posture frequently, 'drumming' with fingers, or other unconscious annoying habits that indicate the therapist is not attending fully
Helping the client understand his or her behaviours and feelings	Judging what the person is saying or doing, making inappropriate comments such as 'What you need to do is…', or worse, contradicting the client
Being present to the client's experience	Mentally 'turning off' from what the client is saying, or thinking about a response rather than listening to what is being said
Staying focused on what the client is expressing and understanding how important it is for that person	Talking about other people's experience, thereby diminishing the experience of the client
Being comfortable with silence, particularly to allow the client to find the words to express him or herself	Filling in the silences with own words
Being empathic to the client's situation	Diminishing the importance of the client's situation by dismissing it: 'You'll feel better tomorrow,' or 'Many people have the same problem'

2. REFLECTING

Reflecting a client's key word or phrase is an effective way to affirm an important statement or feeling. If a client comments that the music has made him or her feel sad, it can be effective to reflect the word 'sad' using a similar tone to what the client has used. The obvious follow-up question then is 'in what way has it made you feel sad?' Reflecting the person's words or feeling state allows the client to stay in the moment and explore it more fully. In many respects this is a unique aspect of therapy – we allow clients the time to uncover feelings at a pace that is comfortable for them.

Reflecting techniques should not be over-used however. If the therapist simply reflects each word or statement the client makes, the client may feel the therapist is mimicking him or her or making fun of what is being said. But used at a time to highlight something important that has been said, reflections can be most effective.

In addition, the word or phrase can be used as a focus for the next improvisation, or for the lyrics of a song, or for some other creative expression. The important point to make is that reflection, as the word implies, allows the therapist to affirm what the client has said or felt.

3. PARAPHRASING

Paraphrasing is used when a client has expressed a number of thoughts, or has unfolded a long story or a complicated incident. Paraphrasing allows the therapist to summarise what has been said, and to check with the client that statements have been heard correctly. It can be useful to clarify what the client has said by prefacing a question with 'It sounds like…' or 'Can I check that I have understood what you have been saying… It sounds like this and that has happened, and you are feeling… Have I understood this correctly?' This enables the client to disagree with you, or to clarify something further. Paraphrasing also helps the client realise that you are listening attentively to what is being said, and it helps the client slow down, or clarify what he or she is saying.

Paraphrasing is also used in music therapy to help client and therapist develop a new theme within the session. It allows the therapist to recapitulate what has already occurred, and to make suggestions for what might follow. For example the therapist might paraphrase what has happened, how the client responded, what has opened up from the experience, and what the therapist suggests might follow.

4. OPEN QUESTIONS

Following a musical experience (whether improvisation, song singing, or listening to music), the therapist uses verbal processing techniques to gain information about what the client has experienced. 'Open' questions are preferable to 'closed' questions (Egan 1998; Nolan 2005). A typical 'open' question following a music experience is, 'What was that like for you?' which leaves the response wide open. A more targeted question would be 'How did you feel about that?' which obviously focuses more on the person's feelings.

A 'closed' question would be 'Did you enjoy that?' The question is closed because it invites a 'yes/no' reply. It is also biased in a sense – it suggests that the therapist wants the client to only think of whether it was enjoyable. A client may unconsciously answer 'yes' because it is implied that the therapist wants the client to say 'yes'.

5. PROBES (TO ELICIT MORE INFORMATION)

Combining open questions with reflection of the client's key words can generate an accurate sense of how the client is feeling. The therapist might also use 'probes' (Egan 1998) to take the discussion further. For example, having understood the client's response to the first music experience of the session it is time to move on to another music experience. The therapist 'probes' for information. 'I get a sense that this is an important feeling for you, shall we explore this further?' is one way to move into a deeper, or more focused exploration. Or the therapist might draw on knowledge of the client's history to probe further 'I recall this was an issue with your family – you mentioned before that this is how you felt with your mother or father. Can we explore this further?' Another example might involve using an observation to suggest an issue: 'You seemed very uncomfortable and distracted when you were listening to that – was that music difficult for you?' or 'I noticed that your playing became stronger and perhaps more aggressive – were you feeling angry when you were playing?' As stated in the previous section, such proposals rely on experience, knowing what is appropriate and timely in the therapeutic process, and drawing on a deeper understanding and a secure relationship with the client.

6. FOCUSED QUESTIONS

Questions can also focus on aspects of the listening (or playing) experience that may help clients to think about their awareness in a more specific way. This is appropriate when a client finds an open question challenging because it is too difficult to find the words or thoughts to answer. Table 1.3 provides examples of more focused questions and what may be elicited in the response.

There can be many variations of these questions. In fact, in order to avoid the pattern of the therapist always asking questions and the client having to explain, sometimes questions can be converted into observations about the client. For example 'You seem more relaxed now than before' instead of 'How do you feel now?' These interpretations still offer statements that can be confirmed, denied or expanded upon by the client.

7. PROVIDING CHOICE

An additional skill used by music therapists is to offer choice within the music experience. This occurs as client and therapist develop a theme for improvisation, or develop lyrics for an original song, or in making a choice of preferred music to be sung or listened to. Choice is one of the hallmarks of music therapy practice – by offering choice to clients we empower them to make decisions that influence the flow of the therapy session. Often clients have few opportunities for choice, particularly if hospitalised or institutionalised where choice of treatment is not a flexible option. Therefore encouraging clients to choose what they wish to do can be a crucial factor in building rapport.

Providing choice, however, can also be confusing for some clients. If the client has poor self-esteem and feels his or her view is not important, making a choice may take some time, and the therapist needs to sit and wait and encourage the client to make his or her point of

Table 1.3 Focused questions and possible elicited response	
Question	**Eliciting**
Can you remember what you were feeling in your body when you were listening to/playing/singing?	Kinaesthetic experiences of a positive or negative type; general physical reactions
What did you notice about the music that you liked or disliked?	Personal preferences; identification of affect
What part of the music you heard/played/sang had a specific meaning for you?	Relationship of part of the music to present or past experiences, or current issues
Were there any moments when the music bought particular images or pictures to mind?	Visualisation experiences that might have symbolic representation of conscious or unconscious issues and themes
Were there any moments when the music bought particular memories or associations to mind?	Past events; significant people; significant places; significant experiences
Were there any moments in the music making (e.g. group improvisational work) when you found yourself connected to another or others in the group?	Group dynamics; interactional experiences with others – positive or negative

view known. The therapist also uses affirming responses to build the client's confidence. At a cognitive level, choice is also important to encourage the client to think through various options, and to make a considered choice.

Providing choice, for clients who have brain impairment requires different skills. O'Callaghan and Turnbull (1987) explain that offering two song titles as a means of choice is effective in working with people who have neurological disorders involving cognitive impairment. For example, they advocate a technique of simplifying the question: 'Would you like to sing "Bonnie" or "Rainbow"?', to indicate 'My Bonnie lies over the ocean' or 'Somewhere over the Rainbow'.

Choice is also fundamental to the process of writing a song with a client. O'Brien's (2005) method of song writing is built on offering choice for all the musical parameters of the song, as well as the lyrics of the song. And in receptive music therapy, the client is often involved in choosing which style of music to listen to.

8. BEING COMFORTABLE WITH SILENCE

There are many instances when a music therapist needs to be comfortable sitting in silence with a client. Therapists who are not comfortable with silence may try to fill the gaps with their own words, or may show signs of anxiety that there is silence in a therapy session.

However, sitting in silence is essential to the development of a strong therapeutic relation-ship. Clients who are depressed or in grief often cannot express how they feel in words, and in that sense they are almost non-verbal. Other clients may be very emotional after a music experience, and may not be able to put the experience into words, a state termed supra verbal.

For the depressed or grieving client the therapist might offer a reflection about the silence with a comment such as 'It seems that it is difficult to talk about how you are feeling at the moment.' The therapist then has a choice of offering another music therapy experience, which might include an empathic improvisation (explained later in the chapter), in which the therapist reflects musically what the client seems to be feeling as a means of supporting and affirming that the client's feelings are beyond words.

For the client who has experienced a deeply emotional response to music, the therapist may sit with the person in silence for some minutes. An intuitive therapist will 'feel' the depth of connection with a client while in silence, and this is part of an effective therapeutic rela-tionship. Rogers (1980) calls this a deeper sense of empathy that involves 'sensing meanings of which the client is scarcely aware' (p.142).

9. ESTABLISHING, DEVELOPING AND MAINTAINING RAPPORT

The relationship between therapist and client is fundamental to the practice of music therapy. Building rapport with a patient/client begins as soon as the therapist meets the client for the first time. Adopting a positive regard and showing genuine interest in the client enables the first meeting to be an encouraging one.

Maintaining rapport during the session requires that the therapist stays 'present' to the client in whatever music experiences are shared. Lapses of attention by the therapist can be detrimental to the flow of the session, whereas genuine engagement with the client's experi-ence enhances rapport. The therapist's attention therefore must be kept constant throughout the session.

10. CLOSING A SESSION

At the closing of the session the therapist reflects on what has happened during the session and brings closure to that experience. The therapist remains 'present' until the client or group has left the session room, or until the therapist has left the client's room. Only then can the therapist allow the focused attention to lapse.

Examples from music therapy practice with adult clients who are verbally articulate

In this section, vignettes from clinical practice will be described to illustrate the use of verbal processing skills. The context for each vignette is an individual music therapy session, using receptive music therapy methods, or, in some cases, singing songs or improvisation. The purpose of the vignettes is to illustrate the flow of verbal processing, rather than to describe the method, and for this reason different music therapy methods are included.

Usually there are different ways to respond to a client's statement or comments. New therapists often feel they have to respond immediately, however clients are often comfortable with short silences while the therapist considers how to respond to a situation. In most situations there is no 'correct' response at all, but several possible responses, each of which can be appropriate and can influence how a session progresses.

Vignette: adolescent client

A 12-year-old girl with a brain injury had burst into tears following an improvisation in which she had been playing drums.

Therapist: Can you say how you are feeling? (*Open question*)

Client: *No response, still crying – pause*

Therapist: It seems like the drumming brought up some strong feelings for you. (*Reflection and cautious interpretation*)

Client: *No response, not crying as much – pause*

Therapist: What was that like, doing the drumming?

Client: Good.

Therapist: Oh that's great! (*Affirmation*) What was good about it? (*Open question*)

Client: *Shrugs her shoulders (Non-verbal)*

Therapist: Was it good to let go? (*Open question / cautious interpretation*)

Client: Yeah.

In this vignette it is important to recognise that young adolescents are often not verbally articulate, and that this is a facet of their development stage. Responses may be monosyllabic, such as 'yeah' or 'no'. So cautious interpretation may be needed.

Vignette: providing choice

A 23-year-old female patient who had a history of superficial suicide attempts was referred to music therapy. The session began with:

Therapist: What would you like to do in music therapy today? (*Open question*)

Client: I don't know.

> Therapist: Well, we could listen to some of your favourite music, or improvise with instruments, or relax with music. How do you feel? (*Offering choice*)
>
> Client: I'd like to relax. I'm sick of talking about myself [in group therapy].
>
> Therapist: We could include some imagery with the relaxing music if you like. (*Choice*)
>
> Client: Yes, that would be good.
>
> The music chosen for the relaxation session (sitting in a comfortable chair) was Debussy's *Prelude to the Afternoon of a Faun*. At the end of the music, the client gradually came out of the relaxed state and opened her eyes.
>
> Therapist: What was that like for you?
>
> Client: *Smiling* I imagined myself on the back of my dad's motor bike. We were riding across paddocks [fields].
>
> Therapist: That sounds great – how did you feel? (*Affirmation and open question*)
>
> Client: It was great – I haven't thought about that for a long time.
>
> Therapist: Can you say more about your dad? How did you get along with him? (*Probe*)
>
> The client then verbalised how close she had been to her dad when she was young, but as she grew older he became more distant.

Providing choice for what music therapy method the client wanted to experience was probably the most important feature in this session. Further discussion of relaxation and imagery is given in Chapter 5.

> ## Vignette: group in aged care setting
>
> The context for this vignette was a nursing home for the elderly. The client was part of a group in which the music therapy method was singing familiar songs (from the 1930s and 1940s).
>
> Therapist: Are there any favourite songs you would like to sing today? (*Direct question*)
>
> Client: I hate those old songs – they make me feel depressed.
>
> Therapist: (*Using reflection*) *in a soft tone of voice* Depressed? What is it about the songs that make you feel depressed?

Client:	They're not very happy songs?
Therapist:	Can you think of a song that you find happy?
Client:	No, not really.
Therapist:	How about 'Oh what a beautiful morning?'
Client:	Yes, alright.

An alternative scenario might occur, however:

Client:	I hate those old songs – they make me feel depressed.
Therapist:	(*Using reflection*) (*in a soft tone of voice*) Depressed? What is it about the songs that makes you feel depressed?
Client:	They're very sad songs.
Therapist:	Which song in particular are you thinking about? (*Direct question*)
Client:	There isn't one in particular, they're just all sad.
Therapist:	So, are you feeling a little sad yourself today, Mrs X? (*Open question*)
Client:	Yes, I guess I am.
Therapist:	Has anything happened to make you feel sad? (*Probe – to seek information*)
Client:	No-one has come to visit me for ages.
Therapist:	Is there someone whom you particularly want to see? (*Probe – seeks information*)
Client:	I wish my son would come and visit.
Therapist:	Can you tell me about your son – what is he like? (*Open question to facilitate the client talking further about her feelings*)

This dialogue draws out the underlying feeling of the client and helps the client (and the therapist) to understand from where the sad feelings come. The sequence of questions is based on a resident in an aged care facility who is articulate. People who have dementia may not be able to respond so directly. The sequence of questions also follows the principles of validation (Feil 1993), where the therapist engages the client to describe what is meaningful to him or her as a means of validating his or her experience.

A third option might be to respond to the statement by focusing on the client's description of the songs being old. If the client's voice tone was not at all depressed, but rather annoyed, the sequence might be:

| Client: | I hate those old songs – they make me feel depressed. |
| Therapist: | Are there newer songs that you would like to sing, Mrs G.? |

In this vignette it is the voice-tone of the client that cues the therapist's response. The feeling component of the statement might suggest she wants to choose a song with more energy and fun, or songs that resonate more with her preferred style or genre.

Vignette: seeking more information

This vignette is also drawn from aged care, where the client has been singing familiar songs:

Client: I refuse to sing songs about war – war is horrific, why should we sing about it?

Therapist: It sounds like you have strong opinions about war, can you say more about how you feel?

This response draws on the earlier discussion about how values and beliefs underpin strong emotions. In this vignette, it is important that the therapist honours the client's beliefs about war. The therapist does this by asking the client to say more about how she feels.

By asking for more information the therapist can determine if the resident is making a value statement, or whether perhaps the resident has family or friends who went to war and didn't return. The therapist may draw out this information by asking, 'Families can suffer when members of the family don't return. Has this happened to you?' (*Probe*) The client may reply in the affirmative, and the therapist can ask what happened. Or the client may not have any experience of losing a family member in a war, in which case the therapist might move on.

Exercises

Outlined below are further examples from music therapy clinical practice, in which the context and scenario are sketched. Each example can be approached from different perspectives, and suggested responses are provided below. Try to work through various responses first, before consulting the suggestions. Note that there is no one 'correct' response.

Example exercises from clinical practice

1. A man aged 75, who is a resident in a nursing home, after singing 'I'll take you home again Kathleen', says: 'I want to go home, but no-one will let me.' What might he be feeling? How might you respond?

2. A 20-year-old male in a rehabilitation unit following a car accident listens to a favourite song, and comments: 'That song reminds me of all my friends – none of them have come to visit me.' What might he be feeling? How might you respond?

3.   A 17-year-old male client in rehabilitation for substance abuse chooses to play a CD of a song with aggressive lyrics very loudly. You ask what he feels about the song, and he says: 'I just want to blast everyone.' What might he be feeling? How would you respond?

SUGGESTED RESPONSES TO EXERCISES:

1.   A man aged 75, resident in nursing home, after singing 'I'll take you home again Kathleen', says: 'I want to go home, but no-one will let me.'

It is common practice in music therapy to use songs that were popular when the client was young, and some of the old songs have lyrics that strike at the core of what some people in residential homes for the elderly are feeling. The main issue for elderly clients is leaving their familiar home and being placed in residential care. Many residents realise that they will not leave the nursing home, and so they grieve for their own home and familiar surroundings, and they may grieve for their own space, their privacy and independence. In addition they may be angry that family members have colluded to place them in a nursing home, and some people feel they have been abandoned, manipulated or tricked by their family. (Note that not all people feel this way.) In the scenario, the man may be responding to the loss of his own home, and that others (staff or family) are stopping him from returning to it. He might be sad, or he might be angry (this would be evident in his tone of voice).

Most therapists abide by the humanistic validation principles outlined by Feil (1993), and would respond to the situation by affirming his memory of his home, for example, 'Can you tell me about your home? What was it like? Did you have a garden? Did you have a pet?' This approach diverts attention away from the reality of the situation and allows the person to reminisce. The therapist might then re-focus attention on singing by saying 'Your home sounds lovely, is there another song that you would like to sing? How about X?'

2.   A 20-year-old male in rehabilitation following a car accident: 'That song reminds me of all my friends – none of them have come to visit me.'

People who are recovering from brain injury and other physical injuries following trauma come to terms with a vast array of losses – loss of physical health, loss of cognitive function, loss of independence, to mention a few. People are required to make adjustments to their dreams and aspirations for the future, their possibilities of having relationships and their sexuality. Often a person with traumatic brain injury has impairment to speech and cognition that may make it difficult to process questions. If the person is unable to express himself or herself verbally, it would be more appropriate to engage the person in improvisation where language can be by-passed.

However, in this scenario the 20-year-old is able to articulate his feelings, and has been reminded of friends that have been lost. This, sadly, is a common occurrence following injury after trauma, and often friends feel uncomfortable about visiting the friend because they do not know what to say, or they are uncomfortable seeing their friend in hospital, in pain and injured. The therapist might:

a) focus on the loss of the friendship, for example, 'It must be difficult not seeing them. Who in particular are you thinking about?' This allows the person to identify a friend. The therapist can then follow up with 'How do you feel about this person not visiting?' If the client is open to reminiscing about the friend, then a verbal prompt might be: 'What did you used to do together?'

b) respond, 'Sometimes friends need time to adjust too. Do you think your friends might visit later on?' (This might prompt a negative reply.)

c) bear in mind people recovering from trauma often have memory loss, and sometimes they do not remember that friends have in fact been to visit. If you know this for a fact, the response might be 'I noticed X visiting you yesterday' with some other comment about the time of day, or what they did, etc., followed by a question about the friendship.

3.   A 17-year-old male client chooses to play an aggressive song very loudly. You ask what he feels about the song, and he says: 'I just want to blast everyone'.

It is common for adolescents to play music (songs) loudly. Often the loudness matches their level of energy, sometimes it serves to fill the silence, and may even serve to keep people away from talking to them! The loudness might send a message to others that the person is angry, frustrated or annoyed at someone, or something. In the scenario the 17-year-old wants to blast 'everyone', which naturally leads on to the question 'Whom in particular?'

a) 'Blast everyone?' (*Reflection*). 'Is there someone in particular you want to blast?'

b) Hone in on the lyrics of the song (in the scenario the lyrics are aggressive). 'The lyrics seem pretty full-on, is this the way you're feeling right now?' Then 'Can you say more about what has happened?'

As you go about your clinical work in the next few days, make a note of any situations where you had options when responding to clients. Write down the client's comment, and work with the options of response. Skills to respond verbally in an empathic way improve with practice, so it is important to gain this practice relative to the clinical situation. It is helpful to realise that there is more than one way to respond, there is no one correct response, and that you can give yourself time to consider whatever response you make.

Empathic improvisation for non-verbal clients

Music therapists work with many clients whose pathologies limit or prevent them from talking, and in some clinical populations language is not developed. Music therapy is often argued as an effective therapeutic medium because it can act as a non-verbal means of communication with clients. In fact, there are three different ways in which music can supplant language for differing reasons.

Pre-verbal

Children and adults with severe or profound intellectual difficulties where the degree of impairment means they have not developed language, may be pre-verbal. For these clients, music can often convey meaning through the mood, dynamic, inflection, character, and sometimes, emotional messages in the musical material, that will gain the attention of the person and encourage some awareness, and potentially lead to comprehension.

Non-verbal

Children and adults with developed language, but whose pathologies or emotional difficulties prevent them from adequately using language, may be non-verbal. Populations here could include those experiencing profound depression, elective mutism, moderate learning difficulty, high-functioning autism and Asperger syndrome and those affected by trauma or neuro-disability. Some receptive music therapy (listening to music) approaches offer a non-verbal experience, where moods and feelings can be presented (or reflected from the attitude of the client) without complicated verbal explanation.

Supra verbal

For children and adults with normal developed language, and no pathologies or limitations to the use of language, music making or listening may provide a medium of expression beyond verbal language. Here, the music played or sung by the therapist, or heard via a CD, can offer an experience (usually an emotional experience) far beyond what can be conveyed through mere words, and where words afterwards may be even redundant.

In all three cases, the music therapist can use his or her own musical skills (in the case of improvised music), or knowledge of the appropriate repertoire (in the case of recorded music) to respond to the client. Playing 'to' the client, using 'empathic improvisation' to reflect the client's feelings is a method originally defined by the pioneer of music therapy in the UK, Juliette Alvin, and subsequently further described in *Improvisation* (Wigram 2004):

'*Empathic improvisation* and *reflecting* require a response that is more specifically connected to the emotional state of the client.' (p.89). Empathic improvisation:

> involves a therapeutic method that was first applied by Juliette Alvin where, typically at the beginning of a session, she would play (on her cello) an improvisation that empathically complemented the client's 'way of being'. In practice this means taking into account the client's body posture, facial expression, attitude on this particular day, previous knowledge of the client's personality and characteristics, and then playing something to the client that reflects a musical interpretation of their own way of being at that moment. It was intended by Alvin as a very empathic technique, not attempting in any way to change the client's feelings or behaviour, but simply to play to the client without any hidden manipulation of their feelings. If a client comes into the therapy room agitated and upset, this mood can easily be incorporated into an empathic impro- visation, whereby the therapist is not trying to ameliorate or reduce the degree of distress which the client is currently experiencing but merely to play it back to them as a supportive and empathic confirmation. (p.89)

The approach of the therapist in using this form of receptive method should rely on the SOLER model, sitting 'Square on', with an 'Open' attitude, 'Leaning toward' the client, with appropriate 'Eye contact', and a 'Relaxed' posture and paying close attention to body language and facial expression. The following examples present typical situations in therapy where empathic improvisation or receptive music therapy may be used. There are no right or wrong answers to these scenarios, because in these circumstances no research shows that one approach is contraindicated while another is indicated. The choice of musical material, live or recorded, and the way in which it is presented will result in different responses from clients – some may relate well to listening experiences, other clients may not be able to attend to listening experiences, and in that situation a different type of music therapy method would be used.

Try to think through how you would use music in each of these three cases – either by improvising something empathic for the client, or selecting a piece to listen to. After the examples are some suggestions:

- **Example 1**: A seven-year-old child with severe autism is rushing round the room, stopping occasionally in specific places in the room to posture and to flap, staring intently at an object. The child rarely comes near to the therapist, who is seated with a drum on her knee, and avoids eye contact. (*Note: avoiding eye contact here is appropriate when working with children who have autism.*)

   How would you create music to empathically capture the emotional and physical state of the child?

- **Example 2**: A 41-year-old man with severe depression sits alone in the room, isolated in his thoughts from the sudden trauma of losing his wife in the recent tsunami in Thailand while on holiday there. He has received much counselling, and is tired of trying to verbalise his current state and how he views his life. The music therapist sits near to him, and thinks about whether to play, or to put on some music to listen to together.

How would you approach playing for the client as a reflection of his state?

What music might you choose to listen to together with the client to resonate with his emotional state?

- **Example 3**: A 22-year-old student has come for music therapy to work on her personal resources, and explore her feelings about life and the future. She wants to work with music because she finds it often catches her mood, provokes her thoughts, or fires her imagination. She has told the music therapist that she listens to a wide range, from classical music to big band and jazz.

  What would you select to listen to together with the client as an opening experience for a session, and why?

Possible approaches

Example 1: Many therapists play what they see, and assume that this is empathic and reflective, as well as wise. In this case, matching the child's movements rushing round the room on the drum, with fast, alternate hand playing, and then stopping and thrumming fingers on the skin when the child stops to posture and flap can demonstrate understanding and empathy that the child will recognise. Alternatively, finding a slower ground tempo to the child's running, accenting occasionally, but providing the pulsed stability, may also stabilise the child while presenting him or her with an alternate identity (musical) of the therapist. Finally, playing or singing some well-known piece such as the 'Can-Can' from Ofenbach's *Orpheus in the Underworld*, or 'Jingle bells' (if it is near Christmas) may provide a context or framework for the child's moving around that will connect him or her to music, especially if he or she recognises the music and identifies with it.

Example 2: Again, many therapists play what they see, and in this case would take an approach that will provide a strong empathic and reflective musical response to the man's distressed state. This may manifest in choosing to play music that is slow, sombre, perhaps even tragic, that may reinforce the client's depressive feelings. Alternatives would be to play music that is thoughtful, not too fast, but may be more nostalgic and tender in character, promoting memories of happier times. Nevertheless this client could be extremely vulnerable and fragile to music that contains either frivolity, or unpredictable changes, so the music should be stable, pleasant and perhaps even slightly uplifting. If using recorded music, the selection should have the same properties – stable, pleasant and slightly uplifting. The reason is that people who have suffered a traumatic event can easily experience flashbacks. The music, therefore, either played live or from a recording, should be very stable and predictable. Perhaps the therapist may encourage the client to sit back in the chair and focus on his breathing during the music. This would help him develop some strategies for coping with flashbacks. Examples of suitable music include Respighi's 'Nightingale' from the *Birds' Suite*, or a selection of quiet relaxing music with few dynamic changes.

Example 3: One way to respond to the student is to ask her what music she would like to listen to (as a starting point). Another alternative would be to ask the student to reflect on how she is feeling in the moment, and to choose some music together that either reflects the mood she is in, or the mood she would prefer to be in.

Conclusion

This chapter has focused on the values and beliefs that we bring as therapists to therapeutic relationships with clients, and some of the verbal skills that the music therapist needs to process receptive music therapy experiences. Therapeutic interventions rely on the sensitive perception of the clients' needs and potentials, and the verbal skills described here begin to explore some of the techniques and skills that therapists need in order to help clients talk about their experiences. In addition, empathic improvisation, as explained in this chapter, is a non-verbal means of receptive music therapy for children and adults to listen to improvised music that has been specifically created to reflect the client's mood and affect.

Chapter 2

Selecting Music for Receptive Methods in Music Therapy

This chapter will describe the process involved in the selection of music for relaxation, imagery and other receptive experiences, across different age groups and in different contexts. First there is a discussion comparing the elements of music used for relaxation with music that stimulates imagery, to show the subtle differences between the two. Different genres are then discussed including music of the Western classical tradition, so-called new age music, meditative and trance music and jazz. In the second part of the chapter, music that is chosen for clients of different ages and in various contexts is described, and an innovative programme for evaluating recorded music in a paediatric hospital is explained, complete with guidelines that can be adopted in other hospital contexts.

This chapter presents an introduction to the criteria used for making selections, and specific suggestions for music selections appropriate to different receptive methods will be included within subsequent chapters of the book.

Differences between music for relaxation and music for stimulating imagery

There are subtle differences between music that is suitable for relaxation and music that encourages and stimulates imagery. The most effective music for relaxation maintains a steady pulse, is quiet in mood and is predictable. There is little dynamic change as the purpose of the music is to enhance deep relaxation of the body.

By comparison, music for imagery is more changeable in instrumentation and in dynamic flow and these changes in the music stimulate imagery through the creation of new and interesting musical ideas. Table 2.1 compares the elements of music that are evident in music selected for relaxation, and for imagery. Although this is presented as a comparative table it should be pointed out that these criteria are not absolute. The purpose of presenting the table is to identify the specific elements that the therapist should consider when making a music selection. This list also functions as a checklist for therapists wanting to assess a new piece of music for its appropriateness for relaxation and/or imagery.

Variation will also occur with regard to age group and the context of the therapeutic encounter. Music that is relaxing for young children will differ in quality and style from music that is relaxing for adolescents, or older adults. Likewise a selection of music for an individual session might be different to music used in a group context, and the therapeutic setting may influence choice. A music selection for use in a busy general hospital will be different to a choice of music for use in a private home.

Table 2.1 Comparison of the elements of music for relaxation and imagery

Music for relaxation	Music for imagery
Tempo is consistent and steady.	Tempo may vary.
Tempo is slow.	Tempo is predominantly slow, but there may be contrasting sections of faster music.
Either duple or triple time, as long as it remains consistent.	Fluctuations between duple and triple time may stimulate imagery.
Melodic line may be predictable, with a rounded shape and small range of intervals (often in step-wise progression). The phrases of the melody may match the intake and exhalation of breath.	Melodic line may include leaps and wide intervals. It might be unpredictable in places to stimulate imagery.
Harmonic structure is typically tonal and consonant, with predictable sequences of chords, or suspended harmonies that resolve.	Harmonic structure may have more variance, sometimes with dissonance.
Instrumentation is likely to include strings and woodwinds, and exclude brass and percussion.	Instrumentation may include various instruments including brass and percussion, although they are likely to be unobtrusive.
Predominantly legato, however some effective music features legato melody line with pizzicato bass line.	Combination of legato, staccato/pizzicato, marcato and other forms of stress and emphasis.
Few dynamic changes.	Larger dynamic changes, but not sudden or frightening.
Repetition is a key feature.	Repetition is less important – variation is needed to stimulate imagery.
Texture likely to be consistent – could be thin or thick texture, but it is mostly consistent.	Texture is likely to change from thin to thick.
Supportive bass line.	Bass line may vary between supportive and not.
Predictable in melodic, rhythmic and harmonic features.	Less predictable in melodic, rhythmic and harmonic features.

Preferred genre

It is well accepted in music therapy practice that the most effective music genre to use is the client's preferred genre, since it is familiar. Therefore in choosing music for individual sessions that include relaxation, imagery and other receptive experiences, individual client preferences can be taken into account. However, sometimes the client's preferred genre may not be suitable, for example if the client prefers hard rock, grunge, etc. In addition, when choosing music for group sessions it is not possible to address individual preferences, and the music choice needs to be made by the therapist.

In order to gain a broader view of suitable music for relaxation and imagery across different age groups and contexts, the music therapists who have contributed to this book were asked to list the music selections they most often use. It was interesting to find that music therapists often choose classical music for clients across most age groups. Other genres used include new-age (such as Enya, Kobialka, Kitaro, Tony O'Connor and, in Denmark, Musicure). When working with adolescent-aged clients music therapists may use trance music or music of India that captures a mystical ambience. In aged care facilities, music therapists may use familiar music, light classical and jazz. In order to appreciate these different genres each will be described in terms of the characteristic features that make the style suitable for receptive methods of music therapy.

The characteristics of music for receptive music therapy

Classical music of the Western tradition

Since classical music of the Western tradition is used so much, it is important to consider the various characteristics that make it effective in receptive music therapy. Helen Bonny, the founder of the Bonny Method of Guided Imagery and Music, has written extensively about the features of classical music and her second monograph is devoted entirely to this discussion (Bonny 2002, pp.301–324). Bonny also lectured extensively on the topic of the relevance of classical music, and one of the lecture outlines (unpublished) lists seven distinctive characteristics. These are listed below with a brief discussion:

1. The structure of classical music is multi-layered; there is (usually) a melodic line, a harmonic structure and a bass line that provides support. These layers interweave and, in parallel with other elements such as texture and instrumentation, create ever-changing layers of musical sound.

2. Classical music is written in various forms, and the most common are: ternary form, sonata form, theme and variations, prelude and tone poem. Each of these will be described briefly.

   - *Ternary form*, mainly associated with the Baroque era, is composed in three sections, ABA, where A is repeated and B represents a different middle section. For therapy work, this form offers a stable and safe musical container, where the repetition of the opening section (as in a Minuet and Trio movement) acts as a familiar ending after a middle period of change.

- *Sonata form*, mainly associated with the classical and early romantic era, is also in three main sections, but with two additional short sections, an introduction at the beginning and a coda at the end. The sections in sonata form are: introduction, exposition, development and recapitulation, which may include a coda. In the exposition there are usually two themes – the first main theme and a second theme that is contrasting in mood or character. In the development section these two themes are developed; a small section of the theme (motif) may be developed, or the theme might be passed from one instrument to another. In the recapitulation, there is a repetition of the beginning (exposition) of the work. The two themes are heard again and there is sometimes a coda (a summation) at the very end. Examples relevant to receptive music therapy methods include the slow movement of concertos or symphonies, which also form many of the music programmes used in the Bonny Method of Guided Imagery and Music (Grocke 1999a, 1999b, 2002). Sonata form is also highly relevant to improvisational music therapy (Wigram 2004, pp.204–206), and in the structure of insight-directed music therapy sessions (Hanser 1999a, p.150).

- *Theme and variations* is a form used variably in different eras of music composition. As the name suggests, there is a theme, followed by a set of variations which are built on the features of the theme, for example, the melody may be played by different instruments, it might be played in different registers (high, medium or low), and it might be elongated by making each note twice its original length, or shortened by making each note half the length. The fundamental feature of the theme and variations form is that there is repetition, and that the theme is embedded in each variation. Purcell's *Chaconne in G minor*, Pachelbel's *Canon in D*, the slow movement of Beethoven's *Symphony no.9*, and the *Enigma Variations* of Elgar are examples of a theme and variations from different eras.

- *Prelude* is a short piece for orchestra that is complete in itself. The most popular prelude used in receptive music therapy is Debussy's *Prelude to the Afternoon of a Faun*, a work inspired by a poem of Mallarmé about a young faun in the forest; Fauré's *Pavane for a Dead Princess* is another example of the prelude form.

- *Tone poem* (or symphonic poem) is a form that emerged in the Romantic era and early twentieth century. As its title suggests this is a form where a story or other artistic work has inspired the composition. Richard Strauss wrote many tone poems including *Ein Heldenleben* (A Hero's Life), thought to be autobiographical. Liadov also wrote tone poems, such as *The Enchanted Lake*. The tone poem has a fairly free structure although it is based on a melodic idea, or series of melodies, and the elements of the 'story' are found in the structure of the music through devices such as leit motifs and variation in orchestration.

3.   The form in classical music is helpful in 'containing' the client's experience. The concept of 'music as container' seems to have emerged from the writings of Winnicott, who developed a theory of containment in relation to the developing child. Winnicott (1971) argued that parents provide containment for the emotional experiences of the young child, so that the child learns to internalise the containment of feelings. This concept is further developed in music therapy (De Backer 1993). In receptive music therapy, the structure and form of the music provides containment so that the client can let go into the experience of relaxation, or imagery. The client senses a level of trust in the music because it moves in a predictable way and there is a musical logic to its changes in melody, harmony, rhythm and instrumentation.

4.   Music conveys mood. The mood may be determined by many factors: the melodic line, the harmonic progressions, modulation points and the timbre of certain instruments. A music piece written in a minor key is likely to suggest a sad, melancholic, or reflective mood, but this is not always so. Associations with particular instruments also influence the emotional substance of the music. The timbre of the oboe for example often suggests sadness because of the reedy quality of the sound of the instrument.

5.   Music creates a sense of movement and flow that enhances both relaxation and imagery. For example, the use of pizzicato in the lower strings may create a sense of stability in music used for relaxation, but it also creates movement, and may influence movement in the client's experience of imagery.

6.   In classical music, rhythmic and melodic fragments and entire sections of music may be repeated, so that the listener may feel secure in hearing the melody each time it is heard.

7.   The quality of the performance is an important aspect in choosing a music selection for receptive music therapy experiences. A performance where the instruments are out of tune, or an ensemble that is not playing exactly together can irritate a seasoned listener, and this can detract from both a relaxation or imagery experience.

In addition, the quality of the recording itself can also affect the quality of the experience. A music performance that has not been mixed well in the recording studio can have a predominance of one group of instruments over another, and this can affect the listening enjoyment of clients. A list of classical music suitable for relaxation and for imagery sessions is given within both Chapters 4 and 5.

New-age music

Another popular style of music for relaxation is so-called new-age music, which often draws on images of nature, the desert, the sea and other nature-scapes, which are enhanced by electronic or computer-generated sounds. For example the music of Tony O'Connor captures nature sounds and the sounds of the Australian landscape. The CDs feature music of pan flutes, synthesised strings, keyboard, flute, didgeridoo and nature sounds (e.g. waterfalls, birds and other sounds of nature). Because the music is created or enhanced through electronic means, the underlying rhythm and pulse can be manipulated to create a surging or pulsing effect to induce a relaxation response.

Another feature of Tony O'Connor's music (and other new-age music) is the tendency to play 'under' the note, then adjusting the intonation into the note. While the sense of resolution can be satisfying, for some classically trained musicians this technique of beginning 'under' the note could be annoying.

Similar features are heard in the rhythmic structure of new-age music, where the instrument carrying the melody may be slightly ahead of the down beat, or slightly behind. The effect can enhance a dream-like state by blurring the precise down beat in the music structure.

Another proponent of new-age music is Kobialka who has produced a large volume of music that includes his violin playing over a background of synthesised sounds. Much of his music is very relaxing due to the seamless quality of the playing. There are few gaps in the music and one track flows into the next so that the flow of playing is not interrupted. The quality of the performance and recording makes for easy listening, and is appropriate across the age-span. Kobialka writes about his desire to create 'spatial' music that 'surrounds and envelopes… [so that] you are soothed, you feel joyfully alive' (Kobialka 2006).

CONTRAINDICATION OF NEW-AGE MUSIC

CDs that include nature sounds may be contraindicated in facilities for people who are confused, for example in facilities for people with dementia. People who are already confused may become more confused by the sounds of birds and waterfalls within the room, and patients have been observed looking around the room seeking the source of the sounds.

Celtic music

Another music genre that is commonly recommended for relaxation is Celtic music. This music is typically modal in character, and vocal selections are often in Celtic brogue, adding to the appeal of the music sound. Enya is an Irish musician who has promoted Celtic songs and music in recordings since 1987. Some of Enya's music is stimulating in character and may not be appropriate for deep relaxation, but could be suitable for imagery, therefore each CD needs to be assessed carefully. The *Watermark* (WEA 2292 43875-2) CD, for example, has four tracks that maintain a deeply relaxed state: tracks 1, 3, 6 and 8 (tracks 3 and 8 are vocal). The combined duration of these four tracks is 12 minutes of music, which makes the combination possible for a full deep relaxation session. Note, however, that the intervening tracks can be highly stimulating, therefore a therapist must monitor the choice of tracks within the CD.

Similarly *Shepherd Moons* (EMI Reprise 9 26775-2) comprises four tracks that are deeply relaxing (3, 6, 9 and 10) and intervening tracks are stimulating. Therefore each CD should be assessed carefully (see the guidelines later in this chapter) to determine the suitable tracks for relaxation, and also the order in which the tracks should be played. However it should be noted that in vibroacoustic therapy (explained in Chapter 9), the entire *Shepherd Moons* CD is used, because there is variety across all the tracks of the CD, and for vibroacoustic therapy this variety is quite appropriate.

Enya was also a member of the group Clannad, a well-known Irish/Celtic group of the 1970s and 1980s. Enya was a member of this group from 1980 to 1982, and their recordings included *Celtic Collection* (Camden 74321 674532), which contains many of their popular songs, some of which were used in British television series such as *Harry's Game* (about the troubles in Northern Ireland) and *Robin (The Hooded Man)*, on the legend of Robin Hood.

Another Celtic artist is Loreena McKennitt (McKennit 2006), who accompanies herself on Celtic harp. Many of the songs are modal and are sung with a haunting quality that inspires reflection, however some tracks include unusual instruments that have a strident tone (e.g. Uillean pipes and sitar), so careful assessment is needed to choose tracks that are conducive to relaxation (or imagery), relative to the age group and the context of the session).

Meditative music

Meditative music has a diverse range of styles and instrumentation. Some meditative music relies on a single-line melody on instruments that model the flow of breath, such as wooden or pan flute. Instruments from Tibet, such as singing bowls, Tibetan bells and small cymbals are also features of music used in meditation. *Music for Zen Meditation* (Scott 1964, Verve 817-209-2) for example features sitar and flute, and is modal in nature. The Eastern sound resonates with meditative practices and often conjures up imagery of the East. It is spacious in sound and generates a feeling of expansiveness. However, the music style may not be familiar to many clients, and the wooden flute melodic line is not predictable as in some Western music (see Chapter 3 for a description of the use of this music with hospitalised adolescents). The spatial and mystical quality of the music may encourage listeners to relax deeply in a meditative state.

Trance music

Music therapists who work with adolescent-aged clients indicate that they use trance music as a means for relaxation.

> Trance is a style of electronic dance music that developed in the 1990s, and is generally characterized by a tempo of between 130 and 160 bpm, featuring repeating melodic synthesizer phrases, and a musical form that builds up and down, often with crescendos or featuring a breakdown. Sometimes, vocals are also utilised. The style is arguably derived from a combination of techno and house as well as being heavily influenced by

Goa trance. Trance got its name from repeating and morphing beats and melodies which would presumably put the listener into a trance. (*Wikipedia* 2006)

It is interesting that trance music enhances a feeling of calmness despite the rapid pace of the notes. The constant movement that is repetitious and monotonous creates a secure foundation for this style of music, and listening to it is calming for those who enjoy this genre.

Jazz music

Jazz music began in the early part of the twentieth century, and originated as the cultural music of black Americans. It is actually a blend of musical elements and styles from Africa and from Europe. The rhythmic structures and style, especially the characteristic syncopated or irregular rhythmic patterns, come from Africa, while the harmonic and melodic styles within jazz emerge from many different influences – mainly originating in Europe. In fact, jazz employs polyrhythmic characteristics, where many different rhythms are employed around a core or basic rhythmic pattern. Alongside jazz, the distinctive musical style of ragtime emerged mainly for piano initially, then for a band. Ragtime is referred to in Chapter 10 in the protocol for music and movement, where a strong, syncopated rhythmic pattern is helpful to promote anticipated, passive movement.

Both jazz and ragtime involve improvisation as a developing style of compositional playing. However, unlike the free improvisation frequently referred to in improvisational music therapy (Alvin 1975; Bruscia 1987), jazz music involves the improvisation or extemporisation of melodic ideas within the safe and predictable framework of a series of harmonic chords (Wigram 2004). The structure of the harmonic sequence can vary, but 8-bar, 12-bar or 16-bar structures are typical, involving a modulation to the dominant or subdominant, with a return to the tonic. The blues, a characteristically slow style of jazz music, is stylistically very conducive to feeling 'laid back', and for gentle relaxation. The blues was truly original to the USA, with such well-known numbers as The St Louis Blues, The Basin Street Blues and countless others. The early proponents of the jazz idiom included such greats as Louis Armstrong, Duke Ellington and 'Count' Basie. Modern jazz emerged in the 1940s and 1950s and the genre exploded with a kaleidoscope of styles on many different instruments. Jazz has a tremendous attraction for receptive music therapy approaches. The idiom, depending on what styles and recordings are used, can promote a wide variety of effects, ranging from meditative relaxation to stimulation, physical reactions, heightened states of awareness and entrained response. Jazz music can therefore act as a stimulant or a sedative in receptive music therapy methods. It can contain a complexity of expression and improvisation that maintains a high level of interest and anticipation from a listener while still providing a predictable and stable harmonic and rhythmic structure. In order to facilitate relaxation the underlying tempo needs to be slow, even if the subdivisions of the metre allow a faster effect. The timbre and quality of instrumentation will also have significant effect. The mellow, gentle tones of the vibraphone or marimba contrast starkly with jazz trumpets. Saxophones can sound relaxing and gentle to some (especially if played with a softer reed) while to others there will always be a noticeably harsh sound to them.

Some of the most evocative music that offers predictability with syncopation can be found in the classic jazz trios of piano, bass and drums – with Jaques Louissier Trio and the Oscar Peterson Trio as very interesting examples. The walking bass, together with the brush sticks effect on the snare drum and crash cymbal provide the gentle ground upon which the pianist can build a harmonic and melodic improvisation or, in the case of Louissier, a jazzed-up representation of Bach's *Preludes and Fugues*. Big band music tends to be generally stimulating, however there are some wonderful slow numbers from the Glenn Miller Band and countless imitators of his style, with close harmony saxophones and clarinets providing the rich harmonic quality for classics such as 'Moonlight serenade' and 'String of pearls'.

It would be impossible to attempt to encompass the vast range of jazz music in this section of a book on receptive methods, and there is no value in doing that, as the diversity is rich and ever expanding. From the greats of the past, a few well-known examples could be mentioned as important starting points for a collection of jazz music used in receptive music therapy, including some of the many jazz compilations with digitally remastered original recordings:

Jelly Roll Morton, *King of New Orleans Jazz* (RCA Victor LPM 1649)

Louis Armstrong, *I Got Rhythm* (Pickwick Music PWK 137)

Duke Ellington, *In a Mellotone* (RCA Victor 1364)

George Shearing, *Jazz Masters 57* (Verve 529 900–2)

The Best of Count Basie (MCA 4050)

Jazz Greats – Swing that Music (MC CD 002A)

Charlie Parker, *The Master Takes* (Savoy JC 2201)

Charlie Parker Plays Standards, Jazz Masters 28 (Verve 521854-2)

The Jazz Ladies, Volume 3, various artists (Prestige CDSGPBJZ10)

The Nat King Cole Trio (Giants of Jazz CD53151)

The Essential Guide to Jazz on CD, various artists (CHARLY JAZZCD 101AAD)

The Oscar Peterson Trio with Herb Ellis and Ray Brown (Giants of Jazz CD53209AAD)

Miles Davis, *Kind of Blue* (Columbia PC-8163)

Other considerations when selecting music for receptive methods

Apart from the genre of the music selection, there are other considerations when choosing music for clients, or with clients.

Associations with music

When making a selection of music for therapeutic purposes, it is important to consider any existing associations with the music selection. Some beautiful pieces of classical music that would be highly suitable for relaxation and/or imagery have strong associations particularly with films, with advertisements, and also with past events in an individual's life. Albinoni's *Adagio in C minor* for example is often included on relaxation CDs. It is a beautiful piece of music with sustained pulse and descending melodic line. However, the piece was used throughout the film *Gallipoli*, a deeply sad movie about the death of Australian and New Zealand soldiers during the First World War. It is also a piece that is commonly chosen for funeral services, and may draw clients back into painful and sad memories. Similarly, the slow movement of Mozart's piano concerto no.21 was used in the 1960s film *Elvira Madigan*, and when clients hear this music, they may have immediate associations with the content of the film, and the feelings that the film aroused for them at the time they viewed it.

Other well-known music may be associated with television commercials. Grieg's 'Morning' (from the *Peer Gynt Suite*), for example, is often used because of the gradual and uplifting shape of the melodic line. Selections of classical music are also used for car commercials, holidays, coffee and other material goods. These associations can affect the enjoyment of the experience, and therefore the therapist might be aware of these possibilities when choosing the selection of music.

A third example of associations with music, which cannot be controlled, is when the client has an existing association with the music that the therapist has chosen. It might remind the client of a former or current relationship, or an event (e.g. a love affair, wedding, death or funeral). These associations are not likely to be known to the therapist, therefore when selecting a piece of music for relaxation or for imagery the therapist needs to be aware that some inadvertent associations might influence the client's experience. This is not necessarily a negative outcome, as the associations elicited might open doors to important memories that can be explored. Should this occur, the therapist could use some of the verbal processing techniques outlined in Chapter 1 to de-brief with the client. The therapist then makes a comment in the post-session notes as a reminder for future sessions.

Music preferences

It is well established in music therapy research literature that the most effective music to use with clients is the music style and genre that is familiar and preferred by the client (or client group). Generally it is easy for the music therapist to ask clients what type of music they like, and then to make choices based on genre or style. Sometimes however the therapist has to make a choice without knowing the client's preferences, and in this instance the therapist must draw on assumptions about the music selections that have been found to be effective in previous sessions, or with previous clients. This is true for clients who are non-verbal, confused, or cognitively impaired. It also occurs at a first session when the therapist has not met a client before.

It is also important not to make assumptions about what style of music different age groups prefer. Most older adult clients like classical music, however some prefer country and western, or jazz, and therefore when choosing music for a relaxation session, the therapist might choose a country and western or jazz piece. There is a wide and varied selection of gentle or slow jazz music that can also be appropriate for relaxation. While most adolescents prefer current high-energy music, some adolescents might like Bach played on synthesiser. Some of the 'jazzed-up Bach' played by the Jaques Louissier Trio (piano, bass and drums) is very predictable, stable and relaxing music.

Length of the music selection

The appropriate length of the music selection will be determined by many factors:

- the length of the whole session
- the amount of time designated to getting the client(s) settled
- whether the music will be played at the same time as the relaxation/imagery script (see Chapters 3, 4 and 5), or whether there will be a relaxation induction with the music played later to deepen the relaxed state
- the concentration span or tolerance span of the client(s)
- the context – in a hospital environment it is likely that shorter pieces of music will be used, whereas in a private room a longer piece might be selected.

Vocal or instrumental?

The solo human voice can have a powerful effect on a client when in a relaxed state. A female or male voice might be heard as nurturing and supportive to one person, but domineering and unsettling to another. Some voices, particularly in classically trained singers, might have a wide vibrato, and this might indicate a more formal or parent voice, whereas a lyric soprano or light tenor voice might depict a younger person. These associations with the timbre of the human voice, and the projections of the client onto the singer, can have a significant effect on the client's experience. Instrumental music on the other hand is typically less problematical as there is less likelihood of the client projecting a human persona onto the music.

However there may be occasions when intentionally choosing a music selection that features a solo vocalist is very apt. For example, working with an adult client in palliative care who has asked for music that will support her religious beliefs might prompt the therapist to choose a female vocalist singing Bach–Gounod's *Ave Maria*. There is a wide repertoire of religious and secular choral music, including popular music for choirs, that can be effective in supporting a relaxed mood state, and to underpin imagery experiences.

Assessing a music selection for suitability

It is advisable always to listen to the music selection yourself before using it with clients, and to find out in both a subjective and objective way what you are hearing. It is important to listen to it under different conditions:

- **Condition 1**: Listen with eyes closed and with full attention on the music selection – that is, do not have the music playing in the background while attending to other things such as driving the car or cooking dinner. Be fully attentive to the music. Listen for the various elements: rhythm, melody, harmonic progressions and instrumentation, and mentally evaluate whether these elements together create the effect you want.

- **Condition 2**: Listen to the selection again, imagining what type of images or feelings might be aroused in the client/client group with whom you intend to use it. Be particularly careful about whether the selection is likely to engender sad or depressed feelings, as many 'relaxation' selections are written in minor key, have a descending melodic line and can easily be depressing for clients who might be in a vulnerable state in hospital or an aged care facility

- **Condition 3**: Listen carefully to the beginning of the selection and to the ending. Does the beginning create the atmosphere that you are wanting? Or is there a lengthy introduction before the section that you really want to use begins? Is the ending of the music well 'grounded', or does the music leave the client with a floating ending that might make it difficult for the client to feel that the music has finished?

It is important that the therapist keeps a note of what selections work well, and which do not work well with individual clients and with groups. This facilitates a self-education process and enables the therapist to build his or her own repertoire of music selections that are certain to achieve what is desired.

Choice of music for particular patient/client groups and ages

In this section the features that influence the choice of music for clients of different ages and in different contexts will be discussed, including infants, hospitalised children, adolescents, adults and older adults.

Choosing music for infants

A wide literature exists about music therapy for neonates, including premature and full-term infants, and sick newborn infants. The music typically used for these infants is very steady, with little or no change in key, tempo or dynamics. An example of appropriate music is the series of CDs entitled *Music for Dreaming*. There are two CDs and a Christmas album, produced by Cherie Ross (see Ross 2006). Each CD of *Music for Dreaming* is almost an hour of continuous instrumental lullabies, performed by select musicians from the Melbourne Symphony Orchestra. The music is played without a break between tracks and the tempo is a consistent 60 beats per minute (the pace of a heart beat at rest). There are no dynamic variations in the music, thereby eliminating the risk of stimulating an alert reaction in the infant.

Another CD cited in the literature is Schwartz' *Transitions* programme, which comprises classical music interspersed with the natural sounds in utero. Schwartz digitally sampled actual womb sounds and then combined the womb sounds with soft, female vocal harmonies and other meditative sounds. *Transitions* provides 'a soothing, sleep inducing environment for newborns, as well as a calming, almost hypnotic effect on mothers during labour and childbirth' (Schwartz 2006). The *Transitions* music has more dynamic variation, therefore *Music for Dreaming* may be more appropriate for vulnerable and fragile infants.

Music for hospitalised young children

Music is often played to young children in hospital to alleviate distress or anxiety. At the Royal Children's Hospital (RCH) in Melbourne, music therapists often play recorded music for children to enable them to relax and, it is hoped, fall asleep. But if the child is distressed or agitated, then the quality of the music initially should match the mood and energy of the child. By adopting this 'iso' principle (Altshuler 1948), the first choice of music may be familiar and energetic. Subsequent choices are less energetic, and gradually become slower in tempo, with less change in dynamics. Beth Dun, senior music therapist at the RCH, explains that music is often used to engage the child's attention, therefore the therapist is likely to draw the child's attention to the music by suggesting the child listens for a certain instrument, or by asking whether the child can imagine anything occurring in the music. Once the child is engaged with the music, the selections can be tailored to help the child relax (see further details in the next chapter).

Dun uses music that is familiar to the child, such as music from television programmes such as Sesame Street, the Wiggles, or CDs of nursery rhymes (personal communication, 11 April 2006). As the child settles, familiar sung lullabies may be effective, and the child may fall asleep. Dun also works with the parents of the child, as the parents may be attending the child in hospital for long periods of time during the day. The parents then learn to select music that is familiar and preferred by their child, and this can be carried on when the child returns home.

Music to enhance a paediatric hospital environment

Helen Shoemark, a registered music therapist who works with sick newborn infants at RCH, describes a project instigated at the hospital to provide recorded music for children in their rooms. The Music Listening Channel (MLC) comprises music that is uploaded into a computer program and is accessible via the television in the child's room. The MLC was created by a husband and wife doctor team, so that parents could have music for their child or for themselves at any time of the day or night. The music therapists were invited to be on the programming committee as there were no established criteria for the selection of appropriate music. Shoemark (2004) trained the music therapy team to use an evaluation protocol for assessing the appropriateness of CDs for the Music Listening Channel.

RANKING OF TRACKS FOR THE MUSIC LISTENING CHANNEL

Shoemark comments,

> one of the most important aspects of assessing the suitability of a CD for music listening, is to evaluate *all* of the tracks. Often a CD that is marketed commercially as being relaxing may have several tracks that are stimulative, or that are sad and/or depressing. Therefore the entire CD should be assessed if the entire CD is to be played. (Shoemark 2004)

Table 2.2 shows the five levels of assessment of an entire CD. Each level is colour-coded so that the predominant level of a CD can be quickly identifiable.

Table 2.2 Ranking an entire CD	
1	Totally sedative – consistent levels for all/most musical elements across the whole CD
2	Predominantly sedative – overall the tracks are sedative or relatively quiet in nature, with occasional tracks that have more energy
3	Mixed – some sedative tracks, but also some more energetic music with elements that are not appropriate to the hospital
4	Up-beat – predominantly tracks that have an energising quality
5	High energy and big variations between tracks

A similar system is used for assessing individual tracks from a CD, as outlined in Table 2.3.

Table 2.3 Assessing individual tracks	
1	Sedative – minimum range/minimum change in all/most musical elements
2	Mostly quiet with clear shifts into more dynamic sections
3	Up-beat but quite consistent in its levels
4	Wide variation in musical elements, with surprising shifts in dynamics

Nursing and allied health staff are educated to identify the suitability of CDs based on the colour-coded system (above), so that they can quickly choose appropriate music if a music therapist is not available on the ward.

Guidelines for using recorded music in the hospital environment

Recorded music is also used in all areas of the hospital, such as treatment rooms and waiting rooms, and staff other than the music therapists often made poor or inappropriate choices for music. The music therapists at RCH were concerned about the unmonitored and indiscriminate use of recorded music generally in the hospital, and they developed *Guidelines for Using Recorded Music in the Hospital Environment* (Shoemark, Dun and Kildea 2004), in response to that concern.

The guidelines are listed in the Policy and Procedure Manual of the hospital and on the Music Therapy Unit web page. The following six key principles formulated by Shoemark *et al.* (2004) in relation to the use of recorded music in the paediatric hospital are reproduced here (with permission), and may be relevant to other hospital environments:

1.   Music affects people differently depending on age, coping abilities, mood, physical and mental state, and previous life experiences.

2.   Clinical evidence indicates that familiar, self-selected music is a more effective support strategy than unfamiliar music.

3.   Music serves as a recreational pastime in the community, but in the hospital environment, sensory stimulation cannot be treated casually. Therefore the inclusion of music must be a conscious choice.

4.   Background music may contribute positively or negatively to the ambient noise level.

5.   Music has strong psychological associations and the capacity to affect physiological change.

6.   Poor quality equipment for playing music limits the benefit.

Mindful of these key principles, individual use of recorded music must account for:

- variation in patient preference
- noise that can be created by too many sources of sound available in one room at the same time
- regular assessment and change of stimuli when appropriate
- detrimental effects of listening to loud music for specific populations such as cystic fibrosis patients and oncology/haematology patients.

Patients should be encouraged to bring and use music that they consider to be supportive.

Clinical applications of recorded music

The Music Therapy Unit should be consulted in providing recorded music to patients in the following situations:

- patients in the intensive care unit
- patients/families in the neonatal unit
- unconscious and sedated patients.

In addition, consultation with the Music Therapy Unit may be helpful in providing recorded music in the following situations:

- patients using music as a supportive strategy or distraction during a procedure
- patients asking to use music for relaxation

- nonverbal patients with whom staff do not have an established mean of communication

- any situation where there is uncertainty about the application of music.

(Shoemark *et al.* 2004, pp.1–3)

Helping parents choose music for their child

The music therapists at RCH also help educate parents in choosing appropriate music for their child. Beth Dun explains that recorded music is a valuable strategy in assisting children to relax and sleep. The music therapists work with families to select music that is appropriate, however if the patient is on the adolescent unit, then the music therapist works directly with the adolescent to determine his or her preferred music. The music therapists use the traditional criteria for sedative music: minimum range and minimum change, and combine these with stylistic preferences of the child or family. There is a library of CDs at the hospital from which the therapists make selections.

Music choices for adolescents

Different styles of music are used with adolescent-aged clients, depending on the context of the therapy. Young adolescent-aged children (about 12–16) tend to prefer music that is currently on the charts, whereas older adolescents (16+) tend to have formed individual preferences for music (Frith 1978). At RCH, adolescents often request particular singers, such as Nora Jones and Pete Murray. In other programmes, such as the one conducted by Katrina McFerran in paediatric palliative care, meditative, new-age, Celtic and trance music, described earlier in the chapter, are used.

Conclusion

This chapter has addressed criteria used to select music of different genres for clients of all ages, situated in different contexts. Further details about choice of music, and description of music used for relaxation, imagery and other receptive methods will be explored in the next chapters.

Chapter 3

Relaxation and Receptive Methods for Children and Adolescents

Introduction

Relaxation methods are used by many professionals – teachers, therapists, nurses, pastoral care workers, yoga instructors, to name a few. Music therapists, however, incorporate music with relaxation inductions for clients of all ages and in diverse contexts. Music therapists may also provide music live, by improvising on piano, keyboard, guitar or voice, to enhance a relaxation session. They may also choose recorded music, utilising knowledge about music structure and form, genre, instrumentation, tempo and quality of recording, to ensure that the recorded music will enhance the experience of relaxation.

Relaxation for child clients varies in many ways, depending on the age of the child, the type of disability or illness, and the context in which the session is conducted. A relaxation session in an acute children's hospital, for example, will differ from a relaxation session for children in the classroom. A relaxation session for a three-year-old child will differ from one for a ten-year-old.

Relaxation for children and adolescents may incorporate many and varied approaches, and in some cases a session is relaxing because the child's attention has been diverted away from pain or anxiety. In some instances relaxation involves engaging in fantasy stories, or creatively imagining scenes. Relaxation may be experienced when a child has his or her eyes open, and the goal might be to calm the child rather than the traditional idea of relaxing muscles and limbs.

This chapter incorporates material provided by music therapists who work with children and adolescents predominantly in hospital settings. Receptive methods include relaxation with music (either live or recorded), imagery scripts used in conjunction with relaxation inductions and music (either live or recorded) and other receptive methods. In each case the context of the session is described and relaxation inductions are written out in full, so that the reader can develop his or her skills in implementing these methods in clinical practice. Inevitably the wording of the inductions may need to be adjusted according to the age of the children, the context and the level of cognitive ability.

The chapter is organised into various sections based on the chronological age group of the children and adolescents. Sections 1 to 5 relate to children and adolescents who are hospitalised:

1.   Receptive music therapy for hospitalised young children (3–8 years)

2.   Receptive music therapy for hospitalised older children (8–12 years)

3.   Relaxation for children with sleep difficulties in a psychiatric setting

4.   Receptive music therapy for children in palliative care

5.   Receptive music therapy for hospitalised adolescent patients

6.   Relaxation and receptive music therapy in the classroom

7.   Relaxation for older adolescents (15+ years)

Receptive music therapy for hospitalised children and adolescents: setting the scene

Theoretical framework

For children who are hospitalised, receptive methods, including relaxation and sometimes imagery, are used for the following therapeutic functions:

1.   to reduce pain (Lathom-Radocy 2002)

2.   to master fear and anxiety (Bishop *et al.* 1996; Nolan 1997)

3.   to reduce distress in paediatric burns patients prior to surgical procedures (Robb *et al.* 1995)

4.   to regulate breathing (Snyder Cowan 1997), particularly in children who have asthma (Lathom-Radocy 2002)

5.   to provide a mental escape from the hospital environment (Loewy 1997)

6.   to provide opportunities for creative thinking and fantasy and engage the imagination (Snyder Cowan 1997)

7.   to promote a positive experience within the stressful environment of the hospital (Loewy 1997).

Beth Dun, senior music therapist at the Royal Children's Hospital in Melbourne, comments that receptive techniques are used for hospitalised children when the child is exhausted, or in palliation. Children who are sedated may be unable to move physically or respond vocally, so receptive music therapy allows the child to rest and listen. Receptive techniques are used therefore to engage the child's attention and to establish rapport (Dun, personal communication, April 2006).

Relaxation for hospitalised children

Relaxation can be used as a segment of a music therapy session, or as an entire session. A music therapist may spontaneously decide to offer a relaxation experience if the child is tense, or stressed, and a child can be referred to music therapy specifically for reducing anxiety or tension. This often occurs if a child is becoming anxious about impending surgery and nursing staff believe that music therapy can help. Both recorded music and improvised music are used by music therapists and need to be of an appropriate style and genre for the age of the child. Familiar songs may be used to capture the child's attention and direct it to the music (and therefore away from the stressful experience). In addition, using imagery is appropriate with young children, particularly if the imagery encourages creativity, the imagination and a sense of the magical world (Dileo 1997). For older children it can be helpful for the therapist to explain and illustrate the process of relaxation if they have not experienced it before, particularly if the child is old enough to use relaxation and imagery for him- or herself after discharge from hospital.

EYES CLOSED?

Young children (approximately 3–8 years old) often do not close their eyes during the relaxation session, partly because there is an association of closing eyes with sleeping. If the therapist suggests the child might 'close your eyes if you want to', the child might close his or her eyes, but then open them again to see what's going on.

EQUIPMENT AND SET-UP OF THE ROOM

The relaxation session (or segment of a session) is likely to take place in the child's hospital bed (or cot, for a younger child). The child may be in a shared ward where it would be impossible to provide a totally quiet environment. The child may be intubated, or in traction, and the music therapist's first task is to make the child as comfortable as possible in the bed. The position of the therapist will also be important, as will the atmosphere of the room. In some wards or shared rooms, it is possible to draw screens around the bed for privacy and to facilitate the child's engagement.

The music equipment

When using recorded music, the CD player needs to be positioned as close as possible to the child. This may be difficult to juggle if the child is attached to a drip, or if there is no space beside the bed, or the power supply is some distance from the bed. The CD player should have simple functions that are easy to manipulate, and should be lightweight in case it has to be placed at the foot of the bed. The volume level should not be loud, particularly if there are other children in the ward. Open headphones may be an option.

Voice quality of the therapist

The music therapist may provide a relaxation 'induction' for the child, or may read an imagery script as part of a relaxation or receptive experience. An effective voice quality is essential in receptive methods and is dependent on the tone, projection, dynamic range and pacing of the therapist's voice.

VOICE TONE

The tone of voice needs to be mid-range, not too high, not too low, and have a warm, comforting tone. It is important to keep the tone of voice fairly constant, so that the quality of the voice itself is effective in inducing trust in the therapist, and engenders a sense of safety – that is, that the therapist has quiet control as conveyed in the tone of the voice. A high-pitched voice, for example, might convey a sense of insecurity or inexperience, and a very low voice might sound too gruff! A mid-range timbre therefore avoids those associations.

VOICE DYNAMICS

For child clients the therapist might use a more dynamic voice quality than with adult clients, and with younger children a greater degree of prosody or 'lilting' intonation. Children have short concentration spans and therefore a more dynamic voice might be needed to keep the child focused on the music, or the relaxation/imagery script.

PACING

It is difficult to relax if a therapist is speaking too fast, as the child has to process the words as quickly as they are said. So a slower pace, with repetition in the instructions given, will enable the child to relax more easily. If the child is anxious and wriggling in bed, it can be helpful to start the induction at a faster pace to match the energy level of the child, then gradually slow the pace down, to match the intended relaxed state.

MODEL THE BREATH

Helping a child to regulate his or her breathing is an important strategy for coping with pain or anxiety (Snyder Cowan 1997). Often the breath is shallow or held in when a person is experiencing pain, and therefore maintaining a regulated breathing pattern that encourages the releasing of held breath will assist in managing pain and anxiety. When directing a child's attention to his or her breathing, the therapist can audibly model the breathing, e.g. 'Breathing in…(audibly take in a breath)…and breathing out…(audibly let the breath out)'.

Receptive music therapy for hospitalised young children

For young children between 3 and 8 years of age, the music therapists at the Royal Children's Hospital (RCH) in Melbourne adopt receptive techniques in three ways:

1.   the therapist sings familiar songs to the child to calm him or her

2.   the therapist chooses a CD that is appropriate for relaxation and helps the child focus on the story and songs on the CD

3.   the therapist uses imagery scripts to activate fantasy.

Singing familiar songs to the child

When a child is very anxious and afraid, the music therapists at RCH sing familiar songs to engage the child's attention until the child has settled or calmed.

Vignette: reducing anxiety in a young child

Beth Dun was called to help a three-year-old child waiting to undergo a lumbar puncture procedure. She found the child with her head buried into her mother's chest. Beth noticed that the mother was also very anxious, and although she was holding her child to comfort her, the mother's anxiety was not providing any containment for the child. Beth sat close to the mother and child and started by singing nursery rhymes, such as 'Twinkle, twinkle, little star', 'Old Macdonald had a farm', and 'Five little ducks'. Beth sang the songs in the same key, at the same pace, with the same accompaniment style, without a break between the songs, and with no dynamic change. Initially Beth could only see the back of the child's head, however, as she continued singing the girl turned to face Beth. Now the child was engaged and Beth asked, 'How many ducks are left?' Having engaged the child Beth could direct the child's attention away from the fear of the procedure, and once the child was engaged the mother's anxiety lessened as well.

In this vignette, the most important skill was to provide song singing that was highly regulated; played in the same key, same accompaniment, same pace and without a break between each song. This regulation not only contained the child's anxiety but also regulated the child's breathing, which released tension, and in turn regulated the heart beat.

CD of songs and dialogue

Another technique to engage a young child is for the therapist to choose an appropriate CD to listen to together with the child, and help the child to attend to the spoken voices on the CD. *Go to sleep, Jeff* is a CD produced by the Wiggles, a group that hosts a very successful children's television show in Australia. The CD *Go to sleep, Jeff* comprises ten songs with dialogue between each song. The therapist sings along with the Wiggles, but then encourages the child to stay attentive by setting up anticipation for the next song. 'What do you think they will sing next?' keeps the child focused on the songs and the dialogue. After the ten songs, there is a repetition of seven songs without dialogue, and by this time the child has often relaxed sufficiently to fall asleep. The therapist then checks that the child is safe in bed, with the sides of the bed/cot up, before leaving quietly so that the child can sleep.

Imagery scripts

In this method the music therapist uses imagery scripts to activate the child's imagination and sense of fantasy.

PREPARATION

The therapist's first task is to make the child as comfortable as possible in the bed, and the following explanation may be helpful:

> We're going to have some quiet time now, when you can relax and listen to some music. First of all, get comfy in the bed.' (The therapist may need to assist the child with pillows, arranging toys to be held or close by.) 'Try and get as comfortable as possible. Feel how warm and comfy the bed is under your body…under your head and shoulders…and your back and your legs… If you want to, you can close your eyes.

MUSIC SELECTION

Soft piano or guitar music is played in the background while the therapist reads one of the following imagery scripts. The music should not be evocative, else it will compete with the therapist's voice. The music should not be stimulative. When the therapist has finished reading the script, the music can be left playing. The music then masks the noises of the hospital and fills the space where the child is lying. Appropriate music selections are listed at the end of the section.

COMMONLY USED SCRIPTS

The imagery script can be quite short, but can be extended if necessary. The flow of the script needs to be smooth (see notes above about voice quality). In the following examples the ellipses indicate slight pauses (3 to 5 seconds) between the phrases.

Favourite place imgery script

This is the most commonly used imagery script at RCH. Focusing on a favourite place enables the child to mentally leave the hospital and imagine being in another place. Beth Dun comments that the most important words in this imagery script are 'I don't know where it is, but *you* do!' Children engage with the idea that they are keeping a secret, and they often smile when Beth says those words.

(Music plays softly in the background.)

> Think about all the places that you like to go to, and choose your favourite place…it might be outside…or inside…it might be a secret place… I don't know where it is, but *you* do!… Think about that nice place and how happy you are to be there…maybe there are other people with you…[add names of family if known]…[add names of the child's pet if this is known]…feel how nice it is to be in your special place.

Warmth imagery script

This induction is not appropriate if the child has a fever, or if the child is feeling hot. Often hospital wards are very warm.

(Music plays softly in the background.)

> Imagine that you are lying on soft sand and the sun is shining down, making you feel nice and warm. Feel the warmth of the sun come over your head…and face…over your shoulders…down your arms…and hands and fingers…feel the warmth come over your tummy…and then over your legs…and down to your feet…feel your whole body warm and relaxed.

Breath imagery script: blowing up a balloon

This imagery script is useful for children who are tense, anxious, or in pain. Instinctively we hold our breath when in pain, or we breathe in a shallow range as if to hold the pain in. Focusing on the breath encourages the child to take in deep breaths, and the lungs expand allowing more room for oxygen. Then, letting all the breath out releases tension from the muscles, and induces relaxation.

(Music plays softly in the background.)

> Imagine that you have a lovely balloon…see what colour it is…now pretend that you are blowing air into a big balloon…you take in a breath and blow it into the balloon…take another breath and blow into the balloon…slowly it is filling up… bigger and bigger…and when it is a nice round shape, gently let the balloon go and watch it float up into the sky.

By the water imagery script

(Music plays softly in the background.)

> Imagine that you are in the country where there are trees and a little stream of water…like a creek or a small river… Imagine you are standing in the shallow water and it is cool, but not cold… Feel the water as it trickles over your feet, making you feel happy inside…feel the water over your toes, making them feel cool and happy. (Extend to other parts of the body if required.)

Fairy garden imagery script

(Music plays softly in the background).

> Imagine that you are in a garden made by fairies… Look around and see the fairy trees and fairy flowers…and little fairy houses… There are fairy people there too…see how they smile at you and make you feel welcome…

MONITORING

While reading the imagery script to the child, the therapist looks for changes in posture, or body language, that might indicate that the child is not comfortable. If need be the therapist might stop the script and ask if the child feels OK. Changes in facial expression may also indicate the child is uncomfortable (frowns or moans), or that the child is becoming very relaxed (smoothing out of frowns, or smile on face).

ENDING THE RELAXATION SESSION

Since the aim of the relaxation session is to help the child feel calm, less anxious, or have less pain, the child may fall asleep during the relaxation. The therapist therefore should not try to bring the child out of the relaxed state, but tiptoe away from the child's bed, leaving the CD playing. The therapist might say, 'Have a lovely rest,' or 'When you wake up you'll feel much better.' The therapist should also check that the child is safe in bed, and that the side of the cot is up (for small children). Often the parents are sitting with the child too, so the therapist can leave knowing the child will stay relaxed with the music.

DOCUMENTATION

At the RCH music therapists document the block of time spent with each child, and they write brief notes about the child's physical and emotional state. The music therapists also keep notes of what music is familiar and preferred for each child, so that they can refer to these notes in future music therapy sessions.

SUGGESTED MUSIC

The Wiggles, *Go to sleep, Jeff* (ABC0328) (Includes narrations between tracks for the first ten tracks, thereafter seven tracks without narrative.)

Ross, C. *Music for Dreaming* (I and II) (SONY-BMG Music Entertainment MDCD001 and MDCD003) (purely music)

Receptive music therapy for hospitalised older children

For older children, between 8 and 12 years of age, music and imagery involves a longer description of a 'journey' or a story, as the children can concentrate for longer periods of time. The preparation, set-up and voice quality requirements are similar to those for the younger child. The choice of music depends on the age of the child, but the CDs listed for younger children are still appropriate for older children up to the age of 12. The therapist can ask the child what music he or she would prefer, e.g. whether he or she would like piano music or guitar music in the background. The child can also be involved in choosing which script he or she would like, for example, 'Would you like a story about floating on a fluffy cloud, or being in a pine forest?' The music can be started while reading the imagery stories. These stories need to be read slowly, pacing them with the music, enabling the child time to bring his or her images to mind. The ellipses indicate pauses (3 to 5 seconds) between the phrases.

PREPARATION

Get comfortable in the bed…if you like you can close your eyes… (then give one of the following inductions)

INDUCTION ONE (GIVEN BEFORE THE MUSIC COMMENCES)

I imagine your feet relaxing and sinking into the bed…imagine your legs relaxing and sinking into the bed…imagine the lower part of your tummy relaxing and sinking into the bed…and now the top part of your tummy, imagine it relaxing and sinking into the bed…and imagine your arms, and your hands relaxing, right down to your finger tips, and imagine your shoulders and head relaxing and sinking into the bed… (Start the music, and begin to read the chosen script.)

INDUCTION TWO (CAN BE READ WHILE THE MUSIC IS PLAYING SOFTLY IN THE BACKGROUND)

Let the music help with your breathing (model breathing in and breathing out audibly)… Let your body feel relaxed…relax your muscles: toes are relaxing…calves are relaxing…knees (are relaxing)…fronts and backs of legs…tummy…back…chest…arms…hands and fingers, right to your finger tips…shoulders…head… (start the music and begin to read the script.)

INDUCTION THREE (CAN BE READ WHILE THE MUSIC IS PLAYING SOFTLY IN THE BACKGROUND)

Let the music help with your breathing (model breathing in and breathing out audibly)… Let your body feel relaxed… Then use the phrase 'Feel the music relaxing' before naming each of the body parts, remembering to pause in between each one: 'Feel the music relaxing: toes… Feel the music relaxing feet…calves, knees, fronts and backs of legs, tummy, back, chest, arms, hands and fingers, right to your finger tips, shoulders, head… (Begin to read the script.)

MONITORING THE CHILD DURING RELAXATION INDUCTIONS

The therapist watches the child throughout the induction to notice any sign of discomfort. If the child begins to wriggle, re-direct the child's attention for example, 'What's coming next?' The therapist also adapts the relaxation induction where necessary, for example changing the words to suggest the music is helping a part of the body to heal.

CHOICE OF MUSIC

Music for this age group includes piano music or guitar music, or a CD of short classical pieces. The following CDs are used at the RCH and are found to be very suitable for this age group. Note: The music is suitable for contexts other than hospital too.

The Wiggles, *Go to sleep, Jeff* (ABC 0328)

Cherie Ross, *Music for Dreaming 1* (Ross 2006)

Cherie Ross, *Music for Dreaming 11* (Ross 2006)

The Most Peaceful Classical Album in the World (EMI 7243 5 67523 0)

George Winston, *Forest* (Windmill 01934 11157-2)

Celtic Twilight (Hearts of Space 14S11104-26)

For a Quiet Evening (Decca 289-472-847-2)

Quiet Time (The Relaxation Co. CD 7511)

Dream a Little Dream (Transitions Music 90806 76422)

Mozart, *Adagio* (Naxos 8-552241)

Peace of Mind (Windham Hill 01934-18105-2)

Acoustic Elegance (2 CD set) (Narada 7 2435-91496-2-2)

Imagery scripts
The scripts are appropriate for children who are hospitalised and are also suitable for general use.

WHITE CLOUD IMAGERY SCRIPT
(Start music)

> Imagine that you are resting on a huge fluffy white cloud… The cloud is like a big pillow and it holds you really snugly and warmly… Imagine that the cloud is moving slowly in the sky…and you can see other clouds passing you by… On the other clouds there are some of your friends… Who can you see?… Maybe the clouds have different colours… What colours can you see?… And now your cloud is coming down from the sky very slowly…and it is coming down to the earth…slowly…slowly…slowly…and now it is resting on the ground…and you can hop off if you want to.

SNOW LAND IMAGERY SCRIPT
This imagery script may be chosen for a child who has a fever and is feeling hot.
> (Start music)

> Imagine that you are in a place called Snow land. In Snow land everything is made of snow… The trees are made of snow…the houses are made of snow… The animals are made of snow…even the people are made of snow…you can feel the snow in your hands…and it's cool to touch… After a while you come to a place where there are many snow people smiling and saying hello to you… They know who you are… They are making a snowman out of the snow and they ask you to give them something to put

on it... You give them a special present and they are very happy... So the snow people give you a present too... It's wrapped up, and it's something you've wanted for a long time... Carefully unwrap the present from the snow people and see what it is they have given you.'

BY THE WATER IMAGERY SCRIPT

Choose 'cool' or 'warm' according to how the child is feeling at the time.

(Start music)

Imagine that you are by a little stream of water that flows over small rocks... The rocks are very smooth...and you can walk on them without hurting your feet... Slowly dip you feet into the water...and feel how cool [or warm] the water is on your feet... The water makes funny patterns as it flow over your toes...and when you move your toes, the water goes in different patterns...watch how the water makes different patterns...now you bend down to feel the water run over your hands and fingers...the water is cool [or warm] and it make you feel really calm...feel how nice the water feels on your feet and your hands...

A PINE FOREST IMAGERY SCRIPT

(adapted from Crook 1988)

(Start music)

Imagine you are entering a pine forest...beautiful tall, green pine trees are reaching up toward the sun...it is a warm sunny day. Feel the peacefulness of the tall trees...and imagine yourself walking toward them...look at the strong trunks of the trees...can you touch them?... Imagine you can hear the breeze as it whistles through the trees... Imagine yourself walking through the trees to a clear space...feel the sun on your body now...warm and gentle...and now you see an animal that has come into the clearing...it is a very friendly animal and it comes up close to you...you can stroke the animal if you like...feel how good your body feels now...

SUNRISE OVER THE OCEAN IMAGERY SCRIPT

(Start music)

Imagine you are looking out over the ocean...it is early in the morning...you see the sun coming up over the water...slowly the yellow sun appears, getting larger and larger...you can feel the warmth of the sun's rays beginning to float over your body...you feel the gentle sun on your head...and across your shoulders...you feel the warmth of the sun down your arms and hands...you feel the sun down your back and your tummy...you feel the warmth of the sun down your legs and across your feet, and you feel the warmth of the sand under your feet. Now the sun is high up in the sky...and your body feels very warm.

CLIMBING A MOUNTAIN IMAGERY SCRIPT

(Start music)

> Imagine that you are standing at the foot of a mountain...look up at the mountain...and see its colour and its shape...you notice there is a small path that begins at the foot of the mountain...you begin to walk along the path...there are flowers by the side of the path and small trees...and it is very green. The path begins to take you up the mountain...you can walk easily and you don't feel out of breath...up you go higher and higher...as you get to the top of the mountain you can see a wonderful view...have a look around you at the scenery from the top of the mountain...you can see forever...and you feel really happy...and now it is time to come down the mountain again... Gently you begin to go back down the path...you feel very relaxed...you get back to the foot of the mountain and there is someone special there to meet you...they are very glad to see you.

Ending the script

If the child is in a hospital bed/cot, and has fallen asleep during the imagery script, the therapist might say 'Dream about it in your dreams,' 'You can stay there as long as you like' or 'You can go there at any time.' The therapist may leave quietly making sure the child is safe in the bed (sides are up). If the child is awake at the end of the imagery script, the therapist might ask what he or she would like to do next: listen to a CD or sing some familiar songs, for example.

If the child is not hospitalised (e.g. is in a schoolroom context), then the therapist must bring the child back to an alert state. An appropriate script is: 'The music has come to an end now...begin to wiggle your toes and your fingers, and begin to stretch your arms and legs...and when you are ready you can open your eyes and look around you...'

Relaxation scripts for children hospitalised long term

Children who remain in hospital for many months benefit from relaxation/imagery scripts that are individualised to include the child's favourite place, or details of the child's home, family members and pets. The script can be recorded onto tape or CD, and the child can use the tape or CD whenever they wish.

Children who are agitated

A 'shaped' relaxation imagery script is used when children are too anxious to settle into the relaxed state. The imagery script begins with stimulative music (e.g. film music such as *Shrek*), and as the child becomes quieter, vocal music might be used, reducing in pace to introduce *Music for Dreaming*. A typical 'shaped' programme for young children might be: *Hi 5*, or *Bob the Builder*, followed by nursery rhymes, followed by *Music for Dreaming*.

Relaxation for children with sleep difficulties in a psychiatric setting

A programme titled 'A Little Night Music' was introduced to address the needs of children with bedtime and sleep difficulties within an inpatient psychiatric setting. Susan Bray Wesley, a board-certified music therapist, describes the programme.

Description of the programme

The techniques described below are an overview of a three-month project at an inpatient psychiatric facility, the Acadia Hospital in Bangor, Maine, USA. The children were aged 5 to 12 and were engaged in music and imagery activities for the purpose of learning how to access and use relaxation and develop positive tone imagery for themselves through the use of music. The intent was that they would learn broader skills to increase self-awareness and reflection, self-regulation and self-esteem, thus providing a sense of personal control, in dealing with personal anxiety around bedtime and sleep. These were small group sessions for one hour in length, offered just before preparing for bed, two evenings a week. No more than four children were assigned per group and each group met for a series of four sessions. Although the children were not met individually, strong attention was given to individual/personal issues, characteristics, and diagnoses.

The initial session provided an orientation to the overall group experience and structure including a short explanation of the centering process; how music would be played; how imagination could be encouraged with a storyline; what materials were available to concretize the imagery; and that a discussion time for processing/integration would also be provided. Thus, all of the sessions provided music, storyline, and an art activity as well as opportunity for discussion. The sessions were provided off the unit in an area of the hospital that was quiet, with softer, more 'family room' like features.

The opportunity for skill building that was provided by the four sessions was a major focus of the project so that the children could become empowered to use such techniques of music and imagery particularly after discharge from hospital. The concrete, consistent, and respectful nature of the activities allowed some children to learn to use relaxation skills for themselves, while still on the unit.

Preparation and inductions

The children arrived at the unit room at 6:00 p.m. with staff. The room was lit with soft overhead light. Each child was invited to comment about the walk to the room and how he or she was doing overall. After each child had a turn to speak, they were introduced to the theme for the session. For example, for session 1 'Today we are going to a bright sunny meadow to explore a big tree with leaves in bright fall/autumn colors'; session 2 'This session we'll return to the meadow and follow a path along a brook'; session 3 'This time we'll return to the pond we saw last session and perhaps see more creatures visit us'; session 4 'In this session we arrive at the pond right after a rain shower. I wonder what we'll find?'

After the short theme introduction, the children were invited to find a place on the floor to 'stretch out' or curl up, in general get comfortable, and the centering or breathing induction began.

> Allow yourself to feel the floor under you – how sturdy it is and the softness of the carpet. As you breathe gently, let your eyes close if you choose and just relax. Feel the air coming into your nose and follow it all the way to your toes. Wiggle your toes if you like and then breathe the air out. Take another breath and follow it to your knees. If you need to move your legs a bit go ahead and then breathe the air out.

Such breathing and centering continued until the children moved their breath up through the tops of their heads.

Starting the music and imagery

The following images and recorded music were used in this sequence with each group of children throughout the project. This sequence continues to be favoured as an introductory series for individuals and groups specifically in institutional settings.

SESSION 1 IMAGINAL SCENE: AUTUMN MEADOW SCENE WITH A LARGE COLORFUL TREE IN CENTER OF A FIELD

Music: 'Cathedral sunrise', *Golden Voyage II*

> As the music begins, we are standing at the edge of the field leaning against a large boulder warmed by the sun. It feels good against our backs as we look out at the full and colorful maple tree in the centre of the meadow. It's autumn and the colors of red, orange, yellow, brown and still some green are glowing in the sunlight. We can hear the brook nearby bubbling along and the sound of the clock tower bell chiming in the distance. There are a few birds in the brush chirping as we ready ourselves to take a walk. As our small group meanders through the grass and wild flowers we breathe deeply the clean sun-drenched air and enjoy seeing a few puffy clouds high in the blue sky. We're closer to the tree now and can see its huge trunk. It must have been growing for decades. Its bark is dark grey and quite smooth in places. We are now at the edge of the canopy and feel the shade cooling the air. Let's go stand under the branches and lean into the trunk. Feel how strong it is. It can hold all of us with its sturdy wood. Look down now at the ground and notice the few leaves that have fallen. Choose one that you like and look closely at it. See its colors and shape. Notice that it looks a bit like your own hand. Turn it over and see the smooth side then the rougher side. Notice its small veins and lines. It came from the branches above. Look up and see how the sun winks at you through the leaves still on the branches. What a beautiful tree and sky. What great air and friends. Just lean back again and feel the strength from the tree as it holds you securely. It's time to be going back to town now. If you like, bring your leaf along to remember the great tree, its colors and strength. We walk back to our boulder now and reaching it we turn to see one more time that glorious tree full of color and delight. (*Music ends with the sounds of the brook.*)

SESSION 2 IMAGINAL SCENE: AUTUMN MEADOW SCENE WITH TREE AND BIRDS AND
WATER SOUNDS IN THE DISTANCE

Music: 'Crystal creek', *Pools of Light* (Harris and Mendieta)

Today we are going to walk again through our meadow but we'll continue on past that
lovely tree we visited on our way to another place in nature. We hear the birds singing
us along, and the stream bubbles on calling us to find it today. As we near the edge of the
meadow opposite the tree a small path can be seen. It's just wide enough to walk one
person behind the other. There is soft moss and small stones at the edge of the path
and looking ahead we can see the small stream. It's not very wide, in fact we could jump
over and back, but look down into the water instead and notice the stones. So many
colors of brown and reds and greys. Maybe you'd like to take one to carry along today.
Looking off to the left a bit further we can see the stream continue on and I think I can
see a very light or sunny opening way down there. As we continue to walk toward that
light area, we come quickly to an opening – a small pond – the stream flows into this
lovely pond. It's not very large, in fact we can walk around it easily. So let's do that and
notice what else is here. There's a small fallen tree. You could use it as a bench to rest
on for a while if you like. And see the turtle – he's sunning himself on the rock at the
pond's edge. Oh – see the robins and sparrows fluttering in the bushes. There are some
lily pads. I wonder if a frog could be in the water below them. Do you still have your
stone? Would you like to find a place to put it here at this pond? Let's just sit for a
couple of minutes before we start back and feel the quiet and peacefulness of this pond
we have discovered today. (*A moment of silence with only music.*) It's time to start back. If
you like you might leave your stone here or bring it back with you to remember this
walk. We pass now beside the stream out into the meadow; pass the colorful tree and
return to the boulder. What a wonderful discovery – this pond.

SESSION 3 IMAGINAL SCENE: AUTUMN SCENE AT THE POND

Music: 'The nightingale', *The Birds* (Respighi)

(*As the music begins*)

Isn't the pond lovely today? The sun is just dancing on the water and it sparkles so
brightly. Yes, today we have returned to that small pond which we discovered and each
of us has found a spot to sit. Looking up into the sky we can see a few white clouds in
the deep blue but look – way off to the right are one, two, three...four, five? Are they
ducks or geese? Let's see where they go. (*Whispering*) Oh, it looks as if they'll land here.
We'll be very still. Here comes the first, now two then three – oh, two more – we're
very still as they come by. They're swimming around very slowly. As one comes toward
you, notice the feather she leaves behind for you. They finish swimming around the
perimeter and must feel very safe with us here, for now they swim to the middle of
pond – and look, they have fallen asleep. We'll leave very quietly today with a feather
that they have given to each of us.

SESSION 4 IMAGINAL SCENE: AUTUMN SCENE AT THE POND AFTER A SHORT RAIN
STORM AND CLOUDS ARE CLEARING AWAY

Music: 'Cradle song' (Grieg)

(*As the music begins*)

> Oh, doesn't the air smell fresh and clean? That short rain shower has made the sky
> seem so much brighter now that the clouds have moved on. Let's look up. Do you
> notice anything different in the sky? It seems a sort of colorful arch is forming. Do you
> see it? Are any of the colors growing brighter? Let's see – I think I see red. Is that pink?
> Then orange, yellow, green, blue, purple – wow, so many colors – I think it's a rainbow –
> take some time to look closely – notice where it stops – can you see to the very end? I
> can't remember ever sitting under a rainbow. It feels pretty good with all of those
> colours up there. Let's just listen. Maybe the colors will tell us something special. (*As the
> music ends*) The colors are very clear and the sky still bright. Bring those colors with
> you now as the trip to our pond closes today.

Concluding the imagery and transition to concretisation

At the conclusion of the music, the following script was used.

> The music has come to an end. Notice the quietness. Let yourself remember: 1. the big
> tree and colorful leaves; 2. the sun sparkling on the pond; 3. the five geese landing then
> swimming in the pond; 4. the colors of the rainbow in the bright blue sky. Bring these
> with you when you are ready to open your eyes. When you are ready find a place at the
> table and begin your picture.

Processing the session and pictures

The children were encouraged to draw a picture, and when they had finished their drawings,
they returned their chairs to the original circle configuration and taking turns shared what
they chose about the picture and their experience during the imagery with music. The
children kept their drawings as a reminder of the positive imagery that they could produce.
This was also intended to reinforce that they indeed could choose gentle, fun and even
adventurous settings for their imagination to explore.

Music details

1. *The Golden Voyage*, Volume 2. 'Golden sunrise' (Awakening Productions, Bearns
    and Dexter, 4132 Tuller Ave, Culver City CA. 90230)

2. *Pools of Light*, 'Crystal creek' (Allyn Harris and Peter Mendiata, 1987 Crystal
    Creek Recordings, Box 277 Stanstead Quebec JOB. 3EO Canada. CCR 8702)

3. Respighi: *The Birds Suite*, 'The nightingale' (CDC-7 47844 2, DIDX-1024,
    1977 EMI Records Limited)

4. Grieg: 'Cradle song' from CD *Music for the Imagination* (CREATIVE 1996
    Barcelona Publishers Licensed by Naxos of America).

★ ★ ★

Receptive music therapy for children in palliative care

In this section, music therapists describe their use of receptive music therapy for children in palliative care, including a multi-modal approach, with recorded music, improvisation and voice.

Improvised music in paediatric palliative care, with children who have chronic illness

Katrina McFerran works with children in paediatric palliative care who may have terminal cancer and diminished cognitive capacity, or may have a long-term neurological disability. Very Special Kids (VSK) is an organisation that supports families throughout their experience of caring for children with life-threatening illnesses, from diagnosis through to recovery or bereavement. Such illnesses include cancer, muscular dystrophy, neuro-degenerative and genetic conditions and rare syndromes. Support is provided through a children's hospice/respite service and family support team. The music therapist works primarily in the hospice but also provides services through the family support team on request.

One of the methods used by McFerran in this setting is a multi-modal relaxation strategy that is intended to communicate through touch, sound and general ambience. This method is based on a strategy of tactile stimulation. It incorporates a range of materials being used on the skin of the young person in order to stimulate sensation. Materials that provide a range and contrast of textures and sensory experiences are selected, with the music being used to emphasise the qualities of the fabrics. McFerran improvises the musical material in response to the texture and movements of the partner carer. Some materials match a state of relaxation, such as lambswool, whilst others are intentionally stimulating, such as steel wool (non-prickly). The method is based on the principle that the skin is the largest sensory organ in the body, and is covered with receptors of varying densities.

McFerran has adapted these ideas for use as a relaxation strategy for children in paediatric palliative care and finds that they are effective. She creates her own music through improvisation.

PREPARATION

This work requires the assistance of a carer or the use of pre-recorded music. When I work with a carer, I improvise music at the piano. The carer and I bring the child into the room, usually in a wheelchair, and gently move him or her to the ground where we have mats covered in warm blankets. We usually remove unnecessary clothing in order to access the child's skin with the various textures and cloths that are incorporated in the session. The room is kept warm for this reason and needs to be prepared at least 30 minutes in advance. The curtains are usually drawn and there is only moderate light in the room so that the child is not inclined to fixate on the light or be disturbed by it.

INDUCTION

We begin with a minute of silence where we all adjust to the space and cease with the prepa-
ratory activities. Following this, the carer gently speaks to the child announcing that he or
she is about to gently massage/tap/rub the fabric/texture onto the child's body or head.
Usually this verbal prompting is more out of respect for the child than an expectation that the
child understands the content. Once each texture has been announced, I begin to play at the
piano.

MUSIC

The musical material is improvised to reflect the texture that is being used. Each improvisation usually lasts approximately five minutes and is followed by two minutes of silence in
order for the child to experience his or her own skin after the cessation of the sensory stimulation.

For lambswool, the music improvisation is gentle and warm – consisting of predictable
harmonic sequences that are cyclic in nature and heavily underpinned by left-hand chords.
The melody is improvised above the chords, usually with a small range of notes and step-
wise intervals. The dynamics are *mezzo forte* and the style is *legato* at a moderate walking pace.

For steel wool (non-prickly) the music improvisation is jagged and unpredictable – the
music is atonal and consists of both clusters and individual notes played across the full range
of the piano. There is no melody, rather there is an emphasis on staccato playing and large
intervallic leaps between different sections of the improvisation. The dynamic is *forte*, but not
overwhelmingly loud. There is no pulse, but the gaps between various fragments are brief
and the texture is continuous.

For the plastic ball the music improvisation is fast moving and constant. The harmony is
represented through arpeggiated chords in the right hand with a bass line being played in
the left hand. Most of the material is in the higher register of the piano and is played *legato*,
but without pedal because the sound is crisp, not blurred. The dynamic is *mezzo piano*, and the
bass line may have a melodic shape at times.

For the wooden beads the music improvisation is flowing and graceful. It is clearly
phrased and relies on melody to outline the shape of the improvisation. The harmonic
framework is rich and includes sevenths and ninths and movement between relative major
and minor harmonies. The dynamics crescendo and diminuendo in line with the phrasing
and the pedal is used to assist in this effect.

For each of these textures, the music is improvised in time with the movements being
produced by the carer and also incorporates any responses by the client, either through
movement or vocalisation.

★ ★ ★

Relaxation with touch / tactile supports and spoken words

Melina Roberts also works with fragile children in palliative care at VSK. She describes a form of relaxation using spoken voice, as well as using recorded music.

I use this approach with the disabled/chronically ill and palliative care children at Very Special Kids (VSK). I often use a blanket and/or touch (hand, feet massage, stroking face, etc.) and voice alone. I describe this as a type of improvised relaxation. I often use story telling or singing the children's names, using soothing singing and lullaby-style vocal improvisation that is very effective. We also have an 'under the sea' themed multi-sensory room at VSK with lights, bubbles, a waterbed and with access to recorded music. When the children are in this room we use recorded music, such as Disney songs, selections from the *Lion King*, or atmospheric music (e.g. Tony O'Connor).

At other times we orientate the child to the items in the room (e.g. fish, octopus) and encourage the child to be aware of these items. We encourage the child to try and relax his or her arms, legs, hands, feet, head and neck using some of the verbal prompts, imagery and story telling [see imagery scripts at the beginning of this chapter]. Pacing is usually very slow with this population.

TYPE OF MUSIC GENERALLY USED

Younger children aged 3 to 8 years

Nursery rhymes, lullabies, *Lion King*, Disney songs, slow-paced Wiggles songs and Hi5.

Older children aged 8 to 12 years

Early rock 'n' roll ballads (e.g. Elvis, Buddy Holly, Roy Orbison, The Beatles), songs like 'Puff the magic dragon', 'The lion sleeps tonight' and slow and repetitive popular ballads on the radio, e.g. 'Beautiful' (Christina Aguilera), 'True colours' (Cyndi Lauper), 'With you' (Jessica Simpson), 'Every time' (Britney Spears), 'Bad day' (Daniel Powter) (or whatever is on the charts).

Teenagers 12–17 years

Chart music with slow tempo, slow popular radio ballads (as listed in the section on children aged 8 to 12 years above), early rock 'n' roll, 1970s' music (e.g. Carole King), Celtic music (e.g. Enya), Luka Bloom, The Corrs, film soundtracks, e.g. *Shrek* and teen movies.

★　★　★

Receptive music therapy for hospitalised adolescent patients

Katerina Stathis describes the relaxation sessions she conducts at CAMHS (Child and Adolescent Mental Health Service at Monash Medical Centre, South Eastern Suburbs of

Melbourne, Australia). Stathis suggests that 'relaxation' takes on a different meaning when working with adolescent-aged clients.

Background

CAMHS is an inpatient and day programme facility that aims to service children and adolescents aged 12 to 18 years with diagnoses of depression, school refusal, eating disorders, anxiety and early onset of psychosis.

Music therapy is included as part of the voluntary treatment programme for the inpatient unit. Sessions run for one hour and are held once a fortnight and usually attract 10 to 16 participants. Due to the varied length of stay with inpatients (usually not more than two weeks), the nature of the group becomes more akin to a 'workshop style' open group aiming to educate the group members about the benefits of using music as a means of coping and to also introduce different styles and cultural concepts and create an understanding of tolerance amongst group members.

PREPARATION

Sessions are held in a large room and group members are seated on large cushions and beanbags placed in a circle prior to group members entering the space. Given that the group is varied in diagnoses, cultural background and tolerance to holistic approaches, sometimes a traditional relaxation induction may not be an appropriate way to either begin a session or help patients relax. It is more appropriate to begin with a casual approach, asking participants to find a spot in the room where they feel most comfortable, and suggest they focus their minds on the music.

MUSIC CHOICE

In one session, the leader chose music from India, which was quite unfamiliar to the group. Initially the unfamiliar sounds were met with curious expressions and disdainful comments. The participants were encouraged to settle into the cushions and beanbags and the session leader again asked participants to find a comfortable position and focus their minds on the music that was playing. After a few minutes, while the music was still playing in the background, the session leader took a ball of string and explained to participants the importance of building connections within the group. The group members were asked to throw the ball of string to another person in the group, but to keep hold of the connection (line of string), both making eye contact and voicing the name of the person to whom they were choosing to connect. This proved to be a successful method in involving all participants as they had choice and control over to whom and how they would connect, and in many situations group members would attempt to make connections with most or all of the group participants. With the added visual effect, almost like a spider web, participants could also visualise where their connections were and began to take ownership of their creation.

As the connectivity process continued the session leader again brought the group participants back to the music by asking them to really listen to the music playing. *Rag Shri with Tintal* is a piece of North Indian classical music and runs for over twenty minutes. The piece begins on a drone instrument or *tambura* (instrument with four strings). A *sarangi* (a bowed stringed instrument) then plays a *raga* for approximately ten minutes before the *tabla-bayan* (a tuned drum) joins in with a *tala* (tintal). The *raga*, a melodic scheme governed by certain traditional rules, provides great freedom for improvisation. The defining and determining notes of the scale and the order in which they should be used give a particular 'colour' to the scheme. The *tala* is a rhythmic arrangement of beats in a cyclical manner that is complete in itself and repetitive (Sorrell and Narayan 1980).

Having established the 'spider web' of connectivity, the group members were asked to lay their connections down on the floor in front of them and choose from a selection of tuned and untuned percussion instruments according to what they would like to play if they were to play an Indian rag and tala. Tone bars in the rag scale consisting of the notes C, Db, E, F, G, Ab and B; a xylophone with the notes C, E, F, G and B; and bells tuned to C and G, were chosen by the 'soloists' of the group. Congas, slit-drums and hand drums were the instruments used by the drummer, and finally, the drone was played on a small keyboard.

This method of group improvisation stemming from a receptive induction proved to work well for the group members. Initially, all group members made a contribution to the improvisation and at times established connections with others in the group, and, as group members became less involved in the music making it appeared that the meditative sound of the notes of the rag scale allowed those who had completed their musical contribution to sit and 'be' with the group as the rag scale provided a structured and grounding aural environment. For the group members who became a little distracted, the process of winding up the spider web of connectivity during the last twenty minutes of the session provided an interesting tactile and visual stimulus for the group members who had finished making their musical contribution.

Finding innovative ways to connect with adolescent-aged clients through 'music making' is a challenge. It is important to note that the adolescents are at an age of questioning and discovery about the world around them, developing their own insights, often far beyond their years. By being completely honest and truthful about trying new ideas, the group was accepting and cooperative. And they seemed to enjoy the unconventional style of music making.[1]

★ ★ ★

Relaxation and receptive music therapy in the classroom

Relaxation may be used for child clients in the classroom context for the following therapeutic goals:

1.   to relieve tension and stress

2.   to educate children about becoming calm when they are overactive

3.   to provide time-out from concentrating on learning tasks

4.   to introduce children to creative thinking in the form of imagery and fantasy and engage their imagination

5.   to provide pleasure.

Relaxation may be incorporated into a music and movement programme (Robbins and Robbins 1988; Wigram and Weekes 1983), where the music therapist is co-therapist with a physiotherapist or special education teacher. The relaxation segment may occur at the end of a music and movement session, to allow the children to calm down before going to the next part of the programme.

SETTING UP THE ROOM

Relaxation as part of a music and movement session is likely to be in a large room, where there are soft mats on the floor. Children are encouraged to find a comfortable space for themselves in the room and to relax on the mats or cushions.

Relaxation can also be carried out in a regular classroom, with children resting their heads on folded arms across the tops of tables or desks.

LIGHT/DARK

Drawing curtains, or closing blinds across windows can reduce the light in the room. However, some children are afraid of the dark, therefore the level of light/dark needs to be monitored by the children's wishes.

The relaxation inductions mentioned above for hospitalised children are also appropriate in the classroom situation. A major difference, however, is that the classroom involves a group of children and it can be difficult to manage a large group of noisy children.

PREPARATION/FINDING A PLACE

The preparation phase of the relaxation session needs more time in the classroom context. The following preparation is based on Rickard's (1992) book on *Relaxation for Children*.

> We are going to have some quiet time now, when we'll be relaxing our bodies and also listening to some music. First of all, find a place in the room where you can make your space…where you can be by yourself for a little while…make sure you won't be touching other children in your own space… (*When the children have found a place in the room, begin with stretching*) now, let's do some stretching…first of all reach your arms over your heads and stretch up high…as high as you can go…feel how your back and your spine get longer and longer as you stretch way up to the sky…now stretch over to one side…and now to the other side, giving your body a big stretch…and now, let's give your body a big shake…shaking your head, and your shoulders, and your arms and your hands…shake, shake, shake, so your body starts to tingle. And now shake out your legs,

one at a time…shake one leg, and the foot, and change legs, and shake the other leg and foot… And now let's get settled in your space where you can relax on the floor on the mat…this is your own space so make sure you have got room around you, and you won't be touching another child/student. This is a time for you to relax your body and have quiet time with some music…let your arms and your legs be still now, and let your body feel floppy and relaxed.

Inductions, visualisations and longer scripts from earlier in the chapter may be used if appropriate to the age range and behavioural and cognitive functioning level of the children. Children with special needs may need language that is simpler, and the language may need to be changed to suit the children's cognitive and/or physical level of functioning.

MUSIC CHOICE
Music selections listed on p.70 are suitable for relaxation sessions in the classroom.

VOICE QUALITY
The same principles of voice quality, tone and pacing apply in the classroom, as with hospitalised children. However when leading group relaxation sessions there is an additional skill required – projecting the voice.

VOICE PROJECTION
When leading relaxation sessions (or segments) with a group of children, it is important to project the voice so that all children can hear the therapist clearly. When leading a relaxation session with an individual child the voice can be softer, but for a group the therapist needs to project the voice so that each member of the group can hear, but without becoming loud. This takes skill. It is possible to project the voice while keeping it relatively quiet. One helpful technique is to project the voice to the child who is furthest away from the therapist, so that all the children between will hear clearly.

Examples from clinical practice
Emily Shanahan is a registered music therapist who works at a special school in Melbourne, for children who have physical and intellectual disabilities. She explains how a relaxation session was introduced at the school.

BACKGROUND
The following vignette details my experiences in working with a group of five young students in their first year at a specialist school. Three students are diagnosed on the autistic spectrum, two have ADHD and an intellectual disability, and all have a mild to moderate language delay.

Relaxation has become an integral component of the music therapy sessions for this group of 4- to 5-year-olds, though it has taken many months for the routine and the activities to work effectively. Initial relaxation attempts seemed futile; students were fidgety and easily distracted, often persisting with their self-stimulatory behaviours such as rocking from side to side or flicking their hands before their eyes, and they were rarely able to lie down independently for more than a couple of seconds. There was barely a calm moment during the relaxation for students to listen.

After a few sessions we began changing the content of the session, focusing more on sensory integration by using music and movement to assist students in developing a better understanding of themselves and their environment. In consultation with an occupational therapist, we incorporated more movement-based activities such as spinning, rocking, jumping, rolling and swinging. These activities were not only highly motivating for the students but also very effective in enabling the students to focus, attend and interact during the sessions.

PREPARATION

Incorporating these activities made an enormous difference to the success of the relaxation. There are also a number of physical considerations we implemented in preparation for relaxation.

1. Initially we used a board-maker timetable of pictures detailing the session's order of activities. The pictures were useful as cues to the children that it was time to get ready for relaxation. Once the students were familiar with the routine the pictures were abandoned.

2. Personal space is very important, as young students enjoy climbing over each other and this is definitely not conducive to relaxation, so individual mats on the floor or pillows are essential. We also use individual heavy blankets that not only denote a space for each child but also provide a weight and warmth that the students find calming.

3. We usually dim the lights and shut the curtains. Initially one student was terrified by this change to the room, and so we introduced slow-moving coloured lights that were not only effective in distracting the student from her fear, but also transfixed the attention of the other students if they were not able to settle. The coloured lights are no longer needed.

4. On occasions when students were having difficulty settling we also incorporated gentle joint compression by gently squeezing wrists, elbows and ankles. The use of touch and proprioceptive input stabilised the students who were experiencing sensory processing difficulties.

MUSIC CHOICE

After many weeks of preparing the students for relaxation, the music could be introduced. Live music is always very effective because it can be tailored specifically to the students, matching their energy closely. Improvisations are created with tubular bells and an ocean drum, improvised piano, and improvised guitar with gentle vocalisations and simple lyrics. The students are now familiar with improvised music and are able to relax to it. A wide range of recorded music, from classical through to contemporary didgeridoo, is effective.

Though diverse, there are underlying features in all of this music that promote the best level of relaxation for the students. It is important that the music is relaxed in its nature, slow in tempo (50–70 bpm), soft in dynamics and simple in harmonic structure and form.

Relaxation time now lasts between five and ten minutes and is an effective way to re-focus the students' attention at the end of a session.

Other ideas for relaxation with children

Children like new experiences, so additional ideas for relaxation include:

1.   *'Parachute' stimulus* Use the canopy of a parachute (these can be purchased from army disposal shops) to create a gentle breeze. Three to four staff members are needed to assist, depending on the size of the canopy. The children lie on the floor and the staff gently raise and lower the canopy to create a gentle breeze. Use music to parallel the timing of the 'breeze'. A script might accompany this activity, for example A Pine Forest (see page 71).

      Precaution Some children may feel frightened if they see the canopy descending on them. Be sure to give the children the option of lying face down or face up.

      The canopy of the parachute can generate a strong breeze (depending on its size) and teachers may need to monitor that it doesn't become too breezy, otherwise the purpose of relaxation will be lost.

2.   *Silk material stimulus* A length of silk material can serve the same purpose as the parachute canopy and the method of application is similar, with conducive music. This may also be easier to manage with fewer staff.

★ ★ ★

Relaxation for older adolescents

The following relaxation induction, adapted from Crook (1988), is a particularly effective induction in that it leads to a deeply relaxed place in which Crook focuses on the person feeling good about him or herself. In a deeply relaxed state it affirms a deeper sense of oneself, and this is important for older adolescents from about the age of 15. It is a longer induction, but the words Crook employs are very positive. As before, the ellipses indicate a short pause between phrases.

PREPARATION

The therapist needs to introduce the experience by preparing the client physically and emotionally for what is going to happen. The preparation will depend on the context of the therapy session, and on whether the adolescent (or group) can relate to the induction and can concentrate for 30 minutes and more. The following preparation script may be suitable for older adolescents:

> Find a place that is comfortable for you (in the bed, or chair or on a mat on the floor). Take some time to get yourself really comfortable in the bed, or chair or mat. If you are lying on a bed or on the floor, lie on your back, so that your body can relax easily. Try and make your body as balanced as you can, so that you are lying straight, without bending your body. When you are in the best position allow your eyes to close, so you block out any annoying distractions (e.g. light or the movement of other people). Feel the support of the bed, chair or mat for your body. Feel the support for your head and shoulders, your back and hips, your arms and hands, your legs and feet, and begin to let your body sink into the bed/chair/mat.

MUSIC

The music can be started at the beginning of the imagery script and be allowed to continue to play beyond the end of the imagery. The volume should be kept low so that the adolescent can hear the therapist's voice reading the script. Familiar, self-selected music is the most effective, given the important relationship between identity and music preference in adolescence. If reading a script over the music, only instrumental music is appropriate. Celtic music, meditative or instrumental trance music is suitable for this age group.

RELAXATION INDUCTION SCRIPT (BASED ON CROOK 1988)

> Become aware of your breathing. Feel what happens when you breathe in...and breathe out... Feel the flow of your breath entering your body and leaving it again, just like a wave washing up onto a beach, and then back down into the sea. As you breathe out, you let go and relax...and allow this relaxed feeling to become stronger and stronger, deeper and deeper... Just as the wave washes the sand down into the ocean, your out breath washes the tensions (or pain) from your body... Now you begin to feel very light, with soft breathing helping you to relax more and more...
>
> Now try to feel your feet and toes...curl your toes under tightly...and now let them unwind, and feel your feet relaxing...feel the tension leaving your feet...your feet feel warm and relaxed. Feel the lower part of your legs, between your knees and ankles...and now as you breathe out, let the lower part of your legs relax...and relax your knees... Now feel the top part of your legs, and the big muscles in the top part of your legs...let them relax...so your legs feel warm and relaxed... Now feel through your hips to the lower part of your back...let your hips sink into the bed/chair/mat...

And now become aware of your back and spine…imagine your spine in the very centre of your back…imagine your spine stretching out…and with your next breath try to stretch out your spine as far as it will go…and then let it relax… Become aware again of your breath and notice how your breath goes right into your back…as you breathe out next time, let your back really relax…let it sink into the bed (or chair, or mat)… Now feel your shoulders and the back of your neck…and as you breathe out next time let all the tension (or pain) flow out of your shoulders…and allow the tension (or pain) to melt away, so that your shoulders are beautifully relaxed… Try to imagine warm water flowing all around your shoulders and the back of your neck, and notice how relaxed they are…

Feel your arms relaxing now…and your hands…and your fingers and thumbs… Be aware of the softness of your breathing…feel the breathing in your chest, and as you breathe out next time, let all the tension flow out from your chest, so it is warm and very relaxed… Feel your breathing right down to your stomach, and now allow your stomach to relax…easily and gently… Feel your breath through your throat, and allow your throat to relax… And now relax your jaw and the muscles around your mouth… Relax your tongue and your cheeks… Notice the flow of air as you breathe through your nose, and feel the gentle breath as it passes down your throat and into your chest and stomach…your breathing has become very soft and very relaxed… And now relax your eyes and the area around your eyes… Feel your forehead, and let your forehead relax…

And now breathe right into the top part of your head and allow the top of your head to relax and be still…your mind is relaxed…floating…very quiet…

Feel your whole body now, deeply relaxed, warm and calm… Feel how peaceful your body is now… Feel how calm your body is now… Feel how comfortable and *good it is to be you…*

ENDING THE RELAXATION SESSION

Depending on the context of the relaxation session, the adolescent (or group) may need to be returned to a non-altered state. The therapist can say:

> The music has finished now…become aware of your body lying on the bed/in the chair/on the mat…become aware of the sounds around you…and the others in the group…give your body a stretch…stretch your arms…your legs…and take a big breath and breathe it out…and in your own time sit up.

There might be a discussion of the relaxation, or the adolescent (or group) might do a drawing about the experience. In discussing the session the therapist might then ask what the relaxation was like for each person. Were they aware of the music, and was it helpful? Did they feel relaxed?

Relaxation for adolescents in a therapeutic community programme

Another effective method of relaxation for adolescent-aged clients incorporates a large flickering candle. The session format described below was introduced for a group of older adolescents/adults (aged 16 to 25 years) with personality disorders living in a therapeutic community. The group members were experienced in group psychotherapy, were capable of concentrating for an hour and were not cognitively impaired.

PREPARATION

The relaxation session is held in a large room that was darkened, by drawing curtains or half-closing blinds. The clients are asked to help in darkening the room, so that they have control over the balance of light and darkness.

Clients are invited to find a place in the room where they feel comfortable, and to choose any of the soft cushions or mats placed randomly in the room. Allowing the clients to find a space of their own is an important strategy – it allows a client to either sit or lie down and it allows the option of being alone or with the group.

In the centre of the room is a large candle placed on a plate. One client is asked to light the candle and the therapist starts the music. Often the clients talk and laugh, but gradually the effect of the music and the mesmerising effect of the flickering candle flame evokes quietness. Some clients may lie down and gradually the talking and laughing stops.

At the end of the music, the therapist quietly comments that the music has finished and invites a person from the group to blow out the candle. There is a group discussion about the relaxation and the effect of the music.

Music selections

The following music selections are conducive to the 'flickering candle' relaxation:

Tony Scott, *Music for Zen Meditation* (Verve 817-209-2)

Celtic Odyssey (Narada 8361-63912-2)

Celtic Moods (Virgin Records 72438-44951-2)

Celtic Twilight (Hearts of Space 0-25041-11042-6)

Further reading

Crook, R. (1988) *Relaxation for Children*. Katoomba: Second Back Row Press.

O'Neill, C. (n/d) *Relax*. London: Child's Play (International).

Rickard, J. (1992) *Relaxation for Children*. Melbourne: ACER.

Note

1   Stathis acknowledges Michalis Tobler and Joseph Moreno for ideas used in the session that were inspired by a presentation at the eleventh World Congress of Music Therapy, Brisbane, Australia, 2005.

Chapter 4

Receptive Methods and
Relaxation for Adults

Introduction

Relaxation is used with adult clients in many different contexts, either as a therapeutic technique in itself, or within a music therapy session where other methods are incorporated, such as singing or improvising. Relaxation is a component of other techniques such as listening to music, imaging to music, or in the Bonny Method of Guided Imagery and Music. Relaxation inductions can be short or long depending on the context and the therapeutic aim.

In this chapter, different types of relaxation inductions will be described. These can be models on which to build a repertoire of favourite inductions. Each induction is written out in full to get a sense of the pattern and repetition that is useful in inducing a relaxed state in a patient or client. These inductions have been developed and honed over many years of clinical practice and teaching, and some aspects have been drawn from training in Guided Imagery and Music (GIM), and ideas from Bonny and Savary (1973), Fleming (1990–1992) and Ventre (1990–1992). The Progressive Muscle Relaxation (PMR) induction is based on Jacobson's *Progressive Relaxation* (1938), and the autogenic inductions based on Schultz and Luthe (1959).

In the first part of the chapter, the theoretical framework and specific skills will be described. In the second section six different inductions are explained in a step-by-step outline, including the preparation, induction, music, return to the alert state and verbal processing. Throughout the chapter various terms will be used to describe the recipients of these methods: patients (for hospitalised adults), clients (for people in health centres, or attending a private practice) or residents (for those in residential care, such as nursing homes). These terms are used interchangeably.

Theoretical framework

Relaxation inductions with music are used in different contexts, where the client (or client group) may be experiencing a relaxation session:

1.   in bed (in hospital or at home)

2.   sitting in a chair (in hospital, home, nursing home or health centre), or

3.   lying on the floor (in health or community centres, or an outpatients unit of a
      hospital).

Relaxation is a vital skill to be practised by clients for physical and mental health. Some of
the benefits of relaxation reported in the literature are as follows:

In medical settings, music and relaxation may:

- reduce stress and tension (Bruscia 1998a; Hanser 1996, 1999b; Kibler and
  Rider 1983; Pelletier 2004)

- reduce anxiety prior to a medical procedure (Metzler and Berman 1991;
  Saperston 1999)

- alleviate pain (Rider 1985) and pain intensity during debridement
  procedures (Barker 1991)

- regulate breathing (Hanser 1996, 1999b).

In mental health settings (based on clinical experience), music and relaxation may:

- reduce stress, agitation and anxiety

- help orientation by focusing the client's attention on the body and
  breathing.

In aged care facilities, music and relaxation can help to:

- reduce agitation in residents who have dementia

- provide a peaceful experience

- enhance the experience of listening to music.

In group settings (e.g. in the community), music and relaxation offers:

- a shared and quiet experience within the group

- an opportunity for group members to learn to relax so that they may use the
  technique at home

- enhanced well-being.

Establishing an environment that is conducive to relaxation with music

There are four major factors that are essential to a successful relaxation and music session,
and these factors apply to all contexts:

1. A comfortable position for the patient / client / resident

Relaxation can be effective while sitting in a comfortable chair, lying in bed, sitting against the wall or lying on a comfortable mat on the floor. The operative word is 'comfort'. The client should remove anything that restricts breathing, for example a tight belt or a tie, and shoes. The chair, bed, or floor must provide a cushioned comfort for the client – it needs to be soft and there needs to be adequate support for the body with pillows to prop the patient in bed or in a chair, and soft pillows to place under the head to support the neck. Finally the client needs to be warm. In an effective relaxation session the client's breathing can slow down considerably and the temperature of the body may drop significantly. Therefore the client may need a warm blanket to maintain body heat. In addition the blanket can provide a psychological blanket, in that the client may feel more protected and less vulnerable if covered. This is particularly true if the client is lying on the floor, as some people feel very vulnerable in this position if uncovered. Even on a hot day, a light sheet or cotton spread can be applied so that the person feels more psychologically protected.

2. Light and dark

In most contexts the ceiling lights need to be turned off completely or at least dimmed. One of the most invasive distractions to relaxation is the flickering of fluorescent lights. Not only are they very bright, they can also pulse. Therefore lights should be turned off. However, many clients will feel unsettled by total darkness, so some filtered light needs to be present. Some lights can be dimmed effectively, or else side lamps can be used to light the room. The therapist, too, must have adequate light in order to manipulate the music equipment (if using recorded music). In some settings it might be appropriate to draw the curtains in the room to darken the room to an appropriate level.

At the end of the relaxation session it is important to prepare the client for a change in the brightness of the room. The therapist might say, 'I am going to turn the lights on again now and you may wish to shield your eyes.' Alternatively the curtains can be opened again, slowly and softly, gradually letting in more light.

3. Uninterrupted space

In busy hospitals it is unlikely that the therapist can find a space that is uninterrupted. Sometimes a therapist provides a relaxation session for a client who is in a ward of four to six patients, and the therapist may only be able to draw a curtain around the bed of the patient. In other contexts it may be feasible to place a sign on the door that says 'RELAXATION SESSION IN PROGRESS. PLEASE DO NOT ENTER' (or something similar). Remember to remove this sign from the door at the end of the session as other co-workers will be annoyed if the sign stays on the door for several hours and no-one is in the room.

The therapist needs to explain to new clients that this is a time to be silent, and to not disturb others (if it is a group context). The therapist may suggest that agitated clients sit close to the therapist rather than disturb others in the group (this might be appropriate, for example, when working with patients in an acute mental health setting).

4. *Monitoring the music reproduction*

When using music as part of a group relaxation session, the volume of the music should be heard evenly throughout the room. This means placing the speakers in strategic positions to maximise the music being heard easily by everyone in the group. For individual clients the CD player may be at the person's head, or feet, or even to one side. The best position should be found before commencing the relaxation induction. The therapist should also check that the equipment is working properly and that the power is switched on! Therapists tell unfortunate stories of carefully preparing a client for a relaxation induction and then finding that the CD player had no CD, or that the power was turned off, or that there was no CD player in the room! So always make sure the equipment is in good working condition.

Therapeutic skills for facilitating a relaxed state in the client

The most important skill in conducting a relaxation session is voice quality, which differs between a) placing a client in a relaxed state, and b) bringing the client out of a relaxed state. Another skill required in conducting relaxation sessions with adult clients is facilitating discussion (verbal processing) at the end of the relaxation to explore and understand the client's experience. These skills are explained in more detail below.

Voice quality

In order to facilitate relaxation for a client, the therapist must have an appropriate voice quality. As mentioned in the previous chapter, music therapists should have a well-modulated voice quality, having developed vocal skill and technique during training, and are comfortable using the voice in many different contexts, including singing songs and vocalising freely. An effective relaxation induction for an individual patient or group is dependent on voice tone, projection, dynamic range and pacing.

1. VOICE TONE

The tone of voice needs to be mid-range, not too high, not too low, and non-seductive. Given that the relaxation induction is necessarily repetitive, it is important to keep the tone of voice fairly constant, so that the quality of the voice is effective in inducing trust in the process of relaxation, and engenders a sense of safety. A high-pitched voice, for example, might convey a sense of insecurity or inexperience, and a low voice may sound gruff, or might conjure up images of an authoritarian figure. A mid-range timbre therefore avoids those associations.

2. VOICE PROJECTION

While keeping the voice at mid-range, it is also important to project the voice, particularly in group sessions, so that each client can hear the therapist clearly. With an individual client the voice can be softer, but for a group the therapist needs to project the voice so that each member of the group can hear, without the need for the voice becoming loud. This takes skill. It is possible to project the voice while keeping it relatively quiet. One helpful technique is to project the voice to the person furthest away while still speaking quietly. In that way, all clients will hear clearly.

3. DYNAMICS

In a normal speaking context, voice dynamics change as important words are emphasised in a sentence, to give the sentence meaning. But for an effective relaxation induction the dynamics of the voice need to be flatter. Dynamic changes in the voice may keep the client wondering what will be said next, whereas the intention is to convey a more stable tone, not varying dynamics as in normal speech. Having said this, it is important that the voice is not unnaturally flat either.

4. SPEAKING PACE

It is difficult to relax if the therapist is speaking too fast, so a slower pace, with repetition in the instructions given, will enable the client to relax more easily. If the energy level of the client or group is high, and the clients are quite active, it can be helpful to start the induction at a faster pace to match the energy level of the clients, then gradually slow the pace down, to match the intended relaxed state.

5. MODEL THE BREATH

When directing a client's attention to their breathing, the therapist can model this audibly, e.g. 'Breathing in... (audibly take in a breath)...and breathing out... (audibly let the breath out).'

Bringing the client out of the relaxed state

At the end of the relaxation induction the client(s) must be returned to a non-altered state of awareness. To do this the voice quality must be different from that at the start.

Tone The tone has a slight 'edge' to it and there is greater dynamic variance.

Volume Volume is gradually increased, initially matching the client's state at the end of the relaxation experience with a soft voice, but then gradually making the voice louder to help the client(s) return to a more alert state.

Dynamics Increase the natural inflection in the voice, to help orientate the person back to an alert state.

The script The typical script at the end of the relaxation is:

> The music has come to an end. Notice how relaxed your body is feeling and remember this feeling. You can allow your body to relax in this way at other times. And now become aware of your body (on the mat/chair/bed). Begin to move your arms and legs. Take in a deep breath (*model this audibly*) and let all the breath out (*model the exhalation of the breath audibly*). Stretch your arms and legs and gently stretch your whole body.

Incorporating the music selection

There are two options for incorporating the music in the relaxation session. The first option is to have the music playing quietly in the background while the therapist speaks the induction. The second option is to present the induction in full and then start the music when the client(s) have achieved a relaxed state and are receptive.

The first option would be more appropriate when there is limited time available, or when it is part of a longer music therapy session and other methods are being used, or if clients are unfamiliar with the relaxation process. The second option would be appropriate for longer relaxation sessions where the intention is to place more focus on the induction itself before moving on to the music experience.

In the inductions that follow, music may be used either during the induction or after the induction is completed, whichever is appropriate to the clinical situation. In this text, the music is placed at the end of the induction, but the option is always open.

Verbal processing of the relaxation experience

It is always important to facilitate a discussion of the client's experience of the relaxation session. When relaxing with eyes closed, the client's attention inevitably turns inward, to thoughts, feelings and possibly memories. It is not possible to know what the person is thinking or feeling during the relaxation, therefore verbal processing is normally essential. Once the client (or group) has returned to an alert state, the therapist can encourage discussion, for example: 'And now let's spend some time talking about what that was like for you… How did the relaxation feel?' It is important to let members of the group express positive and also negative responses. Some clients who have not experienced relaxation before may not feel very relaxed, and the therapist can comment that often the person needs several experiences to feel the benefit.

Other negative comments may be expressed if the client's body is in an awkward position, and feels stiff or painful. Others may have been distracted by unwanted thoughts, or mentally making a list of things to do. In each case the therapist should listen attentively and reinforce that it takes practice for the relaxation to be fully beneficial.

Music selection

There are many options for choosing music that is suitable for relaxation. The most effective is music that the client enjoys, in the preferred genre and style. In fact, research indicates that music and relaxation is more effective when the music is self-chosen (Saperston 1999). Adult clients can often suggest music they would like to listen to, however this music may not be available, or the client may find that the preferred music doesn't sound the same in a hospital context compared to the comfort of the home environment. Inevitably the music therapist may need to choose the music, and in making the choice takes into consideration the age of the client, the level of energy, the physical health state and mood of the client.

For short relaxation inductions, a short selection of music is appropriate (three to seven minutes in duration). For longer relaxation inductions a longer selection of music (10–15 minutes in length) is appropriate. A list of suitable music is given at the end of the chapter. The list will always require updating as new music is released.

Relaxation inductions

In the next section a variety of relaxation inductions are presented in full. Although each induction may seem at times repetitious when you see it printed on the page, it is this very repetition that is the crux of a well-presented relaxation induction.

Each induction is presented in full. The words can, however, be changed depending on the client age, physical state, the context, and what feels comfortable to you.

Note

If you are not experienced in giving relaxation inductions, it is a good idea to record yourself presenting an induction in full, as if you are guiding a group of clients. When you have finished recording, place yourself in a comfortable position, and listen back to your own induction. It is important to do this in a position that is conducive to relaxation (a quiet place, comfortable mat on the floor, or a bed, or a comfortable chair). As you listen to your own voice notice the quality of your voice and the pacing of the induction. This is the most successful way to teach yourself how to give an induction.

The following inductions are presented in full:

1.   Short relaxation

2.   Structured/count-down induction

3.   Autogenic-type induction

4.   Colour induction

5.   'Light' inductions

6.   Progressive Muscle Relaxation (PMR) (based on Jacobson 1938).

Short relaxation

Short relaxations are appropriate in many contexts, for example to help a client settle if she or he is anxious or in pain, or if the client has a short attention span, e.g. in early stage dementia. Short relaxation inductions are also suitable when the client is sitting in a chair, either because lying on the floor is not appropriate, or because there is not enough available space. The short induction is suitable for many different groups, and offers a basic, systematic process for relaxing the body. This example is designed for the client sitting in the chair, but can be adapted for a patient in a hospital bed. As before the ellipses (…) indicate a brief pause between the phrases.

Preparation

First of all take a few moments to get as comfortable as possible in the chair (or bed). (*The therapist may need to support the client's body using pillows as support.*) As you get comfortable try to make your body symmetrical…feet on the floor, arms either in lap or loosely at each side… And now feel the support of the chair for your neck… shoulders…back…hips…and under the legs. Allow your body to sink into the chair, knowing that you are physically supported.

The induction

And now turn your focus to your breathing. Taking in a deep breath and gently allowing the breath to be released, feeling any tension flow out of the body. (*Repeat the phrase 'Taking in a deep breath and gently releasing any tension…', for each statement.*)

from the face…through the forehead, cheeks and jaw

from the neck and shoulders

from the arms and hands

from the chest and stomach

from the back, particularly the lower back

from the hips

from the legs

from the feet

Keeping the body relaxed, allow the music to flow through it and bring comfort. (*Start the music.*)

Music

The music selection may be started after the induction has finished. A short selection (approximately five to seven minutes) is appropriate for clients seated in chairs, or in other contexts where a short relaxation is needed. See the list of suggested selections at the end of the chapter.

Return to alert state

Using voice tone and pacing (as mentioned above), the return can be quite short:

The music has come to an end…stay with the relaxed feeling, knowing you can return to this restful state again…begin to become aware of your body…you might like to gently stretch your legs and your arms…take in a deep breath and fully exhale it (*the therapist can model this audibly*)…give your body a big stretch. (*The therapist can model this stretch, including the audible breathing.*)

Verbal processing

For a short relaxation session you might simply ask, 'What was that like for you?' (There may be a period of silence before clients can answer, as it can be difficult to activate speech when still very relaxed.) Other questions the therapist may put to the client or group are:

- Did you feel relaxed?
- Where in your body did you feel the relaxation?
- What was the music like for you?

Structured/count-down relaxation induction

Context

Some clients need an induction that makes clear what the client is meant to do. The structured induction is suitable for clients who might be confused (e.g. people who have mental illness or are in early stage dementia). It is helpful to give information at the start so that the person understands what will happen.

Preparation

Find a comfortable place in the chair/bed/on a mat on the floor. Find the place that is most comfortable for you. [For groups] While we are involved in the relaxation session please remember not to talk, as this disturbs other people. [For vulnerable clients] If you want to open your eyes at any time, that's OK – you might try closing them again. I will count down from five to one, and with each number you will feel more relaxed. At the end of the session I will reverse the counting, to help you return to an alert state. As soon as you feel comfortable you can close your eyes. This helps block out distracting light, and it helps focus your attention on your breathing, and this helps you to relax. [This information gives a factual reason for closing eyes and can help vulnerable people feel that they are safe and secure.]

Beginning now with the count-down:

Five – be aware of your breathing…notice the breath flowing in and out of your body.

Four – beginning to slow down the breathing now…taking slightly bigger and deeper breaths…feeling your body begin to relax

Three – as you take deeper breaths, begin to notice how your chest fills out with the breath, and as you breathe out how the chest and shoulders fall.

Two – As you breathe out again be aware of releasing any tension in your body and allow the tension to flow out of the body.

One – feeling more deeply relaxed…letting go of any tension…allowing the breath to flow through the body easily, bringing a sense of comfort and relaxation to your whole body… (*At this point start to play the music.*)

Music

The music selection should be short (about five to seven minutes) for clients who are confused or disorientated, or have short concentration spans. For clients who can concentrate for longer periods of time, the music selection might be ten minutes. See the suggestions at the end of the chapter.

Return to alert state

The music has come to an end…begin to stretch your legs and arms…take in a deep breath and exhale…begin to move your arms and legs and have a big stretch.

Verbal processing

The therapist may ask about each client's experience, as for the short relaxation above.

Autogenic-type relaxation induction

The autogenic induction means that the control of the relaxation is with the client, hence auto-genic (the genesis of relaxation is with the self). This induction is useful in many contexts – for groups and for individual adult clients. It is appropriate for clients who are able to concentrate and follow the instructions and can mentally focus on different parts of the body.

In this induction the client may be sitting in a chair, or sitting on the floor leaning up against the wall, or lying prone on the floor. Many adult clients feel vulnerable lying prone on the floor, and it is important to offer people a choice so that they are comfortable. Obviously the induction is more effective if people are lying on a soft bed or mat, or thick carpet. In group contexts, people may prefer sitting on the floor and leaning against the wall, but this limits the experience of relaxation because the body has to support itself in an upright position. This is also true for those who prefer to sit in a chair. It is important not to insist that the person lie on the floor, but better to adjust the induction to the fact that people are in this less than optimal position, and accept that it is more important to engender trust in the process.

Preparation

Find a comfortable place on the floor (or leaning against the wall, or in the chair). Feel the support of the floor (or the wall or the chair).

Feel the support for your head and shoulders…

Feel the support for your back, and for the length of your spine from the top of the spine through to the lower part of the spine...

Feel the support for your arms and hands...

Feel the support for your hips and legs...

Feel your body completely supported [this affirms that the body is physically safe].

Allow yourself to sink into the floor (or chair), beginning to let go of any tension held in the body. Allow the eyes to close gently...

The autogenic induction

And now become aware of your breathing... Notice what your breathing is like... It might be quite fast, or irregular... Notice the movement in your chest as you take in the breath, and as you release all the air from your chest... Notice how your body is feeling...you might feel your body is lighter, or it might be heavier...both of these feelings are fine...gradually allow yourself to take deeper breaths...gently taking in the breath...gently releasing the breath...allowing the breath to fall into its own natural pattern... As you continue to breathe deeply, become aware of the muscles in your right foot...relax those muscles, so that your right foot feels gently relaxed... Become aware of the muscles of your right leg...relax those muscles, so that your right leg feels gently relaxed... Become aware of the muscles of your left foot...relax those muscles, so that your foot is relaxed... Become aware of the muscles of your left leg...relax those muscles, so that your leg is relaxed... Become aware of the muscles through your hips and pelvis and through to the lower back...relax those muscles, so that this part of your body is relaxed... Become aware of the muscles of your stomach...relax those muscles, so that your stomach is relaxed... Become aware of the muscles in your diaphragm and chest...relax those muscles, so that your chest is relaxed... Become aware of the muscles of your shoulders, across the shoulders and the back of the shoulders...relax those muscles, so that your shoulders are relaxed... Become aware of the muscles of your arms through to your hands, and fingers and thumbs...relaxing those muscles, so that your arms and hands are relaxed. Become aware again of the muscles of your shoulders and, moving up now into the neck and throat...relax those muscles, so that your neck is relaxed... Become aware of the muscles of the face...the jaw, across the nose, the muscles of your eyes and behind your eyes, the forehead, to the top of your head...relax those muscles, so that your face is relaxed... And now feel the body fully and deeply relaxed...and now become aware of the music...

This induction can be given in reverse order: from head down to the feet.

Another example of an autogenic relaxation induction is outlined on page 106.

Music

A selection of music that is about 10 to 15 minutes in length is appropriate for the longer autogenic relaxation. See suggested music selections at the end of the chapter.

Bringing the client back to an 'alert' state

The music has finished… Become aware of the sounds around you…the sounds inside the room, and the sounds outside of the room… Become aware of the room we are in… (and the people with you in the room)… Begin to move your body, stretch out your arms…and legs… Take a deep breath…and release (*the therapist might model an audible release of breath*)… And when you are ready, open your eyes…

Verbal processing of the experience

In a group setting the therapist may ask about each client's experience of the relaxation, whether they could relax, and whether anything prevented them from relaxing fully. Typical difficulties might include being uncomfortable on the floor (next time they might use more cushions, or bring something soft to lie on). Some might have difficulty in stopping the mind from thinking about other things (next time they might be aware of the thoughts and just let them go – see also the 'Mindfulness' approach (page 115).

Colour induction

Adding a colour to the autogenic induction above increases the client's awareness of his or her body. It is interesting to note what colour each person chooses, as the colour can indicate the client's emotional state. This induction requires that a colour be breathed into the body. It may not be suitable for people who have difficulty concentrating or difficulty in breathing.

Preparation

Get yourself into a comfortable position…loosen anything that restricts your breathing (belts, tight collars, etc.)… Feel the support of the mat/floor for your body…feel the support for the head, shoulders, the spine and back…the arm and hands…the hips, legs and feet. Allow yourself to sink into the mat/floor and begin to let go of any tension held in the body… Allow the eyes to close gently…

Become aware of your breathing…it may be quite fast and irregular…just notice the pattern of your breathing, following the breath into your body and its release from your body… Gradually allow yourself to take deeper breaths…gently taking in the breath…gently releasing the breath… allowing the breath to fall into its own natural pattern…

The colour induction

As you continue to breathe deeply, bring to your mind a colour that you would like to take into your body… Take a moment to think of this colour…it may be a colour that resonates with how you feel right now…or it could be a colour that you would like to bring into your body right now…take a few moments to think of the colour…notice the shade of the colour, notice its texture… We will be taking this colour through the different parts of the body…allow the colour to change if it needs to… And now take that colour down to both feet… Allow the colour to be drawn in through the soles of both feet, so that the colour fills both feet to the ankles… Now allow the colour to move gently through both legs…through the lower legs…knees…upper part of the legs…to the hips…allowing the colour to bring the body what it needs (*it might be relaxation, or calmness, but it might also be energy, or a feeling of aliveness – for this reason leave 'what it needs' open*)… Now allow the colour to move through the hips and through to the lower back…allow the colour to fill this part of your body…and bring to the body whatever it needs… Now allow the colour to move through to the stomach…allow the colour to fill this part of your body…taking in as much as it needs (*for internal organs suggest 'as much as it needs' so that the person is not overwhelmed with colour*)… Allow the colour to move to the chest…gently taking in as much colour as is comfortable…allowing the colour to bring whatever the body needs… Take the colour into the back…allowing the colour to move gently through the back, bringing whatever the body needs… Allow the colour to move through the shoulders…and down the arms…through the wrists to the hands…and the fingers…and thumbs… allowing the colour to bring what the body needs… And now take the colour upwards from the shoulders…letting the colour move gently through the neck and the throat…into the jaw…across the cheeks…into the eyes…behind the eyes…and up into the forehead…to the very top of your head… And now feel the colour through the whole body…if there is an area that needs more colour, taking the colour there now…and now turning your attention to the music.

This induction can be given in reverse order: from head down to the feet.

Bringing the client back to an 'alert' state

The music has finished… Become aware of the sounds around you…the sounds inside the room, and the sounds outside of the room… Become aware of the room we are in… (and the people with you in the room)… Begin to move your body, stretch out your arms…and legs… Take a deep breath… (*you might model an audible release of breath*) and when you are ready, open your eyes…

Music
A music selection of about 10–20 minutes is appropriate for this relaxation if the clients are in a comfortable position.

Verbal Processing of the experience (see notes under autogenic relaxation, p. 100)
The therapist might ask about the clients' experience of the relaxation, and whether they could relax, and what parts of the body were most relaxed. The therapist also may ask which colour the clients chose, and how the clients experienced the music, whether it helped or not.

'Light' relaxation inductions

There are two alternative inductions here, which are also autogenic scripts. In the first, the focal point is 'light' that travels through the body, or over the body. The various parts of the body may still be mentioned, as this helps the client to calm all areas of the body. In the second, the radiating light induction, the 'light' radiates from a sense of the centre of the person's self. It can be the 'soul' or the 'core of the self'.

Light induction: Preparation

Get yourself into a comfortable position…loosen anything that restricts your breathing (belts, tight collars, etc.)… Feel the support of the mat/floor for your body…feel the support for the head, shoulders, the spine and back…the arm and hands…the hips, legs and feet. Allow yourself to sink into the mat/floor beginning to let go of any tension held in the body… Allow the eyes to close gently…

Become aware of your breathing…it may be quite fast and irregular…just notice the pattern of your breathing, following the breath into your body and its release from your body…gradually allow yourself to take deeper breaths…gently taking in the breath…gently releasing the breath…allowing the breath to fall into its own natural pattern…

The light induction script

And now bring to your mind a sense of a ball of light…take a moment to allow the image to form in your mind…notice if the ball of light has a colour…allow the ball of light to hover over the top of your head…and as you breathe in next, allow the ball of light to move slowly over your head…allowing the light to fill this part of your body…taking in as much as you need… Allow the ball of light to move slowly and gently through your face and neck…taking in as much of the light as you need…allow the ball of light to move across the shoulders…down the arms…through to the hands…and fingers…to the very tips of the fingers…allow the light to move gently through the chest…taking in as much of the light as is comfortable…sensing the light through the chest, and through to the spine…through the lungs…and stomach…taking as much as you need…through to the pelvis and the lower back…taking as much as you need. Allow the light to move through the legs…the upper parts of the legs…the knees, the lower parts of the legs, to the feet and toes. Feel the glow of the light through your body…and now become aware of the music, and what the music brings to your body…

(*Start music*)

The light induction can also be given as radiating through the body. It brings awareness to the very centre of the person's being. Most often this is the solar plexus point in the centre of the breastbone. However it is important not to assume this as the central point – it may be the centre of the face for one person, or the stomach for another. Therefore the induction leaves the actual site of the 'core of being' open. This induction is not suitable for people who may feel overwhelmed by breathing light into the body. It may not be suitable for people who are physically ill for example, or people who are vulnerable (and may feel overwhelmed by it). It is a powerful induction to use in that it focuses on the person's core being, and can be very empowering for clients when used at the right time. In addition the induction fills the body with light, and for some clients the sensation might cause them to feel literally enlarged or inflated. The phrases 'take in as much as you need', or 'take in as much as is comfortable' are important to guard against feeling overly inflated. The induction is best suited to clients who are experienced in using relaxation inductions, and who can monitor the flow of suggestions.

Radiating light induction: Preparation

Get yourself into a comfortable position...loosen anything that restricts your breathing (belts, tight collars, etc.)... Feel the support of the mat/floor for your body...feel the support for the head, shoulders, the spine and back...the arm and hands...the hips, legs and feet. Allow yourself to sink into the mat/floor beginning to let go of any tension held in the body... Allow the eyes to close gently...

Become aware of your breathing...it may be quite fast and irregular...just notice the pattern of your breathing, following the breath into your body and its release from your body...gradually allow yourself to take deeper breaths...gently taking in the breath...gently releasing the breath...allowing the breath to fall into its own natural pattern...

The radiating light induction script

And now beginning to be aware of the centre part of your being...take a few moments to feel where the centre of your being might be...allow yourself to feel that core part of yourself, the very centre of who you are...take a few moments to sense where this centre is in your body...and when you have found that core place, breathe into that core place, allowing it to become alive...and now imagine a ray of light entering this core part of yourself...allow the light to radiate from the core place, gently filling the area around the core of your being...filling it with as much light as you need...gradually allow the light to radiate from this centre...gradually moving through the areas of the body...moving slowly and gradually through the cells...filling the body with the light of your core being...allow the light to radiate through to the head...the arms, hands and fingers...through to the spine...to the legs and feet...feeling the body filled with light...and now become aware of the music, and bring the music into this core of your being...

(start music)

Music
See suggestions at end of chapter.

Progressive Muscle Relaxation (PMR) (based on Jacobson 1938)

The feature of this induction is that it focuses on physically tensing and releasing the muscle groups throughout the body. This induction may be more successful with clients who prefer instructions. It is also very useful for clients who have a high degree of energy, and for whom lying on the floor trying to imagine their muscles relaxing might be difficult. PMR is also useful for people who tend to need more clear and concrete instructions and guidance. Conversely, people who prefer more creativity in their thinking might find the instructions too direct, and they may 'resist' the instructions. As you become more practised with relaxation inductions an intuitive sense of which induction works for which setting will be developed.

The essential skill in the PMR sequence is to use the same timing for the instruction 'tighten'. If you systematically say 'tighten' twice (or three times) for each part of the body, the client can 'time' the tightening of the muscles. If you vary the number of times you say 'tighten', the client will be unsure how long each one lasts.

Preparation

Get into a comfortable position…loosen anything that restricts your breathing (belts, tight collars, etc.)… Feel the support of the mat/floor for your body…feel the support for the head and shoulders…for the spine and back…the arms and hands…the hips, legs and feet. Allow yourself to sink into the mat/floor, beginning to let go of any tension held in the body. Allow the eyes to close gently…become aware of your breathing…gradually allow yourself to take deeper breaths…gently taking in the breath…gently releasing the breath…allowing the breath to fall into its own natural pattern…

Induction

And now focus on the muscles in your right foot…tense the muscles of the foot (by drawing the foot back towards the body)… Tense the muscles tighter…tighter…and relax. Tense the muscles of your right leg, right up to the hip…tense the muscles tighter…tighter…and relax. Tense the muscles of your left foot…tense the muscles tighter…tighter…and relax. Tense the muscles of your left leg…tense the muscles tighter…tighter…and relax. Draw in the muscles through your pelvis, through to the lower back…draw in the muscles, tighter…tighter…and relax. Draw in the muscles of the stomach…tense the muscles tighter…tighter…and relax. Draw your shoulders forward to tense the muscles of the chest…tense the muscles tighter…tighter…and relax. Draw your shoulders back to tense the muscles of your back…tense the muscles tighter…tighter…and relax. Tense the muscles of your hands, by clenching the hands…tense the muscles tighter…tighter…and relax. Tense the muscles of the arms up to the shoulders by stretching them out…tense the muscles tighter…tighter…and relax.

Tense the muscles of your shoulders by pulling them up toward the ears…tense the muscles tighter…tighter…and relax. Tense the muscles of the neck by raising the head off pillow and stretching toward the chest…tense the muscles tighter…tighter…and relax. Tense the muscles of the jaw by clenching your teeth…tense the muscles tighter…tighter…and relax. Tense the muscles of your eyes, by scrunching up the eyes…tense the muscles tighter…tighter…and relax. Tense the muscles of the forehead by making a frown…tense the muscles tighter…tighter…and relax. And now be aware of how your body feels… Feel the body fully relaxed, allowing any last tension to be released from the body… And now listen to the music as it begins to play.

(*Start the music*)

This induction can be given in reverse order: from head down to the feet.

Bringing the client back to an 'alert' state

The music has finished… Become aware of the sounds around you…the sounds inside the room, and the sounds outside of the room… Become aware of the room we are in…and the people with you in the room… Begin to move your body, stretch out your arms…and legs… Take a deep breath (*The therapist might model an audible release of breath*)… And when you are ready, open your eyes…

Verbal processing of the experience
See notes under autogenic relaxation (p.98).

Clinical examples

In this next section various relaxation inductions specific to clinical populations are described. This material has been contributed by Australian and European music therapists, incorporating explanations of how they use these methods with their clients, including a rationale for the choice and including suggestions for music that has been used successfully.

Hospitalised adult clients

Context
Clare Kildea is a registered music therapist (RMT), who worked for a time at the Royal Melbourne Hospital in the bone marrow transplant ward. She describes a relaxation programme with music for people who were going through bone marrow transplant or oncology treatment. She advertised her relaxation session in several wards of the hospital, so that the group comprised people with different types of illness. Some arrived for the session attached to a drip and sometimes an IV pump alarm would start beeping and had to be attended to by a nurse. The induction described here is for patients who are hospitalised and are in comfortable chairs. Kildea played the music throughout the induction, and the suggested music selections are reproduced here, according to the different phases of the session.

This induction ends with an 'affirmation', a statement that the patient can repeat to himself or herself. This comes at the very end of the induction when the person is most receptive to being affirmed. Also in this induction there are no pauses, the script is read quietly and slowly without pauses.

Introduction

As we begin this relaxation, make your body symmetrical so that your arms are resting comfortably next to your body and your neck, spine and legs are in a straight line. Feel your body sitting in the chair, feel the parts of your body that are supported by the chair, your back, your arms and your legs. Feel your feet resting, feel your whole body still and just resting. During this relaxation there will be some music and some silences. Try to follow my voice.

Breathing induction

As you sit quietly, begin to notice your breath, notice how fast or slow it may be, notice how deep it is, gradually begin to deepen your breath, so your full awareness is on the breathing process. Long, slow, deep breaths. On your next 'in' breath I want you to take a comfortable deep breath, and release it with a sigh. Feel your breath, feel the natural rhythm of your breath and listen to the music, slowly let go, sink back into the chair and sink into the music.

Feel your body supported where you are, let your body soften and loosen. This is a time for you, a time for you to care for yourself, a time to nurture yourself, so give yourself the space to use this time in the best way that you can. Allow your body to soften and let go. As you continue to focus on your breath, we are going to move steadily through your body, bringing awareness to each part of your body and then releasing any tension you may be feeling there.

Autogenic induction

So now bring your awareness to the muscles in your right toes, feel the muscles in your right toes and right foot. Your right foot is heavy and relaxing. Now bring the awareness up through the ankle into the bottom half of your right leg. Use the breath to release any tension you may be feeling there. Move the awareness up to the top part of your right leg. The top part of your leg is feeling heavy and soft. Feel the whole right leg now, from the hip down to the toes, soft and loosening.

Now bring your awareness to the muscles in your left toes, feel the muscles in your left toes and left foot, your left foot is heavy and relaxing. Now bring the awareness up through the ankle into the bottom half of your left leg. Use the breath to release any tension you may be feeling there. Move the awareness up to the top part of your left leg and soften and loosen. Both of your legs now are heavy and fully supported.

Now bring a focused awareness into the stomach and lower abdomen area. Breathe into your stomach and feel your stomach softening and loosening and gently releasing. Bring the awareness up now to your chest. Your chest is wide and broad and softening. And your whole back now is relaxing and fully supported. Release any muscles that may be holding tension in your back and allow them to just let go. And now bring the awareness up to the neck and shoulders. Your shoulders are soft and melting. Breathe into your shoulder area and use the exhalation to release any tension you may be feeling there.

Now bring the awareness down the arms and to your hands. Feel the sensations in your palms. And now move your awareness to your face, your jaw is releasing and letting go. You may want to part your lips just slightly to help the jaw relax. Your forehead is broad and smooth, your cheeks are softening and your eyes are resting gently. Your jaw is relaxed and your tongue is resting on the bottom of your mouth.

Now take a deeper breath and allow any last bits of tension to be released from your body.

Listening

Thoughts may come into your mind, but as they come in also let them pass. Imagine your thoughts like passing clouds, as they come into your mind let them pass by. Try not to become attached to your thoughts as they pass through your mind, come back to the breath and back to the sensation of your body softening and letting go, and back to the music.

Feel the natural rhythm of your breath. Feel the ease of your breath moving in and out of your body. Ease the mind, your thoughts are like passing clouds. Right here, right now is a time for you, just relax.

Your mind and your body are working together. Your mind is helping to relax your body and the stillness of your body is calming and focusing your mind. If there is any part of your body that you would like to attend to, go there now, bring full awareness to that area now...breathe into that part of your body, feel the warmth, the healing warmth.

The affirmation

Take this time now to create a personal affirmation. An affirmation is in the present tense... 'I am' ...and is a positive thought that may be repeated, such as 'I am calm and relaxed', or 'I am confident and capable of handling any situation'. Once you have your affirmation repeat it a few times to yourself.

Coming back

Feel your body, your mind, and your spirit. Remember this feeling, know that you can come back to this relaxed state at any time that you wish, through a gentle awareness of your body and your breath.

Slowly now, and with the help of the music, bring your awareness back to the present reality. Feel where your body is supported by the chair, feel where your feet and your hands are resting. Slowly and gently and in your own time begin to move your fingers and your toes, feel your feet, your legs, your back, your arms and your hands and your head, where they are comfortably resting...and then in your own time, open your eyes.

★ ★ ★

Choice of music

Kildea's music suggestions for each stage of the relaxation process are reproduced in Table 4.1 with permission. Her descriptions of the qualities of the music selections match the principles for relaxation outlined in Chapter 2, Table 2.1. Many of the music selections come from the set of CDs developed in 1996 by Bruscia, published by Barcelona publishers and entitled *Music for the Imagination*. These selections are marked with an asterisk (*).

Table 4.1 Choice of music for each stage of the relaxation process (Kildea 1998)

Segment	Music parameters	Music selections
Introduction	Fluid, captivating melody. Moderate tempo. Pleasing harmonies and warm tone in instrumentation	*Walton: Touch her sweet lips and part Morricone: 'Brothers' (from *The Mission* sound track)
Breathing	Regular, moderate pulse. Predictable and fluid melody, lighter instrumentation	Mancini: Moon River *Bizet: 'Intermezzo' from Carmen
Relaxing	Elements of tension and release in the harmonic structure of the cadences. Ternary or rondo form. No sudden changes in tempo or style. Predictable dynamic changes, if any	Mozart: *Piano Concerto no.21*, 2nd movement. Riley Lee: 'Ocean Sunset' Bacalov: 'Il Postino' *Bach: Suite no.3, Air
Listening	Flowing, transportative melody. Rich but tonal harmonies. Steady, predictable rhythm. Smooth dynamic changes. Rich (close) texture in instrumentation, often with solo instrument carrying the melody	*Albinoni: *Oboe concerto*, 2nd movement Mozart: *Clarinet concerto in A*, 2nd movement Morricone: 'Gabriel's Oboe' (from *The Mission* sound track) Riley Lee: 'Reflections'
Coming back	Gentle, soft and predictable melody. No sudden changes. Thin texture. Shorter duration	*Puccini: 'Humming chorus' (from *Madame Butterfly*) Myers: 'Cavatina' *Grieg: 'Cradle Song'

Note: * These selections are published in a set of CDs by Barcelona Publishers entitled *Music for the Imagination*, developed by Bruscia in 1996.

Kildea also compiled relaxation tapes so that patients could listen to the relaxation programmes at any time. She recorded the induction described above, and dubbed it over the recording of the music selection. She also introduced a period of silence between each selection. Kildea documented six compilation programmes and these are reproduced in Tables 4.2 to 4.7 with her permission.

Table 4.2 Relaxation compilation no.1

Composer	Selection	Relaxation section	Time
Pat Metheny (silence)	In her family	Breathing	3:15 (0:30)
Respighi (silence)	*Pines of Rome, 'Gianicola'	Autogenic relaxation	6:39 (2:00)
Mozart (silence)	Clarinet concerto (2nd movement)	Listening	8:05 (1:00)
Delius	* 1st Aquarelle	Coming back	2:28
		Length of programme	24 mins

Table 4.3 Relaxation compilation no.2

Composer	Selection	Relaxation section	Time
Walton (silence)	*Touch her sweet lips and part	Introduction	1:51 (1:00)
Fauré (silence)	*Requiem, 'Pie Jesu'	Breathing	3:28 (1:00)
Mozart (silence)	Piano concerto no.21, 2nd movement	Autogenic relaxation	6:44 (1:00)
Vivaldi	*Gloria, 'Et in terra pax'	Listening	5:19
Puccini	*Madam Butterfly, 'Humming chorus'	Coming back	2:46
		Length of programme	22 mins

Table 4.4 Relaxation compilation no.3

Composer	Selection	Relaxation section	Time
Morricone (silence)	'Brothers' (from *The Mission* sound track)	Introduction	1:30 (0:30)
Mancini (silence)	'Moon River'	Breathing	4:07 (1:00)
Bacalov (silence)	'Il Postino' (theme from the film *Il Postino*)	Autogenic relaxation	4:07 (0:30)
Morricone (silence)	'Gabriel's oboe' (from *The Mission* sound track)	Listening	2:38 (0:30)
Bell (silence)	*New Dawn*	Listening	3:58 (1:00)
Myers	'Cavatina'	Coming back	3:13
		Length of programme	**22 mins**

Table 4.5 Relaxation compilation no.4

Composer	Selection	Relaxation section	Time
Tony O'Connor (silence)	*Eventide*	Breathing	5:15 (1:00)
Riley Lee (silence)	*Ocean Sunset*	Autogenic relaxation	9:11 (2:00)
Tony O'Connor	*New World*	Listening	5:36
Riley Lee (silence)	*Reflections*	Listening	4:28 (0:30)
Riley Lee	*Wave sounds*	Coming back	3:00
		Length of programme	**31 mins**

Table 4.6 Relaxation compilation no.5

Composer	Selection	Relaxation section	Time
Bizet (silence)	*'Intermezzo', from *Carmen*	Breathing	2:32 (1:00)
Bach (repeat) (silence)	*Suite no 3, 'Air'*	Autogenic relaxation	5:15 (5:15) (2:00)
Albinoni (silence)	*Oboe concerto, 2nd movt.*	Listening	5:23 (0:30)
Grieg	*'Cradle Song'	Coming back	4:07
		Length of programme	26 mins

Table 4.7 Relaxation compilation no.6

Composer	Selection	Relaxation section	Time
Bach (repeat) (silence)	*Suite no.3, 'Air'*	Progressive muscle relaxation	5:15 (5:15) (2:00)
Delius (silence)	*1st Aquarelle*	Progressive muscle relaxation (cont.)	2:28 (1:00)
Riley Lee	*Ocean sunset*	Listening	9:11
		Length of programme	24 mins

(compilations from Kildea 1998)

Relaxation for older adults

Adult clients are usually articulate in their discussion and identification of favourite music and their preferred genre. Music preferences are often established when clients are in their 20s and 30s, when music seems to be strongly linked to life events such as love, courtship and marriage, as well as world events that are captured in song.

It is possible therefore to make an informed estimate of the preferred genre of older adults by calculating the decade during which they would have been in their 20s and 30s. The client may also identify performers of that decade, as well as musicals from that period of time. Additional information about the choice of appropriate music can be gained from discussion with family members. Many of the authentic recordings from the 1930s and 1940s convey a nostalgic atmosphere, and can be effective in enhancing a mood of reverie. Listening to these recordings can therefore be relaxing because of the induced mood of reminiscence.

Relaxation induction for clients who are confused

For older adults who are confused, the relaxation induction needs to be short and very predictable. The short relaxation induction (see page 95), or the count-down method (see page 97) are both appropriate relaxation inductions to use for people who are confused and unable to concentrate for long periods of time.

Music

Short pieces of music are preferable and may include music from the client's youth. Relaxation may sometimes induce sleep for some residents. Conversely a resident might become agitated and the therapist can gently guide the person to sit close. The therapist might use gentle stroking down the arm, or hand massage to calm the resident.

Examples of suitable music
CLASSICAL MUSIC

> Grieg, *Peer Gynt Suite*, 'Morning', 4:10
>
> Galway, *Songs from the Sea Shore*, 'Moon on the Ruined Castle', 4:00
>
> Galway, *Songs from the Sea Shore*, 'Lullaby', 3:30
>
> Respighi, *The Birds Suite*, 'The Nightingale', 4:30
>
> Respighi, *The Birds Suite*, 'The Dove', 4:30

(See the complete list at the end of the chapter.)

NON-CLASSICAL SUGGESTIONS

> Enya, *Watermark*, tracks 1, 3, 6 and/or 8 (tracks 3 and 8 are vocal)
>
> Enya, *Shepherd Moon*, tracks 3, 6, 9 and/or 10
>
> Daniel Kobialka albums
>
> Tony O'Connor albums

ENVIRONMENTAL SOUNDS

> Ken Davies, *Early Morning in the Rainforest* (see precaution below).

Precautions in choosing music

Many people with chronic mental illness may not be familiar with classical music; therefore only 'light' classical music selections are suggested. These are easy to listen to and not likely to induce a depressed mood. Some slow movements of Mozart concertos, for example, may induce depressed feelings, although to the therapist they may seem relaxing pieces of music.

Environmental sounds can be very confusing to people who have dementia, and the sounds often prompt the person to look for the source of the sound (e.g. bird call or waterfall). Therefore recordings of environmental sounds may not be suitable for the aged care context, and the therapist should trial the recording before using it for relaxation.

Bringing the session to a close

When the music has finished, allow a moment for the last sounds to drift away.

> The music has come to an end…stay with the relaxed feelings for a little while longer…begin to become aware of your body. (*Increase volume of voice, and use more dynamic range*)…become aware of the room you are in, aware of the sounds outside/inside…(*slightly louder in volume*) become aware of people with you in the room (*this reminds the patients that others are there*)…begin to stretch your arms and legs (*model this if need be*)…taking in a large breath and exhaling…moving all of your body now to wake it up…and when you are ready opening your eyes (*if some still have eyes closed*).

Processing the experience

Ask the clients what the relaxation was like for them – did they feel relaxed? Did anything interfere with the relaxation? Ask them about the music – did the music help them relax? Did they like the music?

Special precautions for people with psychotic mental illness

Sometimes people who have a psychotic illness may feel unsafe. Giving clear instructions is therefore very helpful. Some people may not want to close their eyes during the session, or if they do, may open them to make sure they are safe. If the client is restless, you might gesture to him or her to come and sit beside you, rather than disturb others in the group. If someone wants to talk to you, gesture to stay silent (e.g. placing your fingers over your lips, but not in an accusing way), and gesture for him or her to stay with you.

Relaxation in palliative care: a group context

Karen Hamlett is a registered music therapist at Calvary Health Care, Bethlehem Hospital in Melbourne. She conducts relaxation sessions for patients in palliative care. These patients require special attention depending on the nature of the symptoms of the illness. Karen works with a social worker at the hospital, and describes the approach to relaxation sessions.

Context

The relaxation session takes place in a palliative care day centre for patients with life-limiting illnesses and is facilitated by Karen (music therapist) and Nadine (social worker). Patients vary in age, diagnoses, cognitive and physical function, disease progression, level of experience in the group and circumstance (e.g. inpatient or living at home).

Introduction

Each session begins with a basic introduction to relaxation with music, including an outline of the induction, music listening and verbal or creative processing activities. Given the different diagnoses and ages, patients are encouraged to take part at their own level. This may involve simply sitting quietly and listening to the music through to actively participating in the imagery. Patients are given strategies to manage potential distress such as 'If you begin to feel uncomfortable you can open your eyes,' or 'If you do need to leave, that's okay.'

Induction

The induction involves a combination of breathing exercises, progressive muscle relaxation and autogenic training usually involving colour or a 'white light'. The purpose of combining the techniques is to introduce patients to a wide variety of relaxation techniques in one session and therefore increase the likelihood that patients will find a relaxation technique that they can use at home or on the inpatient ward. During the induction, it is important to consider the physical abilities of patients, as some may be receiving oxygen during the sessions and are unable to take slow deep breaths; therefore a statement such as 'Gradually allow your breathing to deepen to a level that is comfortable for you' is useful. Similarly, patients with oedema or painful joints/limbs may find it difficult to follow a progressive muscle relaxation, so it is important to offer other options, for example, 'If you do not feel comfortable tensing your muscles, just bring your attention to that part of the body and imagine the tension melting away.' Music is not played during the induction as many patients have age-related hearing loss and find it difficult to hear the induction over the music.

Imagery

During the imagery phase, it is important to include statements that address symptomatic issues such as 'Imagine yourself walking along a beach, unaided, free from pain with boundless amounts of energy.' See Chapter 5 for further examples of imagery.

Music

Classical music is most frequently used in palliative care as most patients are older, and classical music is a preferred genre. In addition, carefully selected classical music is calming to patients who are in pain, although some new-age or ambient music, such as Tony O'Connor CDs or *Music for Dreaming* (Cherie Ross), are also used.

Verbal or creative processing activities

A variety of activities are used to help patients process the experience, including facilitated discussion, song writing, collage and drawing. Often these discussions lead to exploration of patients' illness, feelings of loss, issues surrounding death, changes within the family or living situation, etc. Patients are able to explore their circumstances and receive emotional support from the facilitators and other group members.

★ ★ ★

Adaptation of relaxation in palliative care: case example

Matt Holmes is a registered music therapist who works at Calvary Health Care, Bethlehem Hospital in Melbourne. He adopts a 'mindfulness' approach in the relaxation sessions he uses with clients. Mindfulness practice and principles have their origins in many contemplative and philosophical traditions. For example, Buddhism contains many traditions of meditative training with a mindfulness perspective. More recently, psychologist Jon Kabat-Zinn has brought pioneering attention to the clinical and psychotherapeutic benefits and applications of mindfulness. In essence, mindfulness involves paying attention to the present moment in a non-judgmental way. The emphasis is on seeing and accepting things as they are without trying to change them. This is in contrast to our normal perceptive attitude of 'being on automatic pilot', yet paradoxically striving for rigid, goal-directed expectations (Kabat-Zinn 2003; Melbourne Academic Mindfulness Interest Group 2006). In the following vignette Matt Holmes uses the mindfulness approach to assist a man with Huntington's disease.

Background

David, a 54-year-old man with Huntington's disease (HD), normally lives with his wife but was admitted to the clinic due to increased anxiety and an increased level of delusional thoughts concerning his perceived lack of affection for his wife. He was not a physical threat to his wife during these ongoing delusional thoughts.

Patient's music preferences

The music used during these sessions was chosen by the patient from a selection of nature sounds CDs. The client had previously insisted that 'no love songs' were to be played, and therefore the music therapist decided that nature sounds would offer the least likely association to either love themes or his wife. David chose forest sounds from the series *Echoes of Nature*. The CD consisted of approximately an hour of morning songbirds, the natural sounds of the wilderness.

The induction was adapted from Smith's (2005) ABC2 Relaxation Theory, and began with a progressive muscle relaxation (PMR).

In this exercise we are going to relax by gently squeezing and letting go of various muscle groups. First make sure you are seated upright and in a comfortable position, and that your feet are flat on the floor. When you are ready you may close your eyes.

Let's begin by focusing on the hands. Squeeze the fingers together by making a fist. Tighten up the muscles, and let the tension grow. And let go. Release the tension. Let your muscles begin to go limp. Let all the tension begin to flow out, as your hands sink into relaxation. (*Repeat instruction in full.*)

This time focus on your arms. Squeeze your lower and upper arms together, reaching to your shoulder. Let the tension grow. And then let go. Allow the tension to melt away, as your muscles become more deeply relaxed. (*Repeat instruction.*)

This time, focus on your shoulder muscles. Squeeze your shoulders, bring them up to your ears in a shrug. Let the tension grow. And then let go. Allow the tension to melt away, as your muscles become more deeply relaxed. (*Repeat.*)

This time focus on the muscles of your face. Squeeze them all together now. Let the feelings of tightness grow. And let go. Let the tension melt away, as you become more deeply relaxed. (*Repeat.*)

This time focus on the muscles of the feet. Point your toes to the floor and tighten the muscles. Let the tension grow. And let go. Let the tension flow away out through the toes, as you become more deeply relaxed. Far away from the world.

Mindfulness section

We will now begin our mindfulness relaxation. The room is alive with sounds and sensations. Allow yourself to quietly reflect on what passes by. There is no need or reason to think about anything. Whenever you notice something, gently name it, put it aside, and continue attending with an open mind until you notice something else. Perhaps you can hear the sounds of distant traffic...or the sounds of normal activity around you...or the sounds from the nature CD in the room. Whatever it is, gently name it, allow it to pass with an open mind, and continue listening to the sounds and the moments that come and go. For the next few minutes, allow yourself to listen to all the sounds around you with an open mind, as you become more deeply relaxed...

And now, let go of what you are attending to. Take a deep breath and stretch your legs and arms. And in your own time open your eyes. We have completed our mindfulness relaxation.

Special considerations

1.   The PMR was shortened due to the chorea movements that are the primary symptom of Huntington's disease. The music therapist did not want these choreic movements to inhibit the client's efforts at relaxation. Additionally this shortened version was easier for the client to comprehend due to his restricted cognitive functioning abilities. The shortened version of the PMR was successful, as it allowed the client to have a degree of physical control over relaxation of his body, in contrast to the extensive physical limitations placed on

him by Huntington's disease; and it took account of cognitive deficits including any difficulty in comprehension of simplified commands.

2.   The mindfulness technique was more amenable for a cognitively impaired client than a lengthy imagery or autogenic script, as both require a degree of concentration that may have mitigated against any relaxation effect.

3.   The use of nature sounds was useful for two reasons: first, it deflected and absorbed all ambient and industrial white noise from the hospital ward. Second, the nature sounds provided something concrete for the client to focus on and listen to during the mindfulness section, as well as an anchoring point for the RMT to re-direct the client towards if required.

Relaxation and music for patients in cardiac rehabilitation

Karin Schou is a qualified music therapist researching in Denmark with patients who have had heart valve repair surgical procedures as a single procedure, or a double procedure involving valve repair and heart bypass procedures. Schou's PhD dissertation is a random-ised controlled trial on the effect of guided relaxation on agitation levels in cardiac rehabili-tation. For this chapter, we are incorporating the protocol for Schou's guided relaxation and music.

Introduction

The guided relaxation is based on principles described by Bonny and Savary (1973) and focuses on relaxation of the body in parts and as a whole. The progressive relaxation (Jacobson 1938) is one method of meeting the cardiac patient's need for rest, and guides patients' awareness from their feet and progressively through their body parts. The guiding contains no suggestions of imagery. At the end of the session the patient is encouraged to seek physical assistance from the staff if needed.

Protocol: guidelines for the guide (music therapist) during guided relaxation and music

The following guidelines outline the role, attitude, and quality of voice of the music therapist in sessions of guided relaxation with music, and how the tempo may be organized.

ROLE

The role of the music therapist is primarily supportive. Disturbing sounds or other disturbing elements from outside the room are contained by the music therapist and are commented on if necessary. It is the responsibility of the music therapist before the session to put a sign 'Session in progress' on the door (starting and ending times are marked), in order to avoid interruptions from others.

ATTITUDE

The music therapist relates to the patient empathically and observes his or her responses. The music therapist follows the relaxation in her own body while guiding the patient. Thus she listens both from within herself, and by 'listening' to the patient.

QUALITY OF VOICE

Depending on the patient, the music therapist colours her voice to make it sound warm, supportive and with a rounded, soft timbre. The music therapist uses her voice in its middle to lower register. At the same time it is important that her voice sounds relaxed and slightly airy. The pronunciation must be sufficiently distinct for the patient to be able to hear and understand the words.

TEMPO AND TIMING

The period for guiding relaxation lasts 30 minutes, which allows time for pausing between the given instructions. The pauses are marked by ellipses (...).

The tempo of the guiding is calm and is as much as possible attuned to the patient's breathing and/or the music. Instructions describing action in the patient, e.g. moving awareness from one body part to the next by saying 'Now, be aware of...', may follow the patient's in-breath. When the patient is given an instruction beginning with 'Let...', the music therapist may follow the patient's out-breath. The music therapist may match the shift of awareness to changes in the music when it seems natural.

USE OF THE TEXT FOR GUIDING

The word 'now' is parenthesised to allow for variation. The music therapist decides when to include or exclude it. It is recommended to use 'now' regularly (e.g. every other or every third time) in order to support the patient in being aware of the present time (here and now).

PROCESS

As the purpose of the guided relaxation and music is to support the patient in relaxing, the music therapist does not engage in conversation regarding deeper emotional aspects. The music therapist must refrain from asking opening questions that may stimulate processing. If the music therapist observes or senses signs of pain or discomfort in the patient (e.g. grimaces, voice sounds, tight fist, irregularities in the breathing pattern), she may support the patient by commenting on these signs with words such as 'If parts of your body need further attention this is ok. Try to let it be, while you listen to the music. I will guide you.'

Guided relaxation and music

(For a first session, pre-operatively, during which the patient chooses his or her preferred music.)

The client lies in a bed in a position comfortable for relaxation.

PROCEDURE FOR CHOOSING PREFERRED STYLE OF MUSIC

The following describes the procedure by which the patient is assisted in choosing his or her preferred style of music for relaxation. The patient is asked to make a choice between four different styles of music using the examples shown in Table 4.8 (excerpts from the main music selection).

Table 4.8 Music examples 1–4				
CD number	Music style	Title	Duration	Source
1	Easy listening	'Why worry'	0:40	Here Comes the Sun no.6 Kaare Norge (RecArt 5941032)
2	Classical	'Air'	0:40	Bonde *et al.* 2001, CD no.25 Orchestre de Chambre Jean-Francois Paillard/Paillard (RCA Viktor 09026654682)
3	Specially composed	'Secret path'	0:40	Fairy Tales no.2, Gefion Records (GFO 20136)
4	Jazz	'Cinema Paradiso' (love theme)	0:40	Beyond the Missouri Sky no.11, Charlie Haden and Pat Metheny (Verve 537 130-2)

The music therapist follows the procedure with the following wording (translated from Danish).

Before the start of your rest period I will ask you to choose which music you prefer to listen to for your relaxation. There are four different styles of music to choose from. I will play four examples (excerpts) for you, before you decide.

Now, this is example number I which sounds like this. (*Play example number I.*) Now, example number 2 sounds like this. (*Play numbers 2, 3 and 4 till you have played all four examples.*)

Which music do you prefer for your relaxation? (*The music therapist may play the example of the chosen style of music for the patient if he or she needs to listen to it one more time.*)

Before starting to play the music the patient is asked if the volume if is suitable. The same 35-minute music programme of the chosen style of music is used for all the (four) sessions that the patient receives.

Draw the curtains if the room has windows and turn off the lights (leave enough light for the guide to manage the equipment). Start the music.

PREPARATION

It is now time for you to relax. I will guide you.

You may take off your glasses and shoes. Make yourself comfortable in the bed. Make sure that your clothes are comfortably loose. Do you need anything else to lie comfortable?' (The bed may need adjusting; the patient may need pillows under their knees and arms, and a light blanket or duvet to keep him or her warm.) 'Take your time to make yourself comfortable.

Let your thoughts pass by – be prepared to relax. Now, be aware of your breathing – take a deep breath – breathe as deeply as it is comfortable for you right now – in your own rhythm and at your own pace. Now, let the breathing take care of itself.

INDUCTION

Let *your body* sink into the mattress…almost as if the mattress holds you…feel the support of the mattress…let the mattress hold you…let the mattress support you…you are fully supported by the mattress beneath you…let your body and mind relax as it is comfortable for you right now.

(Now) be aware of your *toes* and *feet*…let your toes and feet sink into the mattress…as if the mattress holds them. Be aware of the sensation in your feet and toes…feel this sensation…let go and let your toes and feet sink into the mattress…let the mattress hold your feet and toes, while they sink into the mattress.

(Now) be aware of your *lower legs*…let your lower legs sink into the mattress…as if the mattress holds your lower legs. Be aware of the sensation in your lower legs…feel this sensation…let go and let your lower legs sink into the mattress…let the mattress hold your lower legs, while they sink into the mattress and relax.

(Now) be aware of your *thighs*…let your thighs sink into the mattress…as if the mattress holds your thighs. Be aware of the sensation in your thighs…feel this sensation…let go and let your thighs sink into the mattress…let the mattress hold your thighs, while they sink into the mattress.

(Now) be aware of *both your legs*…let both your legs sink into the mattress…as if the mattress holds both your legs. Be aware of the sensation in both your legs…feel the sensation in both your legs…let go and let both your legs sink into the mattress…feel the support of the mattress…let the mattress hold both your legs, while they sink into the mattress and relax.

(Now) be aware of the *lower part of your body*…let the lower part of your body sink into the mattress…as if the mattress holds it. Be aware of the sensation in your lower body…feel this sensation…let go and let the mattress hold your lower body, while it sinks into the mattress and relaxes…let the lower part of your body be supported fully by the mattress beneath you.

(Now) be aware of your *hips*…let your hips sink into the mattress…as if the mattress holds your hips. Be aware of the sensation in your hips…feel this sensation in your hips…let go and let your hips sink into the mattress…let the mattress hold your hips, while they sink into the mattress and relax.

(Now) be aware of your *bottom*…let your bottom sink into the mattress…as if the mattress supports your bottom. Be aware of the sensation in your bottom…feel this sensation…let go and let your bottom sink into the mattress…let the mattress support your bottom, while you sink into the mattress and relax.

(Now) be aware of your *abdomen*…let your abdomen sink into the mattress…as if the mattress holds your abdomen. Be aware of the sensation in your abdomen…feel this sensation…let go and let your abdomen sink into the mattress…let the mattress hold your abdomen, while it sinks into the mattress and relaxes.

(Now) be aware of your *fingers and hands*…let your fingers and hands sink into the mattress…as if the mattress holds them. Be aware of the sensation in your fingers and hands…feel this sensation…let go and let your fingers and hands sink into the mattress…let the mattress hold your fingers and hands, while they sink into the mattress and relax.

(Now) be aware of your *forearms*…let your forearms sink into the mattress…as if the mattress holds your forearms. Be aware of the sensation in your forearms…feel the sensation in your forearms…let go and let your forearms sink into the mattress…let the mattress hold your forearms, while they sink into the mattress and relax.

(Now) be aware of your *upper arms*…let your upper arms sink into the mattress…as if the mattress holds your upper arms. Be aware of the sensation in your upper arms…feel the sensation…let go and let your upper arms sink into the mattress…let the mattress hold your upper arms, while they sink into the mattress and relax.

(Now) be aware of *both your arms*…let both your arms sink into the mattress…as if the mattress holds both your arms. Be aware of the sensation in both your arms…feel the sensation in both your arms…let go and let both your arms sink into the mattress…feel the support of the mattress…let the mattress hold both your arms, while they sink into the mattress and relax.

(Now) be aware of *the upper part of your body*…midriff and chest…let the upper part of your body sink into the mattress…as if the mattress holds the upper part of your body. Be aware of the sensation in the upper part of your body…feel this sensation…let go and let the upper part of your body sink into the mattress…feel the support of the mattress…let the mattress hold the upper part of your body…let it sink into the mattress and relax.

(Now) be aware of your *back*…let your back sink into the mattress…as if the mattress holds your back. Be aware of the sensation in your back…feel this sensation…let go and let all your back sink into the mattress…feel the support of the mattress…let the mattress hold your back…let it sink into the mattress and relax.

(Now) be aware of *the upper part of your back, your shoulders and back of your neck*…let your shoulders and neck sink into the mattress…as if the mattress holds the upper part of your back, your shoulders and your neck. Be aware of the sensation in the upper part of your back, your shoulders and your neck…feel this sensation…let go and let the upper part of your back, your shoulders and your neck sink into the mattress…feel the support of the mattress…let the mattress hold you and let the upper part of your back, your shoulders and your neck be supported fully by the mattress beneath you and let them relax.

(Now) be aware of your neck and throat…feel your neck and throat…try to let go and let your neck and throat relax.

(Now) be aware of your *jaws*…your *mouth*…your *nose*…your *cheeks*…your *ears*…*eyes*…your *forehead*…your *temples*…and *the bones of your head*. Be aware of the sensation in your jaws…your mouth…your nose…your cheeks…your ears…eyes… your forehead…temples…and the bones of your head…feel the sensations…let go and let them relax.

(Now) be aware of your *face*…let your face relax. Be aware of your *head*…let your head sink into the pillow…as if the pillow holds your head…let go and let the pillow hold your head, while it sinks into the pillow and relaxes…let your head be fully supported by the pillow.

(Now) be aware of your *whole body*…let go and let your whole body sink into the mattress…let the mattress hold you…let your body be fully supported by the mattress beneath you, while your body relaxes. If there are still areas in your body that need more attention…let go…let all your body relax while listening to the music.

I am sitting here with you while the music continues to play until it finishes.

The music therapist stays quietly next to the client; pays attention to the client's breathing and any observation relevant to the client's relaxation. Possible signs of discomfort or tension may be commented on in the following way, for example, 'If there are parts of your body that need more attention in order to relax, it is all right – if you can, try to let it stay as it is now while you listen to the music.'

WHEN THE MUSIC IS OVER

The music has ended now – be aware of the sounds around you. Move your feet and hands gently and other parts of your body as much as you need – you may need to stretch a little – take your time. When you are ready open your eyes slowly (*if the patient has closed his or her eyes*) – gradually adjust to the light and calmly take a look at the room around you.

Conclusion

All of these examples of clinical applications with specific populations, together with the relaxation inductions described at the beginning of the chapter, should be carefully considered in terms of the client's needs, how appropriate the model is, and what adaptations may need to be made for individual or population-specific applications. Nevertheless, there are still interventions that might result in adverse responses, and so potential contraindications need to be addressed responsibly by therapists.

Contraindications

There are no studies reporting contraindications for relaxation inductions, however, the following points should be taken into consideration when planning relaxation sessions for adult clients:

1. Patients/residents who are confused may have difficulty understanding abstract concepts, and may engage better with relaxation scripts that are short or have instructions to follow.

2. Patients/residents who are confused may have difficulty relating to relaxation scripts that involve embodied experiences, for example, breathing a colour through various parts of the body.

3. Clients who feel vulnerable or feel they are being watched may have difficulty closing their eyes during relaxation experiences, or may need to open their eyes to make sure they are safe.

4. Patients following cardiac surgery may feel discomfort unless correct positioning and support is in place. It may be appropriate with post heart surgery patients to stress that they breathe only as deeply as is comfortable for them. Due to chest pain, a more upright position may be more comfortable to a patient in the first phase of post heart surgery rehabilitation.

5. Similarly, when using relaxation procedures with older adults who have physical disabilities, discomfort may occur unless correct positioning and support for the body (usually with pillows) is provided.

6. Patients who need physiological support (e.g. oxygen, breathing support) may experience pain or restriction to deep breathing during relaxation, and the relaxation script should either avoid instructions about deep breathing, or include a comment to 'only breathe as much as is comfortable'.

7. Residents in care homes for the elderly may feel uncomfortable or embarrassed when paying attention to various parts of their body in the presence of another person.

Music selections

The list below contains a collection of music from the classical tradition or other genres, that have been used in clinical settings and found to be effective. The reader is reminded that before choosing a selection of music for use with clients to assess the music carefully, using the three-stage process outlined in Chapter 2. There are many different recordings of these works and therefore it is important to choose one that is appropriate. For example, recordings of Pachelbel's *Canon in D* can vary from 4 to 11 minutes, indicating that some performances are very fast, others slow. Many of the selections below can be found on *Music for Imagination*, a 10-CD compilation developed by Bruscia, and produced by Barcelona

Publishers in agreement with Naxos records (www.barcelonapublishers.com). *Music for the Imagination* contains many of the pieces most suitable for relaxation with adults, and these selections are indicated by an asterisk (*). Tracks without asterisks come from the following compilation CDs:

From Winter's Stillness, ABC (Aust) (ABC 461 728-2)

Meditations for a Quiet Night (Nimbus NI 7007)

Meditations for a Quiet Dawn (Nimbus NI 7009)

Music Therapy (Erato 0630 11943-2).

Short selections (note: duration timings will differ between different recordings)

*Albinoni, *Concerto for oboe in D min*, 'Adagio', 5:23

*Bach, *Suite no.3*, 'Air', 5:15

*Bach, *Brandenburg Concerto no.6*, 'Adagio', 5:29

*Bach, *Christmas Oratorio*, 'Shepherd's song', 5:55

*Bach, *Concerto for Two Violins*, 'Largo', 8:56

*Beethoven, *Piano Concerto no.5*, 'Adagio', 7:45

Beethoven, *Romance no.2 in F major* 9:47

*Bizet, *Carmen*, 'Intermezzo', 2:32

*Borodin, *Symphony no.1*, 'Andante', 6:12

Butterworth, *On the Banks of Green Willow*, 6:07

*Chopin, *Piano Concerto no.1 in E min*, 'Romance, Larghetto', 9:19

Debussy, *Dances Sacred and Profane*, 8:00

*Dvořák, *Czech Suite*, 'Romance', 4:32

*Fauré, *Requiem*, 'In Paradissum', 3:17

Gluck, *Orfeo and Euridice*, 'Dance of the blessed spirits', 2:44

Grieg, *Peer Gynt Suite*, 'Morning', 4:00

Grieg, *Peer Gynt Suite*, 'Solveig's song', 5:00

*Grieg, *Holberg Suite*, 'Air', 5:44

*Grieg, *Cradle Song*, 4:07

*Haydn, *Cello Concerto in C*, 'Adagio', 9:45

*Holst, *Planets Suite*, 'Venus', 8:07

*Holst, *Planets Suite*, 'Neptune', 7:01

Korngold, *Much Ado About Nothing*, 'Garden scene', 4:38

*Liadov, *The Enchanted Lake*, 7:58

Mascagni, *Cavelleria Rusticana*, 'Intermezzo', 2:59

Massenet, *Thais*, 'Meditation', 5:47

Mozart, *Eine Kleine Nachtmusik*, 'Romance', 6:03

Mozart, *Concerto for Flute and Harp*, 'Andantino', 9:40

Mozart, *Piano Concerto no.20 in D minor*, 'Romance', 9:00

Mozart, *Piano Concerto no.21*, 'Andante', 7:15

Pachelbel, *Canon in D* (from Music Therapy CD), 7:07

*Puccini, *Madame Butterfly*, 'Humming chorus', 2:46

Rachmaninov, *Songs op.34*, 'Vocalise', 6:51

*Ravel, *Pavane for a Dead Infant*, 7:44

Respighi, *The Birds Suite*, 'The Nightingale', 4:30

Respighi, *The Birds Suite*, 'The dove', 4:30

*Respighi, *The Fountains of Rome*, 'Villa Guilia at dawn', 4:28

*Respighi, *The Fountains of Rome*, 'Villa Medici at sunset', 5:45

Saint-Saens, *Carnival of the Animals*, 'The swan', 3:07

Sor, *Etude op.35 no.2 for guitar*, 2:20

Stamitz, *Cello Concerto no.2 in A*, 'Romance', 6:51

Strauss, R., *Oboe Concerto in D*, 'Andante', 8:00

Tchaikovsky, *Romance in F minor*, 5:46

*Walton, 'Touch her soft lips and part', 1:51

*Warlock, *Capriol Suite*, 'Pieds en l'air', 2:21

Longer selections (approx. ten minutes +)

*Debussy, *Prelude to the Afternoon of a Faun*, 10:30

Dvořák, *Romance in F minor*, 12:46

Pierne, *Concerstücke for Harp and Orchestra*, 15:30

*Ravel, *Introduction and Allegro for Harp and Orchestra*, 10:17

Light classical

Galway, *Songs from the Seashore*, 'Moon on the ruined castle', 4:00 (RCA GD80117)

Galway, *Songs from the Seashore*, 'Lullaby', 3:30 (RCA GD80117)

Film music

Out of Africa (MCA Records MCAD-6158)

The Mission ('Gabriel's oboe', 'Brothers') (Virgin Records CDV 2402)

New-age

Stephen Halpern, *Soft Focus* (Halpern Sounds HS 385)

Stephen Halpern, *Natural Light* (Halpern Sounds HS 834)

Daniel Kobialka (see list of CDs at www.danielkobialka.com)

Tony O'Connor, *Mariner* (sounds of waves, seagulls)

Tony O'Connor, *Tales of the Wind* (pan flutes)

Tony O'Connor, *Summer Rain* (birds, cicada sounds)

Tony O'Connor, *Rainforest Magic* (bird calls)

Tony O'Connor, *Windseeker* (flutes)

(See list of CDs at www.tonyoconnor.com.au)

Chapter 5

Music, Visualisations and Imagery

There are diverse methods used in receptive music therapy that incorporate visualisations and/or imagery in a relaxed state, with music. Bruscia (1998a) defines 'imaginal listening' as 'the use of music listening to evoke and support imaginal processes or inner experiences, while in a non-ordinary state of consciousness' (p.125).

Why use visualisations/imagery in conjunction with music?

One of the most commonly reported difficulties that clients express when engaged in relaxation sessions is the presence of insistent and intrusive thoughts. These thoughts can change rapidly, such as scanning a list of activities that need to be done, for example, compiling a shopping list of items that need to be purchased to make a meal. Thoughts can be intrusive if they pass quickly, as the brain speeds up to process them, and this is counter-productive to being in a relaxed state. Similarly a rapid flow of images (termed stream of consciousness) may interfere with a state of relaxation.

Including a simple visualisation helps the brain become focused. As the therapist directs the client's attention to the visualisation, and invites the client to look more deeply into it, the visual field literally narrows in order to focus. Focusing or centring is a necessary part of the relaxation process where the therapeutic intention is for the mind to be quiet and still.

Another technique for engaging a busy mind is to adopt the 'mindfulness' approach, which is designed to notice the flow of images and thoughts and to let them pass (see also discussion in Chapter 4). The mindfulness approach accepts that thoughts and images need to be noticed and let go, rather than trying to dismiss or stop them (Kabat-Zinn 2003).

In addition, imagery and visualisations have been shown to help hospitalised patients in the management of pain and stress. As will be explained, inviting a patient to recall a favourite place enables the person to mentally move out of the confines of a hospital bed, to 'escape' for a period of time to a place that is pleasant and less stressful.

Finally, imagery enhances the aesthetic enjoyment of listening to beautiful music. Imagery is expressed in dream material and is activated each time we recall a pleasurable event. Thus imagery is important to our emotional health and well-being.

Crucial to the effective use of imagery in a therapeutic context is the client's understanding of what imagery is, and the ability to differentiate between what is imagined and what is real. Most clients will be able to imagine a warm sunny day and the sun in the sky making the body feel warm. There is a logical flow of imaginal ideas, built on a common experience. However, more complicated imagined scenes can become problematical if the client cannot distinguish fantasy from reality, or if the client has difficulty in concentrating on the image. Therefore the following methods vary in the depth of the experience, and the role of the therapist and the client. For a client who has limited concentration and for whom the therapist should provide a safe experience by eliminating extraneous thoughts, visualisations and directed music imaging are appropriate methods.

For clients who are capable of differentiating between fantasy and reality, who can concentrate on the process and who can gain understanding from the images, unguided music imaging, in individual sessions or group sessions (group music and imagery), and guided music imaging are appropriate methods.

This chapter is organised into three sections. In the first, visualisations and directed music imaging are described. These methods belong together because in both cases the client follows the directions or script of the therapist. The client does not need to generate the imagery him- or herself, and the client does not report any imagery experiences verbatim to the therapist while listening to music. These methods are useful for clients who need structure but they can also be used quite freely with all clients.

In the second section of this chapter, methods that require the client to generate imagery are described. These methods include unguided music imaging (UMI), practised in individual sessions, and group music and imagery (GrpMI), practised with groups of clients.

In the third section of this chapter, guided music imaging (GMI) is explained. GMI is a short form of the more complex Bonny Method of Guided Imagery and Music, which can only be practised after completing three levels of training. The short form (GMI) however can be practised with just level 1 and 2 training (see below for details). Table 5.1 sets out the differences between the methods in relation to the context, the role of the client and the therapist.

Visualisations and directed music imaging

Before introducing visualisations and imagery for a client, or client group, it is essential to assess whether the method is suitable. The following points should be considered.

Assessing a client's suitability for music and imagery methods

An assessment of suitability of music and imagery methods is necessary to determine how a client views his or her creative imagination. Samuels and Samuels (1975) comment that when people close their eyes, and there is silence:

> images and thoughts come to them that appear to be within their mind. In their mind's eye they 'see' memories of past events, imagine future situations, daydream of what may or may not be… [yet] many people deny that the experiences are real. (p.5)

Table 5.1 The differences between the methods in relation to the context and the roles of the client and the therapist

	Context	Role of the client	Role of the therapist
Visualisations	Individual or group	Follows instructions of the therapist	Provides a script for the visualisation
Directed music imaging	Individual or group	Follows instructions of the therapist	Provides a script for the imagery
Unguided music imaging (UMI)	Individual	Generates imagery in response to the music	No active role during the music listening time
Group music and imaging (GrpMI)	Group	Each group member generates his or her imagery in response to the music	No active role during the music listening time
Guided music imaging (GMI)	Individual	Engages with the therapist in dialogue describing imagery experiences as they occur	Asks questions (interventions) to gain a sense of what the client is experiencing

For some people the external reality is safe, and they know little about their inner world. An initial session therefore should be designed to assess whether imagery methods are suitable, and should include a short relaxation induction and a visualisation experience, with a short piece of music. This will provide the therapist with sufficient information to enable an informed decision about whether these imagery methods are suitable for the client.

The therapist should monitor and assess whether the client can:

1. listen to the relaxation induction and follow the instructions

2. concentrate on the therapist's voice when giving the visualisation

3. return from the relaxed state

4. discuss the experience and gain some benefit from it.

Visualisations

For the purpose of this book a visualisation may be defined as a relatively static image, or a short sequence of images, that are used to deepen or enhance a relaxed state of mind. Examples of visualisations include looking into the centre of a flower, the sun setting, a bird in flight, a waterfall, and the sea lapping onto the beach. The music therapist provides a relaxation induction that focuses on the breath and the rhythm of breathing (see Chapter 4 for examples of relaxation inductions). A selection of music is used to enhance and parallel the relaxation. The music may be played throughout the induction and visualisation (as background). Alternatively the music can be played after the induction.

Examples of visualisations
1. A FLOWER

> Bring to your mind an image of a flower…it might be a favourite flower…take a moment to allow the image to come to your mind…notice the shape of the flower…trace the outline of the petals in your mind…notice the colour of the flower and how the colours might change at different places…be aware of the scent of the flower if it is there…and now focus on the centre of the flower…take your attention to the very centre, and enjoy the colour and beauty of the flower.

2. BY THE SEA

> Bring to your mind a favourite place by the sea…take a moment to allow this image to come to your mind…notice the colour of the sea, and the shapes of the waves…notice the warm sand under your feet…feel the warm sun on your body…you might like to lie down on the warm sand listening to the gentle sound of the waves on the shore…notice how it feels in your body…

3. BIRD IN FLIGHT

> Imagine you are watching a bird in flight…take a moment to allow the image of the bird to come to your mind…notice its shape and form, and watch its wings as it moves through the air…notice the freedom of the bird in flight…and feel that freedom for yourself…

Choice of music

Because the visualisation is quite short, the piece of music may also be quite short (see examples on p.142). Selections of five to ten minutes may be appropriate, particularly if the visualisation is introduced as a segment of a longer music therapy session. The music therapist can also determine the music preference of the client, and use that music choice during the visualisation, making sure that the music matches the intention of the visualisation.

Bringing the visualisation to an end

When the music has finished playing, an appropriate ending is: 'now the music has come to an end allow the image to fade, knowing that you can return to this image at another time.' If this is the end of the therapy session, the therapist may leave the client in the relaxed state. If the visualisation is part of a longer music therapy session, the therapist then moves on to the next segment of the session.

Applications

Short visualisations with music are appropriate in aged care facilities, for people who have chronic mental illness, for hospitalised patients where the therapy session is of short duration, or patients in physical rehabilitation, where there may be cognitive impairment.

Vignette: individual session – aged care

Mr T. was a member of the Salvation Army, and had led a very structured life. He had been placed in an aged care hostel, where he had his own room. Staff were concerned about how isolated Mr T. was, and that he always appeared very tense and uptight. He was referred to music therapy for relaxation training. In the first session a breath relaxation was used, however Mr T. could not understand the idea of breathing deeply and instead became more tense as he took in short audible breaths that did not have any ease in flow or rhythm.

In the second session a progressive muscle relaxation (PMR) induction was used, and this suited Mr T. very well. He responded well to instructions, and followed the logical progression through the body easily. PMR was used in subsequent sessions effectively, but the therapist (DG) wondered if imagery might enhance the relaxation even further. In discussion with Mr T. he described a favourite place in Northern Australia, in the desert where the earth is red. The image of the 'red centre' became the focus image used at the end of the PMR session. Mr T. reported that he used this imagery to help him sleep at night, and staff reported that he seemed less tense.

Directed music imaging

Directed music imaging is defined by Bruscia (1998a) as:

> The client images what the therapist presents while listening to music, usually in an altered state of consciousness. The image may be selected by the therapist or the client, and may be mental or physical in nature. The image may be specific, personalised, or general, and the therapist's guiding may be spaced at various intervals. (Bruscia 1998a, p.125)

Directed music imaging is an effective method for clients to experience a longer imagery script that incorporates a 'journey' of some kind. It is presented as an imagery script that the therapist reads to the client while the client is relaxed. The therapist provides a relaxation induction for the client. At the end of the induction the music therapist introduces a guided script. The music may be played in the background while the therapist reads the script, or the music can be started at the end of the script. Suggested scripts are:

1. You are walking through a field of grass…it is a pleasant day, and the grass feels soft under your feet…you see a house ahead of you…notice what the house looks like…as you get close to the house you see a path leading to the

front door…as you get closer you walk along the path up to the door…notice what the door looks like…you open the door…inside there is a special person waiting for you…be glad to see them…

2.   You are sitting on the beach in the late afternoon…the sun is setting…the birds fly across the sky…it is becoming quieter…the sun sets over the water…it makes beautiful reflections in the water…you start to walk along the water's edge…you watch the colours in the sky…and reflected in the water.

Creating individualised scripts

The imagery script can be created for the client based on a special place. For example, for a hospitalised patient who is missing the garden at home, the therapist may ask about the garden – what does it look like? What flowers are growing in the garden? What are the colours of the garden? What are the favourite perfumes of the flowers for the client? An imagery script can then be created from the information, and the music therapist then provides a relaxation induction (see Chapter 4) and either reads the script while the music is playing, or starts the music at the end of the script. Using the example of a client's garden at home, an individualised script might be:

Imagine that you are entering your garden at home…you are walking down the path…you come to the bed of roses that is your special place in the garden…notice the colours of the roses…move closer to the pink roses that are your favourite flower in the garden…bend down to smell the sweet perfume of the flower…now look around you again and notice other flowers in your garden…take in the beauty of this place that you have created at home.

The details of the script may change based on what information the client tells the therapist in subsequent sessions.

A second example is that you might discuss a favourite place with a client/patient, and then write a script to include all the descriptive words used. It might be a place in nature, or it might be a special place within his or her home, for example, a favourite room. Using the example of a favourite room in the house, a hypothetical script might be:

Imagine yourself in the front room of your house…notice the colours of the room…and notice your favourite parts of the room…the big comfortable chair, the books on the shelf, the mirror that was given to you by a special person…take a few moments to find a place in this room where you would like to rest…and now allow the music into that scene to help you rest. (*Start music here.*)

Music selections appropriate to the length of the therapy session are listed on p.142.

Managing a negative experience to an imagery script

Although the therapist carefully selects an imagery script for a patient/client's situation, there can be occasions when a client reacts in a negative way to the imagery. An example of this is described in Clair's *Therapeutic Uses of Music with Older Adults* (1996). A music therapy student was reciting a script to a resident in a hospice. The script was one that was commonly used and it began:

> 'Picture yourself in a beautiful, cool meadow. It is high in the mountains. The air is clean and fresh and it feels cool as it blows against your skin. There are wildflowers every-where, and they are all colours of the rainbow.' (Clair 1996, p.127)

The resident, who was agitated about leaving her home without having made sufficient preparation for leaving, experienced a negative reaction to the script, saying 'Get me out of here! I can't stand being in the meadow! All I can think about is lying beneath the sod in my grave. I can't breathe with the dirt on my face. Help me! Stop!' (Clair 1996, p.127).

The music therapy student wisely asked the resident if there was something she would rather think about while listening to the music, and the resident then described everything in the house that had not been cleaned. The student's response was very appropriate in this situation. It is possible that even though the script speaks of beautiful images, the client may experience unwanted, spontaneous and involuntary images that are contrary to the script. In these situations the therapist calmly asks, 'What would you rather do?' or 'Where would you rather be?' The therapist then follows the lead from the client, for example, if the client would rather be in her own house rather than in a meadow, the therapist follows with 'Can you describe what the house looks like?' and 'Where are you in your house?' The therapist 'walks beside' the client's imagery, being present to the client's experience and helping the client calm down.

Unguided music imaging (UMI) and group music and imagery (GrpMI)

In these two methods the client's imagery is self-generated, that is, the imagery is created in the client's inner awareness in response to the music.

Self-generated imagery can be illuminating to the client (and the therapist), in that the images emerge from the client's unconscious, and may depict issues that the client is facing in his or her life. Carl Jung wrote extensively about Active Imagination, a method he used to encourage patients to describe in greater detail and depth what they were feeling, 'giving form, giving expression in outer reality, of an inner image or reality' (O'Connor 1990, p.100).

Jung encouraged his patients to explore what the images might mean, as distinct from him providing the interpretation. He also had high regard for the content of dreams and the images within dreams to help his patients understand their inner life.

Hans Carl Leuner (1969) developed a method termed guided affective imagery (GAI), which inspired Helen Bonny in the development of the method now called the Bonny Method of Guided Imagery and Music (BMGIM). In GAI, Leuner used a set of ten images that he presented to the patient as a means of gathering diagnostic information. The ten scenarios were:

- relaxing in a meadow
- climbing a mountain
- following a brook upstream to its source, and downstream to the ocean
- imaging a house (a symbol representing the personality of the patient)
- visualising a close relative (quality of the patient's emotional relationships)
- visualising a situation that represents sexual behaviour and feeling
- visualising a lion
- saying the name of a person of the same sex (representing the patient's ego ideal)
- imaging situations that facilitate the appearance of symbolic figures (e.g. looking into a dark forest)
- imaging a swamp in the corner of the meadow (representing the 'shadow' figure) (Leuner 1969).

Bonny took six of these images to form the basis of one of her music programmes called 'Imagery'. Leuner's ten scenarios, however, are important because they represent the range and variety of experiences people have during unguided and guided music and imagery sessions, in individual sessions and group contexts.

Types of imagery experiences

Clients experience a wide range of experiences while listening to music in a deeply relaxed state. Some experiences are visual in form, but other senses are also activated. Based on her clinical experience, Grocke (1999a, 2005a) developed a comprehensive list of the different types of experiences that clients have during BMGIM. Table 5.2 is an extension of that list.

Table 5.2 Types of imagery experiences	
Visual experiences	Colours, shapes, fragments of scenes, complete scenes, figures, people, animals, birds, water (lakes, streams, oceans, pools)
Memories	Childhood memories, significant events, significant people and feelings, reminiscences
Emotions and feelings	The full spectrum of emotions and feelings, including: sadness, happiness, joy, sorrow, fear, anger, surprise
Body sensations	Parts of the body may feel lighter, or heavier, parts of the body may become numb and feel split off from the body, there may be feelings of floating or falling, sensations of spinning, feelings that the body is changing in some way

Body movements	The client may make expressive movements of the body in relation to the imagery being experienced – e.g. hands create a shape, arms reach up in response to an image, fists may clench in reaction to feelings of anger
Somatic sensations	Changes within the internal organs of the body may be experienced – e.g. pain felt in the chest or heart, exploring an internal organ for its shape and colour, a surge of energy felt through the entire body
Altered auditory perception	The music sounds like it comes from far away, the music is very close, or one particular instrument stands out (which can also be transference to music)
Pure music transference	The client is fully engaged in the music (Summer 1998)
Associations and transference to the music	Memories of when the music was last heard (e.g. wedding, funeral), memories of playing the music or that the music is being played especially for the client, or that the client is actually playing the music being heard
Abstract imagery	Mists, fog, geometrical shapes, clouds, etc.
Spiritual imagery and spiritual experiences	Being drawn toward a light, feeling a presence very close, being in a cathedral, a spiritual person: a monk, priest, or woman in flowing robes
Transpersonal experiences	The body becoming smaller, or larger, a change felt deep in the body (cells changing, parts of body changing shape), or the person becomes another form – e.g. the person becomes the bird in flight, or becomes one with a significant feeling or event
Archetypal figures	Figures from legendary stories, or film characters may appear, e.g. King Arthur, Robin Hood, the Vikings, Aboriginal man/woman, a witch, or Merlin; figures from movies, such as Superman, ET, Luke Skywalker, Darth Vader; also Mickey Mouse, Donald Duck, Homer or Marge Simpson!
Dialogue	Significant figures from the client's life may appear in the imagery and often have a message, so that dialogue may occur e.g. with parental figures. Aspects of self may be symbolised in human form (a baby or adult figure), or significant companions (e.g. an albatross or an eagle) and dialogue may occur with these aspects
Aspects of the shadow part of the self	A person of the same gender may appear that the client immediately dislikes. It is helpful to find out what aspect of the person the client is reacting to, as this may be a part of the client that he or she does not like to recognise in him- or herself
Symbolic shapes	A long tunnel, a black hole, seeds opening. These shapes or images can be symbolic of moments of change or transition. Symbolic images such as an ancient book or the trident shape often have specific meaning to the client

Assessing a client's suitability for methods that involve self-generated imagery

Before encouraging a client to engage in music imaging, it is important to determine whether the method is suitable, and whether the client's mental and physical state will allow him or her to benefit from the method. Summer (1988) developed guidelines for the use of guided imagery and music in institutional settings, and these guidelines are accepted universally as a template for screening a client's suitability for music and imaging. A client is suitable for music and imaging if he or she:

1.   is capable of symbolic thinking

2.   can differentiate between symbolic thinking and reality

3.   can relate his or her experience to the therapist

4.   can achieve positive growth as a result of GIM therapy (Summer 1988, p.32).

The fourth criterion is an important one. Some clients engaging in imagery experiences may be confronted with negative images, for example. While the purpose of therapy is to understand these negative experiences, for some clients they may be overwhelming, or may be part of the pathology of certain conditions (e.g. autism, psychotic illness, confusion, etc.). Therefore music and imagery experiences with these clients may be contraindicated.

Procedure

In the two methods described below (unguided music imaging, and group music and imagery), the client(s) is in an altered state of consciousness, meaning that the therapist has provided a relaxation induction, and that the client is deeply relaxed. There is a music-listening period, during which the client is engaged in self-generated imagery. At the end of the music the therapist brings the client, or client group, out of the altered state of consciousness, and there is either discussion of the experience, or the client/clients draw a mandala, or free drawing, or other creative expression of the imagery experience (for example, creating a form from moulding clay). The role of the therapist, however, requires an understanding of symbolic thinking and skill in facilitating discussion of the client's experience, and it is recommended that the therapist undertakes further training to learn these skills. The most appropriate training is at least level 1 (Introductory) training in the Bonny Method of Guided Imagery and Music (BMGIM). Training programmes in this method are offered throughout the world (see www.bonnymethod.com/ami/training.html).

Unguided music imaging

In unguided music imaging (UMI), 'the client images freely while listening to music while in an altered state of consciousness without direction or dialogue with the therapist, with or without a focus. The music is usually short' (Bruscia 1998a, p.125). This method may be used for hospitalised patients, or in other contexts where dialogue with the therapist is not warranted – e.g. if the client is tired.

Marr (1998–1999), a qualified BMGIM therapist, provided unguided music and imagery sessions for a woman who was terminally ill, and over 15 sessions the client resolved a number of issues about the ending of her life. The music selections came from the Bonny music programmes used in BMGIM, however each session contained only 15 minutes of music, and the patient did not engage in dialogue. Marr provided a short relaxation induction for the woman, and then played the music selection. At the end of the music, Marr brought the client back to a non-altered state of consciousness, and then discussed the imagery the woman had experienced.

Procedure

Unguided music imaging (UMI) can be practised in diverse contexts – hospitals, aged care facilities, mental health centres, rehabilitation centres or any other similar setting. The therapist may make decisions for all aspects of the UMI session, or may consult with the client about the type of relaxation induction he or she would like, what the focus of the session might be and even what selection of music to use.

For the UMI method, the procedure follows seven steps:

1.   make the client comfortable

2.   determine a focus for the session

3.   select appropriate music (with or without the client)

4.   provide a relaxation induction

5.   monitor how the client is engaged with the music

6.   bring the music and imagery experience to an end

7.   facilitate a discussion of the client's experience.

1.   The comfort of the client depends on the context of the session – whether the client is in a hospital bed, or seated in a chair, or lying on a padded mat on the floor. The environment should be conducive to the music and imagery experience, for example, a quiet place, a sign on the door (if appropriate) requesting no interruptions, and dimmed lights in the room (this may not be possible in a hospital ward). The client needs to be kept warm, as the body temperature drops during relaxation, therefore the client should have a blanket to cover the body, which also provides a 'psychological' protection so that the person does not feel vulnerable. A pillow for the client's head is also necessary, if the person is lying on the floor or in bed.

2.   The therapist discusses with the client what the focus might be for the UMI session. It is helpful to develop a theme of some kind. If the theme is left open (e.g. 'let's see what happens'), it is often difficult for a client to engage with imagery in this abstract way. In addition it is difficult for the therapist to monitor what the client might be experiencing. Finding a theme (or focus) such as 'releasing pain', or 'healing for a part of the body', or 'having time to myself' will allow the therapist to match a relaxation induction and choose music that matches the focus/theme. The therapist can begin this discussion by asking, 'What would you like to focus on today?' Using some of the verbal skills outlined in Chapter 1, the therapist can develop a sense of what is important to the person, and then check with him or her what the focus for the session will be.

3.   The therapist might also ask the client about the type of music he or she would like for the imagery experience, e.g. slow or moderate, bright or mellow, classical or ambient. Alternatively the therapist may make a choice based on the CD collection available (with or without the client's input). See the list of suggestions at the end of this section, p.142.

4.   Chapter 4 outlines a range of relaxation inductions to suit a short session where there might be five minutes set aside for the relaxation induction, or a longer induction if the session is of longer duration. The main features of the induction include making sure the client is as comfortable as possible, that appropriate voice quality and tone is adopted, that the induction flows smoothly, using repetition in the directions. At the end of the induction the therapist introduces the focus image: 'And now become aware of [the part of the body needing healing] and allow the music to bring healing to your body,' or 'Allow an image of a place where you can have space for yourself – it may be a favourite place, or a special place of some kind. Take a few moments to bring an image of that place to your mind, and now allow the music into that feeling of space for yourself.'

5.   Monitor the client's experience of the music and imagery by noting any changes in body movements, or changes in facial expression. The therapist can get a sense of what the client is experiencing by noting whether the body seems relaxed or tense, or whether the client frowns, or whether the face is very relaxed and calm. These observations will help in the discussion that follows the end of the music.

6.   In order to bring the music and imagery experience to an end, when the music has finished, the therapist waits for 30 seconds or so to allow the last strains of the music to fade way, and then says 'The music has come to an end...allow yourself to remain with the imagery for a few moments longer [this encourages the client to note the imagery he or she has experienced], and then gradually

allow the imagery to fade.' The therapist then brings the client out of the deeply relaxed state, saying 'Become aware of the room we are in, the mat (or chair) under your body...begin to wiggle your toes, and hands, and give your body a big stretch...and opening your eyes when you are ready...'

7. Conclude with a discussion of the experience. Allow several minutes for the client to come out of the relaxed state before asking questions about the experience. During relaxation the analytical part of the brain slow down, and finding words to explain the experience might be difficult. When the client appears ready the therapist might ask an open question such as 'What was that like for you?' Later the therapist might also ask about the music: 'What was the music like for you?' This question is very helpful so that in future sessions the therapist is aware of the client's music preferences and how he or she relates to certain types of music. Alternatively the therapist might suggest that the client creates a drawing of the imagery experience. It may be a free drawing, or a mandala drawing (a circle is drawn in the centre of the page, and the client either draws within the circle, or uses the circle as a reference point for the drawing).

Group music and imagery (GrpMI)

In this method, a group of clients listen to music in a deeply relaxed state, without direction from the therapist, but usually with a focus for the experience. At the end of the music listening period, the group discusses imagery that has occurred.

GrpMI is used for groups that have a common purpose or identity, for example, indigenous peoples (McIvor 1998–1999), high school students (Weiss 1996–1997), youth at risk (Marek 2002), in aged care facilities (Short 1992; Summer 1981), in spiritual retreat (Holligan 2004a, 2004b; Marr 2003), psychiatry (Erdonmez 1977; Goldberg 1994, 1995) and treatment programmes for clients who have chemical addictions (Borczon 1997).

Procedure: setting the scene

The GrpMI should be held in a large room with carpeted floor, to enable sufficient space between group members when lying on the floor. Alternatively, clients may be sitting in comfortable chairs in a large circle. Usually the music is played immediately after the induction (see Chapter 4 for fully written inductions). The duration of the music selection will vary according to the context of the session. The selection needs some dynamic changes to stimulate imagery, but be well contained at the end, that is, have a definite ending to the music, e.g. a definite concluding cadence. At the end of the music each member of the group draws a mandala or writes about their experience.

Procedural steps

The procedure is similar to the seven-step model presented above for the individual session, however in the group context there are additional points to consider.

1. Assess the suitability of the clients in the group for the method. In the group context each member should be able to respect the others in the group and not disrupt the group process.

2. The set-up for the session follows the guidelines above – a quiet place, a sign on the door to prevent disruption, a comfortable floor with mats, or comfortable chairs, a sound system that reproduces music well and is positioned so that all members of the group can hear equally well.

3. Start with a discussion with the group to determine a theme for the session (see following examples). It is helpful if the group has a common goal that they may be working toward, or perhaps a common goal that has brought them together. The therapist facilitates a discussion about the focus/theme, and then summarises the views of the group and suggests the focus, or theme. This helps the group have a sense of where the imagery might start and provides an anchor for the imagery experience.

4. Suggest the group members find a place in the room (or a chair) that is comfortable for them, and encourage the clients to take some time to get as comfortable as possible. Usually the group members need a blanket to keep them warm during the session, and a pillow for their head. Dim the lights in the room. When the group members are as comfortable as possible the therapist begins the relaxation induction. The therapist might begin by suggesting that each person turns his or her attention to how his or her body is feeling, and to 'let any other distractions be attended to by another person'. This statement helps if a member of the group is unsettled, or if there is noise outside the room. At the end of the induction the therapist focuses the group on the theme: 'and now bring your attention to…and as the music begins to play, allow the music into that image, allowing the image to change as the music suggests'. This latter point is important in the group context, because the therapist has chosen the music for the group, not for an individual, therefore the match may not always be a good one. Sometimes group members comment that they had an image in mind, but when the music started it didn't match the image, and therefore the imagery stopped. So it is important to say 'allow the image to change as the music suggests' – which indicates to the clients in the group that they can change the image, since the music cannot be changed to suit each person's experience.

5. Monitor the group's experience. While the music is playing, the therapist carefully observes each person in the group, noting any changes in body posture, facial expression or other indication about each person's experience,

e.g. tears, a client turning on his or her side and moving into a foetal position. During the post-music discussion, the therapist might check with the client about his or her feelings to ensure that each person in the group leaves the session in a safe frame of mind.

6.   When the music has finished, the therapist says 'The music has finished – allow any imagery to come to a close – allow the imagery to fade.' In the group context the therapist needs to project his or her voice so that it reaches to the person furthest away. The therapist also needs to remind the group of the physical place they are in, since some group members may be still in an altered state of awareness.

> Become aware of the room we are in, your body on the floor (or chair)… become aware of the other people in the room…aware of the sounds within the room (or outside the room if there are noises that are audible)… gradually begin to wiggle your toes and fingers, move your legs and arms, and give the body a big stretch…and open your eyes…

Sometimes group members do not 'return' at the same pace, and the therapist continues to project the voice giving it an 'edge' so that people hear more acutely what is being said. If a client is still not alert, the therapist might approach close to the person and mention his or her name 'Mrs J., becoming aware of your body now, begin to move your legs, Mrs J.' etc.

7.   In GrpMI sessions it is common for the clients to draw a free drawing or a mandala in response to their experience. The therapist can facilitate the drawing by saying:

> you might like to draw something of your experience – it does not have to be a replica of your imagery, but rather capture the essence of what you have experienced. You might want to draw a shape, or you may be drawn to a colour that will start your drawing.

These instructions help a client who feels unconfident about drawing. The group draws in silence, and after a period of time the therapist may say 'Let's have another two to three minutes on the drawings and then we can share together.' This provides enough warning for those who are taking a lot of time over their drawing to bring some closure to the drawing. If there are time restrictions for the group the therapist might also say 'If you haven't finished your drawing at this point we might start our sharing while you finish,' or 'You might like to finish the drawing at home, but for the moment let's share the experience you have had.' The therapist then facilitates the clients' discussion of their imagery experience via the drawings, viz 'Can you tell us something about your drawing – what stands out for you?'

Music selections for unguided music imaging and group music and imagery

Music selected for UMI and GrpMI, has more dynamic variation than music used in pure relaxation sessions. As described in Chapter 2, music for imagery requires variation in tempo and instrumentation (and other elements) in order to stimulate imagery in the client. The purpose is to make changes to, or shift, the imagery to maintain the flow of creative ideas. The following list comprises music that has been used successfully with clients to evoke imagery. (Selections identified by asterisk (*) are found on *Music for the Imagination*, Barcelona Publishers.)

Short selections (four to ten minutes in length)

*Bach, *Concerto for two violins*, Largo, 7:00

*Beethoven, *Piano Concerto no.5*, 'Adagio', 6:36

Boccherini, *Cello Concerto in B*, 'Adagio', 6:57

*Brahms, *Violin Concerto*, 'Adagio', 8:38

Butterworth, *On the Banks of Green Willow*, 6:07

Debussy, *Dances Sacred and Profane*, 8:00

*Dvořák, *Czech Suite*, Romanze, 5:12

*Fauré, *Pavane for a Dead Princess*, 7:44

*Haydn, *Cello Concerto in C*, 'Adagio', 8:36

*Holst, *Planets Suite*, 'Venus', 8:07

*Liadov, *Enchanted Lake*, 7:58

Pachelbel, *Canon in D*, 7:04

Respighi, *The Birds*, 'The dove', 4:34

Respighi, *The Birds*, 'The nightingale', 4:39

*Respighi, *The Fountains of Rome*, 'Valle Guilia', 4:28

Respighi, *The Fountains of Rome*, 'Villa Medici', 5:45

Longer selections

*Brahms, *Piano concerto no.2*, 'Andante', 14.29

*Brahms, *Symphony no.4*, 'Andante Moderato', 12:40

*Debussy, *Prelude to the Afternoon of a Faun*, 11:15

*D'indy, *Symphony on a French Mountain Air*, 11:40

Pierne, *Concertstüke for Harp and Orchestra*, 15:30

*Ravel, *Introduction and Allegro for Harp and Orchestra*, 11:00

Smetana, *Ma Vlast*, 'The Mouldau', 12:29

*Vaughan-Williams, *Fantasia on a Theme of Thomas Tallis*, 16:15

Applications of group music and imagery

Indigenous women

McIvor (1998–1999) developed a four-session GrpMI programme for Maori women, based on the stages of the Hero's Journey, an archetypal story. Her choice of music for each stage was:

Hearing the call:	Strauss, *A Hero's Life*, Section 6 (excerpt)
Setting out:	Beethoven, *Piano Concerto no.5*, 'Adagio'
Obstacles and helpers:	Beethoven, *Symphony no.9*, 'Adagio'
Reaching the goal:	Brahms, *Violin Concerto*, 'Adagio'
	Bach, *Concerto for Two Violins*, 'Largo'
Bringing back gifts:	Shostakovitch, *Quartet no.3*,
	Wagner, *Lohengrin*, 'Prelude' 1st movement
	Sibelius, *Scaramouche*

Youth at risk

Marek (2002) also incorporated the Hero's Journey concept in GrpMI sessions for youth at risk, during a youth art camp. Six young men were involved in the sessions, which took place in caves near to the site of the camp. Walking through the bush to the caves served as a type of induction and a mood of silence had already descended on the group as they took up positions either lying down or seated against the rocks in the cave.

The first session was a Naming Session where, during the imagery, each man found a warrior name for himself (e.g. Adventurer, Amos the Pirate, Lionheart, Fisherman and Hercules).

The music chosen included:

1.   Djam Leelii (African drums), *Unwired – Acoustic Music from Around the World*, NCOS ROOTS

2.   Strauss, *Death and Transfiguration*, 'Transfiguration'

The second session was 'The Journey and the Battle', and the music chosen was:

1.   Smoking music, African male voice unaccompanied, 'Red Ribbon', *Unwired – Acoustic Music from Around the World*, NCOS ROOTS

2.   Blakey, *Orgy in Rhythm*, 'Elephant Walk'

The two GrpMI sessions empowered the men with strong masculine identities that they took forward to other experiences within the camp, for example, deciding to sleep in the caves for the remainder of the camp.

High school students

Weiss (1996–1997) conducted GrpMI sessions with female high school students. At the beginning of the class the girls wrote about how they were currently feeling, and then either reclined on the floor, or rested their head on the desk (the choice was theirs). The therapist led them through an induction and proceeded to the music listening segment, which comprised a single music selection. After the music ended the girls wrote a postlude about how they were feeling. The session fitted within the 40-minute class schedule of the school. The music choices were:

Session 1:   Pachelbel, *Canon in D*

Session 2:   Copland, *Appalachian Spring* (excerpt)

Session 3:   Pierne, *Concertstücke for Harp and Orchestra*

Session 4:   Elgar, *Enigma Variations* no.8 and no.9

Session 5:   Brahms, *Piano Concerto no.2*, 'Allegro non troppo'

Session 6:   Britten, *Simple Symphony*, 'Sentimental Saraband'

                    Vaughan-Williams, *Prelude on 'Rhosymedre'*

                    Berlioz, *L'Enfance du Christ*, 'Shepherd's Farewell'

                    Puccini, *Madame Butterfly*, 'Humming chorus'

Session 7:   Beethoven, *Piano Concerto no.5*, 'Adagio'

                    Vivaldi, *Gloria*, 'Et in terra pax'

Session 8:   Haydn, *Cello Concerto in C*, 'Adagio'

The girls found the GrpMI sessions relaxing and helpful, and the sessions impacted positively on their daily life. Significant images were remembered and recurred and one girl commented that she could understand her dreams more. The girls commented that all high school students should have access to GIM.

Group music and imagery with elderly clients

Short (1992) conducted 18 GrpMI sessions with a group of elderly residents who had physical disabilities, including stroke, visual impairment, heart disease, arthritis and mobility impairments. She used Western art music for the sessions, ranging in duration from 4 to 12 minutes, and the group members imaged 'vividly', addressing issues such as bereavement, sexuality and the aging process. Summer's (1981) groups consisted of 15 residents who met for one hour for GrpMI. She used a five-minute progressive muscle relaxation, followed by seven minutes of music of the classical tradition. Summer also found that elderly clients gained self-awareness and self-acceptance from the imagery experiences, and that 'in addition to the psychotherapeutic benefits of GIM, it exposed residents to classical music, which was enjoyed without exception' (Summer 1981, p.41).

Group music and imagery for retreats

Marr (2003) conducted a series of four GrpMI sessions for a church community, based on the words of the Lord's Prayer. She divided the prayer into four segments, and each session progressively added more segments – i.e. the first session was based on the first segment of the prayer, the second session focused on the first and second segments, the third session on segments 1, 2 and 3, etc.

The session format comprised seven stages:

1. discussion of the week's events (bringing the group together)

2. reading of the words that were the focus for the session

3. relaxation induction

4. reading the words again (as the focus)

5. music

6. return to an alert state

7. processing of the experience (drawing, verbal discussion).

Music selections

Marr suggests the following music selections (all from *Music for the Imagination* CDs)

Session 1: Borodin, *Symphony no.1*, 'Andante'

Session 2: Chopin, *Piano Concerto no.1*, 'Romanze'

Session 3: Rodrigo, *Concierto de Aranjuez*, 'Adagio'
and Delius, *1st Acquarelle*, 'Lento ma non troppo'

Session 4: Strauss, *Death and Transfiguration*, 'Transfiguration'.

The structure outlined here for spiritual retreat can also be used for other programmes where there is a themed series of GrpMI sessions. The seven-step session format outlined above can be used to explore all types of inspirational writings, or for themes such as the four seasons of the year, or the four elements (earth, water, air and fire).

Holligan (2004a) used the seven-stage format (see above) for a three-session programme on 'Peace'. In the first session she used 'Being peace': the words of Thich Nhat Hanh, a Buddhist monk. In the second session the Gaelic blessing 'Deep Peace' was the focus, and in the third session the 'Desiderata' was read. The music she used to accompany these three sessions was:

Session 1:   Massenet, *Orchestral Suite no.7*, 'Sous les Tilleuls'
and Bach, *Suite no.3*, 'Air'

Session 2:   'Deep peace', ABC (Australia), Swoon Collection
and Elgar, *Cello Concerto*, 'Adagio'

Session 3:   Beethoven, *Piano Concerto no.5*, 'Adagio'
and Vivaldi, *Gloria*, 'Et in terra pax'.

In another series of three sessions, Holligan (2004b) used the inspirational writings of Vivian Elisabeth Glyck, '12 Lessons on life I learned from my garden' to structure reflections on 'Women, wisdom and the world'. The session, and music selections were:

Session 1 Appreciate the growth of winter: Haydn, *Cello Concerto in C*, 'Adagio'

Session 2 Patience is a virtue: Bach, *Concerto for Two Violins*, 'Largo'

Session 3 Balance is the key: Rodrigo, *Concierto de Aranjuez*, 'Adagio'.

Group music and imagery with clients in treatment for chemical addictions

Borczon (1997) adopts a different model for group music and imagery sessions with his clients. First there is a warm-up activity to settle the clients into the session. The clients then recline on beanbags for the listening experiences. Borczon provides a relaxation induction of between eight and ten minutes and plays the first piece of music. When the music finishes, Borczon asks each person to report on any imagery he or she may have experienced. At the end of the reporting, Borczon provides a brief re-focus into the relaxed state, and then plays the second selection. At the end of the music the clients report any imagery, then re-focus into the relaxed state for the third selection of music, and so on. Borczon uses a range of music styles and moods, and the selections are of approximately two minutes duration, for example:

Selection 1:   Michael Jones, *Mexican Memories* (first 2 minutes only)

Selection 2:   Bernstein, *West Side Story*, 'Cool'

Selection 3:   Chaquico, *Acoustic Highway*

Selection 4:   Enya, *Watermark*, 'River'

Selection 5:   Stravinsky, *The Firebird* (final two minutes).

Borczon (1997) monitors the imagery experiences of each person in the group and is able to reflect on any themes that emerge in each person's imagery experience over the five music selections (pp.89–116). He comments that the sessions can be 'relaxing, powerful, insightful, and fun' (p.115). He also notes that because the clients have similar issues relative to chemical addiction, there are similarities in the clients' imagery experiences that help the whole group gain insight.

Adaptations to GrpMI

The GrpMI method can also be adapted where necessary and Goldberg (1994) outlines adaptations required for psychiatric inpatients. In order to provide maximum psychological safety Goldberg modified the session in the following way:

a) Patients sit in chairs, rather than lying down

b) The type of music and its dynamic range are limited

c) The music phase is limited to five to ten minutes

d) The entire experience, including the induction, is contained within the music phase

e) After the music begins, a very brief relaxation is given

f) There is a much longer period of focus to provide verbal structure during the music phase

g) Patients record their images immediately as the music continues. (Goldberg 1994, pp.26–27)

Goldberg used the following music selections for patients in acute psychiatry:

Daniel Kobialka CDs

Pachelbel, *Canon in D*

Bach, *Air on a G String.*

Similarly, Blake and Bishop outline adaptations for patients with post-traumatic stress disorder. The adaptation required:

a) short duration of relaxation (1–2 minutes),

b) remaining in a sitting position,

c) high level of specificity of image and goal for the induction,

d) short duration of music [no more than 10 minutes],

e) experiencing the imagery with eyes open, and supported by writing, drawing, or movement, and

f) emphasis on safety, validation and reinforcement of efforts. (Blake and Bishop 1994, p.128).

Guided music imaging (GMI)

Bruscia defines this method as 'the client freely images to music while in an altered state of consciousness and dialoguing with the therapist' (Bruscia 1998a, p.125). GMI is an adapted form of the longer BMGIM session that lasts about one and a half hours. The GMI session usually involves a short discussion, a relaxation induction, and a short selection of music (approximately 10–20 minutes) during which the client dialogues with the therapist about what is happening in the imagery. At the end of the music the client might draw a mandala. The session usually fits within an hour.

GMI differs from a full-length BMGIM session in that the selection of music is shorter, thereby limiting the depth to which the client can go in the imagery experiences (the BMGIM music programmes are typically 30–40 minutes duration).

Table 5.3 compares the role of the client and therapist in unguided music imaging (UMI), outlined above, and guided music imaging (GMI), explained below. The essential difference between the two methods is that in GMI the therapist engages the client in dialogue about the imagery experiences. Making appropriate interventions requires skill, and it is strongly recommended that the music therapist complete at least level 1 and 2 of BMGIM training before embarking on GMI sessions with clients.

Table 5.3 Comparison of unguided music imaging and guided music imaging

	Client's role	Therapist's role	Level of expertise required
Unguided music imaging (1:1 session)	The client listens to the music and may have imagery or other experiences in response to the music	The therapist does not dialogue with the client, but observes the client's response to the music	Music therapists trained in receptive techniques can implement this method, although training at level 1 of BMGIM is recommended
Guided music imaging (GMI) – a shortened form of the BMGIM session	The client self-reports any imagery or other experiences in response to the music	The therapist engages the client in dialogue, by asking simple interventions, and observes the client's response to the music and imagery	At least level 1 and 2 of BMGIM training is recommended

Procedure

The therapist discusses with the client what the focus for the session might be. If the therapist is not trained in the Bonny Method of Guided Imagery and Music, then the focus should be a 'safe' experience, such as a place in nature, or a favourite place. The therapist and client might choose a selection of music that matches the scene or the experience, and the therapist then provides a relaxation induction for the client. At the end of the relaxation induction the therapist directs the client's attention to the image: 'Bring to your mind the image from nature/favourite place.' The therapist then guides the client's attention to the music: 'Allow the music to join that image.' Once the music has played for a minute or so, the therapist can ask questions (interventions) about what is happening in the client's imagery. The client describes what is happening for him or her, and a dialogue continues between the therapist and the client. Four examples are given below: these interventions are suggestions only and are intended to illustrate the types of interventions used. They should not be taken as literal sequences of questions.

At the end of the music, the therapist says 'The music has come to an end, allow any imagery to come to a close for the moment, knowing you can return to it at another time.' The therapist then verbally processes with the client about his or her experience, or the client may draw about the experience.

Example 1

Focus: In a nature scene

Music: Respighi, 'The Nightingale'

Relaxation induction: A short induction that concludes with 'Allow the music to join the image, letting the image change as the music suggests...'

Allow 30 seconds to 1 minute after the music begins before making an intervention.

Intervention suggestions:

- Can you describe the scene? (shapes and colours – try to get a good description of the place)
- What does it feel like to be there?
- What else do you notice around you?
- Can you describe it? (colour, shape)
- Is anyone there with you?

Whenever the music changes, such as getting faster, softer, louder, ask:

- What is happening now?

Example 2

Focus: A path (notice what it looks like; how it feels to be there)

Music: Debussy, 'Prelude Afternoon of a Faun'

Relaxation induction: A short induction that concludes with 'Allow the music to join the image, letting the image change as the music suggests…'

Intervention suggestions:

Allow 30 seconds to 1 minute after the music begins before making an intervention.

- What does the path look like? (colour, shape)
- What is the path made of?
- How does it feel under your feet?
- Are you moving along the path?
- What do you see?

If the path divides, and there are two paths at any time, ask:

- Which path do you want to take?

Whenever the music changes, such as getting faster, softer, louder, ask:

- What is happening now?

Example 3

Focus: By water (the sea, a lake, a stream, a waterfall)

Music: Grieg, 'Morning', from the *Peer Gynt Suite*

Relaxation induction: A short induction that concludes with 'Allow the music to join the image, letting the image change as the music suggests…'

Intervention suggestions:

Allow 30 seconds to 1 minute after the music begins before making an intervention.

- What does the water look like? (small stream; huge ocean; cool)
- What is the colour of the water?
- Do you notice anything else? (sun might be hot; blue sky; ferns growing along the bank of a stream)
- What does it feel like? (restful, peaceful, etc.)
- Where in your body do you feel it? (whole body, in chest)

Example 4

Focus: A place in nature, perhaps in the hills or mountains

Music selection: Respighi, 'The dove'

Relaxation induction: A short induction that concludes with 'Allow the music to join the image, letting the image change as the music suggests…'

Intervention suggestions:

Allow 30 seconds to 1 minute after the music begins before making an intervention.

- What do you see?
- Can you describe this place?
- How does it feel to be there?
- What else do you notice?

Interventions for short pieces of music

Interventions should match the client's imagery experience. If the client reports visual imagery, then the interventions should be in the same modality, asking for a description of the visual imagery. If the client is feeling alone, or sad, then the interventions should ask about the feelings. The therapist, however, should not over-intervene, otherwise the client will feel he or she is answering too many questions. Therefore the therapist can use supportive affirmations.

Affirming interventions

Uh-huh

Hmmm

Oh…

Interventions for visual imagery

What does it look like?

Does it have a colour?

Does it have a shape?

Interventions for feelings

What is the feeling like?

Where in your body do you feel it?

Interventions if a person appears in the imagery

Is this someone you know?

Is there anything you want to say to this person?

Is there anything the person says to you?

Group of people

Is there one person that stands out?

(if so, then go to questions under 'Interventions if a person appears in the imagery')

Interventions when the client has no imagery

Can the music help?

Does the music say anything?

Stay with the music and enjoy it.

Applications of GMI

GMI differs from a full-length BMGIM session in that the selection of music is shorter, thereby containing the depth to which the client can go in the imagery experiences. GMI therefore can be considered an adapted form of the longer BMGIM, and may be chosen because of time restrictions – for example, a GMI session can be carried out within one hour (Ritchey-Vaux 1993). If the session has to be contained within the hour, then GMI is a suitable method. Some BMGIM therapists refer to GMI as an adaptation of BMGIM, and Ritchey-Vaux describes how this short form of BMGIM can fit within the hour, relative to a psychotherapy session.

GMI, as an adaptation of BMGIM, is also effective for patients who have post-traumatic stress disorder (Blake 1994; Blake and Bishop 1994), in short-term acute psychiatry (Goldberg 1994), for a patient with brain damage (Goldberg, Hoss and Chesna 1988) and a client with dissociative disorder (Grocke 2005b). In all four contexts the full-length BMGIM session was modified; the relaxation induction was either lengthened to allow the patient more time to enter a relaxed state, or conversely the induction was shortened to prevent the patient from becoming too deeply relaxed in an altered state of consciousness. In all four cases the music selection was shortened and the form and style was not complex. During the music and imagery dialogue the therapist was often more directive, even suggesting the imagery scene in a last session (Goldberg *et al.* 1988). Often the client opens his or her eyes in order to feel safe (Blake 1994: Blake and Bishop 1994; Grocke 2005b). In the post-music discussion the therapist helped the patient to make connections between the images and the recovery process.

A single GMI session (as an adaptation of BMGIM) was effective in helping an elderly woman with dementia to address unresolved emotions about her husband's death, while also confronting her own fears of death (Colegrove 1995). Interestingly, the GMI session incorporated longer selections of music, but no relaxation induction. The woman was in a 'time confused' (Feil 1993) state late in the afternoon and was fearful that people were coming for her. Colegrove used six pieces of classical music (the 'Imagery' music programme devised by Bonny) during which the woman confronted the people coming for her, and went quietly with them. She 'came face to face with...her core fear – her fear of death' (Colegrove 1995, p.45).

GMI can also be practised in a short series of themed sessions. The purpose is to set a series of topics associated with a theme so that the client is aware of the overall plan of the therapy. Rachael Martin conducted a series of six GMI sessions with five healthy music students who were experiencing performer anxiety in their music examinations. Martin developed a six-session programme where each session had a specific theme:

- Session 1: Assessment session, which included filling out questionnaires and an introduction to GMI (favourite place imagery)

- Session 2: What first inspired the participant to become involved with music

- Session 3: Remembering one of the best experiences of playing music

- Session 4: Remembering one of the worst experiences of playing music

- Session 5: Presenting feelings about playing music and plans for the future

- Session 6: Discussion and closure.

Focus images for entry into the music phase were specifically chosen for each student drawn from the earlier discussion of the session theme. Each session lasted approximately one hour and comprised 1) a discussion, 2) relaxation induction with focus image, 3) guided imaging to a short selection of music (10–15 minutes), 4) return to an alert state, and 5) integration via drawing a mandala or verbal processing.

Music selections

The music selections came from the Bonny music programmes, and were chosen to reflect the anticipated nature of the specific theme. They included:

Session 1:   Debussy, *Danses Sacree et Profane* (9:49)

Session 2:   Ravel '*Introduction and Allegro for harp, flute, clarinet and string quartet* (10:25)

Session 3:   Debussy, *Prelude to the Afternoon of a Faun* (10:30)

Session 4:   For this session there were three choices of music, to cater for anticipated differences in the focus image (the worst experience of playing music). The three choices were:

Holst, 'Mars' (to match a memory of feeling angry) (7:18)

or Debussy, 'Andantino' from *String Quartette* (for anxiety) (8:09)

or Dvořák, 'Larghetto' from *Serenade in E major* (for sadness) (6:49)

followed by Warlock, 'Pieds-en-l'air' from *Capriol Suite* (2:21)

Session 5:   Delius, 'La Calinda' from *Koanga Suite* (4:07), followed by Bizet, 'Intermezzo' from *Carmen* (2:59)

Session 6:   Verbal discussion only (no music and imagery experience).

Images that were common across all five students included:

- solid barriers or blocks, e.g. a wall, stage curtains closed, wall of faces
- feelings of anxiety or being uncomfortable
- reassurance or nurturing, e.g. protective or encouraging figures, nature scenes
- mastery of playing or performing
- recurring colours, e.g. light blue, red, yellow.

The students found the GMI method gentle though intense. They engaged in the imagery quickly and were dealing with serious issues by the second session. Processing the experience by either talking or mandala drawing was valuable for understanding their imagery and enabled a sense of connection to it. Participants found the themes covered a broad range of performances at different stages of life, and the themes were approached from a positive point of view. Benefits gained in performance also transferred to other areas, i.e. confidence, self-esteem, coping with difficult situations and self-awareness. Students also noticed a sense of increased relaxation and mood after the GMI sessions lasting up to a few days. They all thought it was a valuable method and recommended others to try it (Martin 2006).

Unguided and guided music and imagery in medicine

Music and imagery methods are well recognised as important vehicles to bridge the mind, body and spirit (Bush 1995, p.48), and therefore these methods have been used effectively in the treatment of many conditions where stimulation of the immune system is advocated. There is convincing evidence that music, and music-imagery, enhance immune function and reduce the perception of pain (Reilly 1996; Rider 1985; Rider and Achterberg 1989; Tsao *et al.* 1991).

Achterberg (1985) writes convincingly about the use of imagery for cancer patients. She incorporates imagery to help patients combat pain and gain a sense of control over the disease.

Procedure

1. The patient is encouraged to find an image for the disease.
2. The patient is then encouraged to find an image that represents healing.
3. The patient is then guided in visualising the treatment image interacting/attacking the disease image.

Achterberg works with her patients several times a week, to assist them in strengthening the imagery process as part of treatment. Her research identified images that signified illness, and those that signified healing, and she noticed a pattern relative to prognosis and the potential for activating the immune system. Healing images indicating good prognosis tended to be strong images of heroic or archetypal figures, such as Superman, Robin Hood, Vikings and others. A poor prognosis was indicated when the images for healing were weak or amorphous (e.g. white fluffy clouds, that lack strength to fight the 'disease' images). There were poor outcomes when images of the cancer were immutable, such as lumps of coal, submarines, etc., that were difficult to 'attack' or break down.

Rider (1985) and others (Dileo and Bradt 1999) have adopted Achterberg's procedure and modified it to incorporate the use of improvisation as an entrainment mechanism. The therapist asks the patient to describe the pain – its intensity, shape and rhythm. The patient chooses an instrument that represents the image of the pain. There is an improvisation with this instrument, until the patient has played 'through' the pain by confronting it and letting go.

A similar process is used in BMGIM, where the patient develops an image that represents the pain in the body and the therapist chooses a selection of music that resonates with the qualities of the image. As the client/patient engages with the illness image (or image of pain), the therapist guides the client to explore the dimensions of the illness/pain – the shape and colour, and how the client feels about the image. The client is encouraged to engage with the image and to find an 'antidote' for the illness/pain, using interventions such as:

Is there anything that the (part of the body) needs?

Can you bring that to the (part of the body)?

What does that feel like?

What is happening now to the image?

Is there something else that you need?

Contraindication

However, in clinical practice confronting the pain is not always successful and sometimes the pain is exacerbated by focused attention on it (Grocke 2003). An alternative is to use music and imagery to divert attention *away* from the pain. It is not clear when each of these options should be used; for some clients addressing the pain and focusing on it can be helpful in moving 'through' the pain, for others the pain is exacerbated. The therapist therefore should assess the client's level of physical and psychological resilience to address illness/pain and his or her manner of engaging with imagery before attempting to address pain issues. A client who does not have the resilience needed to follow through with the imagery experience may find the pain is exacerbated, whereas a client who is committed to confronting the pain and working through it is more likely to find relief from the pain. These issues are explored in detail in Dileo and Bradt (1999) who differentiate acute from chronic pain, and advocate five treatment options for patients, including relaxation enhanced by 'a warm soothing voice' (Dileo and Bradt 1999, p.203).

Conclusion

Methods of music and imagery are used in various ways with adult clients. The imagery session may be guided or unguided, and may be an individual session or a group experience. The duration of the music selection varies depending on the context and the therapeutic intention of the session. Music and imagery methods can also be modified or adapted, according to the specific needs of different patient populations. Of great importance is that the therapist should seek further training in these methods before applying them, and at least level 1 and 2 of BMGIM training is strongly recommended.

Chapter 6

Song Lyric Discussion, Reminiscence and Life Review

Songs express who we are and how we feel, they bring us closer to others, they keep us company when we are alone. They articulate our beliefs and values...and they bear witness to our lives... Songs weave tales of our joys and sorrows, they reveal our innermost secrets, and they express our hopes and disappointments, our fears and triumphs. They are our musical diaries, our life stories. They are the sounds of our personal development. (Bruscia 1998b, p.9)

Introduction and definitions

Different terminology is used to describe the method of music therapy where the client brings to the therapy session a song (or recorded instrumental music) that is meaningful in some way, for discussion with the therapist, and/or with a therapy group. The rationale for this method is that the client expresses him- or herself through the lyrics of the song (or piece of music) and there is a projection of feelings onto the music, or the song lyrics. This method is referred to variously as:

Song sharing

CD sharing (Skewes 2000)

Song analysis (Erdonmez 1977)

Song-based discussion (Holligan 1995)

Song (music) communication (Bruscia 1998a)

Song (lyric) discussion (Bruscia 1998a)

Song reminiscence (Bruscia 1998a)

Songs can also form part of the music life review method, discussed later in the chapter.

This chapter will focus on the methods and techniques involved in song (music) communication, song (lyric) discussion, song reminiscence and music life review.

Bruscia's (1998a) definitions of song (music) communication and song (lyric) discussion are very similar, and both are presented here for the purposes of clarifying the subtle differences. Song (music) communication is defined as follows:

> The therapist asks the client to select or bring in a recorded song (or other piece of music) which expresses or discloses something about the client that is of relevance to therapy, or, the therapist selects a recording that communicates something of relevance to the client. Then both parties listen to the recording and explore what the music communicates about the client, the client's life, or therapeutic issues. (p.124)

The definition of song (lyric) discussion is as follows:

> the therapist brings in a song that serves as a springboard for discussion of issues that are therapeutically relevant to the client. After listening to the song, the client is asked to analyse the meaning of the lyrics, and to examine (in dialogue with the therapist or other clients), the relevance of the lyrics to the client or the client's life. (p.124)

This chapter combines these two discrete methods to develop a three-stage working method that is applicable to individual and group therapy sessions, and includes both methods. The three stages are:

Stage 1: The client or clients choose the song (or piece of music), either by bringing a CD to a session, or by choosing a CD from a collection in the therapy room.

Stage 2: The therapist and client(s) listen to it together.

Stage 3: There is a discussion about the song and its meaning to the client (and the group), and an analysis of the lyrics of the song.

The term song lyric discussion (SLD) will be adopted for the remainder of the chapter to refer to this method. A summary of the theoretical and historical basis, and what constitutes this method follows.

Song lyric discussion (SLD)

Basic theory and history

One of the earliest descriptions of this method was published in the *Journal of Music Therapy* in 1973, under the title 'Psychiatrist as music therapist' (Baumel 1973). In this article, Baumel outlines several ways of using songs in a group context as a stimulus for the discussion of therapeutic issues:

1. The client selects a song that reflects something about him- or herself and presents it to the therapist or group.

2. The client selects a song that reflects a feeling for someone else in the group.

3. The client selects a song for the group.

4.   The therapist selects a song that conveys his or her feelings to the client or group.

5.   The therapist selects a song that represents his or her response to the perceived emotional or therapeutic issues of a particular client.

6.   The therapist selects a song that will facilitate the group process when members of the group are reluctant to make their own choices, because of resistance or vulnerability after long periods of silence, or some other reason.

It is the first of these options that will be described in detail here, although similar principles apply to the other presentation options as well.

Song meanings

Songs become 'popular' when the lyrics speak of everyday situations that people experience, for example:

- relationships – including the tentative beginnings of relationships (e.g. 'Does he or she like me?'), difficulties with relationships (e.g. 'You said this, and I'm hurt'), issues of trust (e.g. 'I saw you with someone else'), the ending of relationships (e.g.'Now it's over', or 'How can I live without you?')

- identity, e.g. 'I want to be me', 'True colours' (Cyndi Lauper)

- peace – songs that talk of world peace (e.g. John Lennon's 'Imagine')

- drugs – e.g. 'Heroin' (Lou Reed), 'Mama's tripping' (Ben Harper)

- aggression – explicit lyrics that can speak of anger and aggressive acts.

Plach (1996), in his book *The Creative Use of Music in Group Therapy*, provides an extensive list of songs popular in the 1970s and 1980s and the possible life issue the song represents. Altogether some 46 different issues are listed for the songs, and these range from intimate relationships, family relationships, friendships, identity, self-acceptance, lifestyle, the full range of emotions to addictions and substance abuse, memories and looking forward to the future.

Standley (1991a) also provides a comprehensive list of songs by counselling topic. Her themes include: active change, addictions/substance abuse, adolescence, aging, anger, child abuse, crisis intervention, decision making, depression/loneliness, disappointment, emotional involvement, marital issues, problem solving, relationships, suicide and terminal illness/catastrophe (pp.155–161). Baker and Tamplin (2006) provide a list of songs used in rehabilitation for patients with brain injury, for song comprehension (2006, p.117), abstract thinking (2006, p.125), self-reflection and self-exploration (2006, 208–214).

There is no doubt that popular songs speak of human life and human frailty, and there is no doubt that people of all ages relate to the lyrics of songs, because the lyrics describe aspects of life that are common to all people, irrespective of age, culture and upbringing.

Artists

It is also common that clients are attracted to popular artists, particularly during adolescence, when young people are forming a sense of their own identity. People form attachments to recording artists for various reasons:

1.   The artist is a role model, in that the artist represents characteristics that the person wishes she/he has.

2.   The artist's life story impacts in some way on the person. These stories are told (either accurately or inaccurately) through the media, and 'popular' magazines and through interviews. Sometimes the life story of the artist is inspiring, particularly if he or she has overcome some significant hurdle in life. Delta Goodrem (an Australian female artist) contracted Hodgkin's disease in 2003, and for a period of time she underwent chemotherapy and radiation therapy. She lost her hair during treatment, but eventually recovered and returned to the music scene. Many young women who are hospitalised for cancer conditions or related diseases identify Delta as a role model in that she represents the recovery that the client is also hoping to achieve, and she models an attitude to adversity that is admired.

       Similarly Kylie Minogue's struggle with breast cancer has been an inspiration for many young women throughout Australia and England. Kylie's attitude of 'I'm going to get through this' was widely conveyed through the media, prompting women in similar situations to adopt a similar attitude.

       Equally, from an adverse perspective, people may identify with a pop artist's drug addiction, or episodic aggressive acts (such as trashing a hotel room or outrageous behaviour on and off stage). Or they may identify with the image of the artist, e.g. Marilyn Manson (alternative/gothic) or Heavy Metal (skulls, black and death images).

Table 6.1 provides a list of current songs, including the recording artist(s) and the issues expressed in the song. Music therapists who use this method in clinical practice have contributed their interpretation of the song's issue, based on clinical experience. The issues listed may not be universal, that is, clients will interpret songs in different ways, based on their own views of the song, and it is this dynamic that makes the method therapeutically valuable.

Table 6.1 Songs, artists and issues explored in the song lyrics

Title of song	Recording artist	Issue(s) expressed in the song
Thankyou	Dido	Appreciation of good times in a relationship
My lover's gone	Dido	Sadness after ending of a relationship
Honestly OK	Dido	Feeling lost and lonely
I hope you dance	Ronan Keating	Expressing hopes and dreams for child
Good riddance (Time of your life)	Green Day	Unpredictable changes in life
Boulevard of broken dreams	Green Day	Loneliness, feeling lost
American idiot	Green Day	Political statement about the media, and alienation
Wake me up when September ends	Green Day	Depression, death (lead singer's father died in September)
Stand by me	Ben E. King	Friendship
Nothing else matters	Metallica	Friendship and trust
Teenage dirtbag	Wheatus	Feeling excluded, wanting to be accepted
Affirmation	Savage Garden	Expression of beliefs and hopes
Yellow	Coldplay	Love
Fix you	Coldplay	Friendship and support
Complicated	Avril Lavigne	Inauthenticity and teenage frustration
Goodbye	The Spice Girls	Coping with loss
Hit me baby one more time	Britney Spears	Loneliness and regret
Smells like teen spirit	Nirvana	Self-hatred expressed through arrogance
Wishlist	Pearl Jam	Expression of beliefs and hopes

Continued on next page

Table 6.1 continued

Title of song	Recording artist	Issue(s) expressed in the song
Six feet from the edge	Creed	Suicidal thoughts
Under the bridge	Red Hot Chilli Peppers	Loneliness, reflecting on life; using drugs
Am I not pretty enough	Kasey Chambers	Self-questioning, identity
Time to come home	Matchbox 20	Trying to resurrect a lost relationship
Bitter	Jill Sobule	Critique of critical people
Born to try	Delta Goodrem	Striving and achievement
Beautiful	Christina Aguilera	Self-affirmation
As long as you love me	Backstreet Boys	Love and acceptance
I'll be there for you (*Friends* theme)	The Rembrandts	Friendship
Superman	Five for Fighting	Wanting to be something that you're not
Please do not go	Violent Femmes	End of a relationship
Better man	Pearl Jam	Unhappy relationship (often presented by women who have been battered)
Hero	Mariah Carey	Following your dreams, self-belief
Drive	Incubus	Taking control of life, fear and uncertainty
Everybody hurts	REM	Survival; universality
Nothing compares	Sinead O'Connor	Relationship break-up
Walking away	Craig David	Misunderstood
My heart will go on	Celine Dion	Death and loss
Tired of sleeping	Suzanne Vega	Depression

Table 6.2 lists some of the classic songs from 1970 to 1990, that are still presented in therapy groups because of the timeless relevance of the lyric content.

Table 6.2 Classic songs from 1970 to 1990		
Title of song	Recording artist	Issue(s) expressed in the song
The way we were	Barbara Streisand	Reminiscence, nostalgia, memories
I am a rock	Simon and Garfunkel	Emotional withdrawal
You've got a friend	Carole King	Relationship support
I never meant to hurt you	Barbra Streisand	Relationships – feeling guilt for causing hurt
Yesterday	Paul McCartney	Nostalgia, loss, regret
Imagine	John Lennon	World peace
Just the way you are	Billy Joel	Relationships – accepting the other person as he or she is
Tears in heaven	Eric Clapton	Death and loss
Knockin' on heaven's door	Bob Dylan	Suicidal thoughts; funeral
Father and son	Cat Stevens	Family relationships
Wind beneath my wings	Bette Midler	Appreciation and 'hero' worship of another; often used at funerals to depict gratitude
Satisfaction	Rolling Stones	Striving

Looking at the prospective issue that each song raises is likely to engender discussion in a group session. There may be many different perspectives on what message the song portrays, and these differing interpretations make the song lyric discussion a dynamic therapeutic modality. For example, consider the song 'Wind beneath my wings', sung by Bette Midler in the film *Beaches*. In the film, Midler plays the role of a successful music star and the song is sung for her friend who is in the terminal stages of cancer. The meaning of the song in the film is one of acknowledging the support of the friendship, and that Midler would not have succeeded without her friend's support ('Didn't you know you were my hero?', and 'I can fly higher than an eagle, because you are the wind beneath my wings'). The song, however, has come to have many meanings. It is often sung at funerals to depict acknowledgement of a life, it is sung at weddings to depict romantic love and support, and it can have meaning for clients who are struggling with life-threatening illness, or serious chronic illness (such as schizophrenia) to depict the strength needed to overcome life's challenges and difficulties.

Similarly the song 'Imagine' by John Lennon was originally written about world peace, but is now played at both funerals and weddings, and is chosen by clients who are facing major challenges in their lives (to reflect the sentiment 'imagine a world without illness'). Therefore, although the songwriter may have wanted to depict a certain meaning in the lyrics, the empowering factor for therapy is that clients can project into the song any meaning that is relevant to their life at the time. In this sense, song lyric discussion can be a projective technique (Erdonmez 1977).

Therapeutic purpose

The purpose and objectives of this method are to:

- provide an opportunity for clients, particularly young adults, to enjoy their preferred genre and preferred artist(s)

- promote a projective technique whereby difficult emotions can be expressed and discussed via projection onto the artist, or the lyrics of the song

- promote music as a catalyst for discussion of issues pertinent to the client(s)

- encourage insight by discussion of the song's lyrics

- provide opportunities for choice and self-expression

- assist clients to understand feelings associated with current issues.

Procedure

MATERIALS

Depending on the context of the therapy setting a client may either bring a favourite song on CD from her or his private collection, or the client can choose a song from a collection of CDs held in the music therapy session room.

A CD collection should contain a range of song material so that the client can choose something that is preferred. CDs can be stored in boxes and arranged (as in music stores) by female and male artists, or by groups (in alphabetical order). It is important to have a wide range of artists represented, including current solo artists, popular groups, and also seasoned favourites, such as The Beatles and the Rolling Stones.

Good audio equipment is needed so that the client(s) can hear the music at its best, and gain full aesthetic pleasure. Speakers should be located appropriately in the room so that the sound is projected to all areas of the room equally. For group sessions, chairs are arranged in a circle so that each member of the group can be aware of others and discussion can be facilitated. The therapist may position himself/herself near to the CD player, to monitor the volume level.

In individual sessions the therapist may sit close to the client, and may or may not be facing the client. The sitting position will be determined by the depth of the therapy, the rapport between the client and the therapist, or the context of the therapy, e.g. whether the patient is hospitalised and the therapist is facing the patient lying in bed.

PREPARATION

The first time an SLD session is facilitated for clients, the therapist should provide information about what will happen, and why the method is useful in the therapeutic context. There are different levels of therapeutic intent in this method. The first level is an 'activities'-based level, where the clients choose a song or selection of music based on their liking it. A deeper level of this method is when clients choose a song because it has meaning to them, and the intention is that the client will discuss the meaning with the therapist or the group.

For the activities-based level the explanation could be as follows:

> Songs can be important to us in our lives because they tell about the experiences of life that are common to all of us – disappointments, losses, difficulties in relationships, searching for identity, etc. What we are going to do is to choose songs that you enjoy listening to, and that we can share together. We can listen to the song first and then discuss anything about the song that you think is important. Can you choose a song for us to listen to?

It could be important to just suggest choosing one that a client 'likes' rather than making more overt the therapeutic intention of asking the client to choose one that has a 'special meaning' for him or her.

Once the client(s) has chosen the CD then the therapist suggests that the client chooses one track to play. The therapist may also ask the client to say something about the song before listening to it, or may ask why the client has chosen that particular song. Decisions about this part of the procedure need to be made based on the therapist's knowledge of the client(s), and could be informed by a number of issues:

- It may not be wise to ask for such explanations if this is the first session, or the first time you have used SLD with a client or group of clients.

- Conversely, it may be important for there to be an understanding that this approach has a clear therapeutic direction.

- It may not be wise to ask the client to talk about the song at all before playing it, as it is in the listening to the song that all the important emotional reflections and meanings will emerge. In addition, suggesting the client makes a comment prior to playing the song might result in a defensive comment, e.g. 'You probably won't like this song.'

- Conversely, it may help both client and therapist to have a focus of meaning while listening.

Further distinctions between 'activities-based' and 'insight-oriented' sessions are discussed later in the chapter.

PLAYING THE SONG

It is advisable for the therapist to have control over the volume setting. The song needs to be played loud enough to hear the words, but not too loud that it is distressing to others (in the case of group work). A client who chooses a very loud song and is clearly aggressive will want the song played very loud. If the therapist has control over the volume, it can be adjusted. If the client has control it is difficult to reduce the volume once the song is playing without a reaction from the client.

The therapist should make the comment that while the song is playing the group will listen, and not talk. To create the atmosphere of listening the therapist can establish a quiet space before starting the CD. This can easily be done by first saying 'Let's listen to the song now,' and waiting for silence before starting the music, thereby creating an anticipation of what is to come.

MONITORING

During the playing of the song there can be a tangible connectedness in the group, as the clients reflect on the words, and are moved by the music. The therapist makes periodic observations of how the client or the members of the group are relating to the song. The person who has chosen the song may show signs of feeling vulnerable. After all, in choosing the song the client is disclosing something of him- or herself that could become apparent, or be interpreted in a certain way by the therapist, or by others in a group situation. The therapist also scans the body language and facial expressions of others in the group to get a sense of whether the song is meaningful to other people. This will be helpful during the discussion of the song.

MANAGING THE ENDING OF THE SONG

When the song has finished, there is usually a period of reflective silence before the therapist asks the client to share what is meaningful about the song. The therapist can stimulate discussion of the song by asking questions. These questions (suggested below) can be graded to deepen the level of discussion, however they should not be asked in a series, otherwise there will be an unnatural flow to the discussion. Balancing questions with supportive comments or reflections (as described in Chapter 1) will allow the discussion to flow freely.

First-level questions ask about the music

- What do you like about the music/song?
- What do you think about the performer, or the band?

These questions keep the discussion at a level relevant to the music. The therapist can gain information about the client's preference for genre and performing artist, and can sense whether the client would like to explore the lyrics of the song.

Second-level questions probe the meaning of the song to the client

- Are there particular lyrics that stand out as being meaningful to you? In what way?

- Is the song meaningful to you in some other way (apart from the lyrics)? In what way?
- Does the song remind you of anyone or anything special in your life?

These questions focus on the meaning of the song, and can uncover information about the client from the lyrics, as these are likely to pertain to the client's current life situation. If the context of the therapy session encourages further exploration, the therapist may ask about the relevance to the person's life.

Third-level questions probe the connection of the meaning of the song with what is happening in the client's life at the moment

- Is there something about the song that relates to your life at the moment?
- Why did you bring that song today?
- How does the song make you feel?
- What images or thoughts came to you when you were listening to the song?

Sometimes a client may want to talk immediately about the relevance of the song to his or her life, however for others there may be a feeling of vulnerability, so that easing into the more personal questions can occur via the first- and second-level questions above.

It is important to remember that listening to songs is not a cerebral experience but often a very emotional and embodied one, and clients may realise that the song says a lot about their current life situation and they may feel undefended in the discussion. It is essential then to 'read' the body language of the client to determine what level of questioning is appropriate.

WIDENING THE DISCUSSION

If the song lyric discussion is within the group context, the questions may be opened up to the group, for example:

- How do others in the group feel about this song?
- Are there other meanings about the song?
- Does anyone have something further to say about the song?

Clients can feel particularly vulnerable in the group situation where others in the group can comment about the song. If the group is insensitive in their comments, or sarcastic or cynical, this can affect not only clients' attitude to the song they have chosen and its meaning for them, but potentially their position within the group. As stated previously, songs are very powerful, and can be profoundly meaningful.

If the group is a 'closed' group (meaning the members of the group do not change over a period of time), then the group will be familiar with challenges by the therapist or by the group members, and they will anticipate challenges to their choice of song. For other groups, where the membership changes frequently, the therapist may need to actively direct the discussion if a client is in danger of being challenged. The therapist can model appropriate responses by indicating the need for group members to be tolerant of others' beliefs, values and preferences. This can achieved by statements such as 'It is important in this group that we respect each others' point of view,' or 'It seems that the song has been meaningful to Jo, and therefore we need to show respect for her feelings.' These statements can educate the group members about sensitivity, as well as help contain the group process.

At the end of the discussion, it is helpful to acknowledge the person who has presented the song:

> Thank you for bringing the song and sharing it with the group.
>
> I can see why this song is so important for you.
>
> Talking about this song has helped me to understand you better.
>
> It seems this song has meaning for several people in the group, thanks for bringing it.

VIDEO CLIPS

Discussion of the song may also include impressions of the song conveyed via video clips. Video clips leave an indelible impression or set of images that are associated with the song. During discussion it may be the visual image conveyed in the video clip that has meaning for the client.

Vignette: Sally

The vignette of Sally demonstrates the process involved in SLD, and illustrates the powerful role that a song can have in a client's life. In this case the client was electively non-verbal, yet her choice of song was clearly indicative of her emotional and psychological state. Not only was the song itself transparent in meaning, the manner in which Sally presented it each session indicated that the song was an alternative means of self-expression, that is, the song was a projection of Sally's feelings that she could not divulge or disclose to the group.

Sally was admitted to a psychiatric ward, aged 16, following suicide attempts. She was a successful student in year 12 of high school, however her family situation was quite unstable with two brothers and two sisters all fathered by different men. There was no stable parental figure in the household. Sally made frequent suicide attempts and was described clinically as passive aggressive, i.e. she responded to all attempts to interact with her in angry silence. This occurred in interview situations, in individual therapy and in all group therapy sessions. She did however seem to enjoy the weekly song lyric discussion session, but would not participate in improvisation or music relaxation sessions.

Each week Sally chose the same song to present to the music therapy group – a little-known song written by Richard Carpenter and John Bettis ([1969] 2006), and sung by Karen Carpenter, entitled 'Eve'. The song lyrics illustrate a low self-image, and this gave a clear picture of how Sally possibly viewed herself:

Eve, I can't believe
that you could mean what you just said.
Think of what you are
how very far you are from being real.
Look into the mirror, nothing there to see,
Eve, I can't believe you'd really leave him.

The lyrics express a poorly defined sense of identity ('nothing there to see', and 'how far you are from being real'). The music portrays a sad quality; it is slow with an accompaniment of repeated chords, however the melody has quite a lyrical flow to it.

The second verse expresses more negativity:

Eve, I wouldn't lie, the open sky is not your home,
Wide as it may be, reality is here among the stones
Thorns among the roses add to what is real
Eve you are a rose among the thorns here.

The lyrics 'you are a rose among the thorns here' puts Eve in a more positive light, but still among the thorns. And 'reality is here among the stones' suggests a lifeless reality, one that is barren and hard.

The bridge in the song adds:

Notice how her image saddens, how lonely she's become
Just once I'd like to see her happy, before the winter comes.[1]

The lyrics express a depressed mood, with themes of loneliness and loss of happiness, and it is possible that 'before the winter comes' hints at successfully ending life.

Each session Sally played this song to the group, and each week she remained silent about what the song portrayed. The lyrics themselves clearly express the poor self-image and sadness that Sally was projecting. In the session however she would not speak about the words, and interventions to encourage her to express feelings were completely ignored.

Working with passive aggressive clients who elect to remain mute is difficult work. Inevitably the therapist (and group) become frustrated at the lack of responsiveness, and if not well trained, the therapist can get annoyed. The interventions that were used are listed below. They illustrate the usual trajectory of interventions – how one leads into the next – although in Sally's situation none broke through her defence of silence.

The first intervention was always 'What do you like about the song?' Or, 'This seems to be an important song to you, could you tell the group a little about why it is important to you?'

Then, to explore the meaning of the lyrics typical interventions were: 'Some of the lyrics in the song seem a little sad, do you think so?'

'I remember that Karen Carpenter had to struggle with her self-image, is there anything you would like to say about Karen's music, or the way she dealt with problems in her life?'

Another option was to make an interpretation about Sally's lack of willingness to talk about the music. This type of intervention challenges the behaviour, e.g. 'It seems that you are not willing to talk about the song, and sometimes this happens if a person is not feeling comfortable within the group – is this what you are feeling?'

At this point the interventions can seek help and support from the group, e.g. 'Would anyone in the group like to make a comment about the song that Sally has presented?' Members of the group would often comment about the similarity between the song lyrics and how they saw Sally as sad and lonely. When invited to respond to members of the group however, Sally would stay mute.

Over a period of a few weeks Sally continued to present the same song and continued to say nothing about it in the discussion. The group tired of trying to make supportive comments, particularly as Sally ignored their sensitive efforts. The group began to make more hostile comments to Sally, saying they were tired of trying to engage in discussion with her. And so the pattern continued.

Eventually the dynamic that changed Sally's attitude had nothing to do with a therapeutic intervention at all. A new patient was admitted to the ward. She was the same age as Sally and had similar issues with poor self-esteem and suicide attempts. The two girls formed a pact and kept closely together. The new girl however was open in her communication with others, and slowly Sally began to open up.

Sally chose a new song to present to the group – 'True colours', a song that highlights identity and 'your true colours shining through'. Finally Sally started talking about her situation and that the catalyst that brought her to hospital was the death of her grandmother who had been the only nurturing and stable person in her life. Without her grandmother she felt completely alone. Finally Sally talked about the song 'Eve' as being important to her because it said everything she wanted to say about herself – in fact she didn't need to talk about herself at all, because the song said it all. Although Sally was not capable of speaking about the song and the lyrics, this is not a typical response. Normally clients are eager to share the song that they bring to the group. If others in the group also relate to the song, it can be an empowering experience for the client. If group members are challenging about the song, the therapist may be required to support the client, although ultimately the therapeutic goal would be that the client can speak for himself or herself.

Who can benefit from song lyric discussion?

Song lyric discussion can be structured to suit a diverse range of people, by adjusting the level of the discussion from basic to insight-orientated. The three levels of music therapy practice as outlined by Wheeler (1983) are important here.

Activity-based sessions might focus only on the music – the band, the singer, and what clients like about the music.

Insight-oriented sessions might focus on the meaning of the lyrics to the person and how the person feels about the songs.

Re-constructive sessions might look at the significance to the person's life and the embodied experience of the music.

It is important to emphasise that the therapist should listen carefully to the cues from the client in order to approach and engage in the discussion at the appropriate level and depth. If a client immediately wants to discuss the significance of the song to his or her life, then that is the level at which the therapist should engage.

It is also important to emphasise that the 'levels' outlined above are not rigid, and that clients may function at different levels even within a session. Much depends on the client's needs in the moment, and the nature of the client–therapist relationship, and the relationship of the client to the group.

Responding to aggressive clients/aggressive lyric content

One of the most difficult therapeutic challenges is when a client becomes verbally aggressive when choosing and presenting a song, or when the lyrics of the song are offensive. If a client is choosing a CD from the therapy room collection then the content of the songs can be controlled by the therapist. But if clients are encouraged to bring in their own music, it is possible that songs that have offensive lyrics might be presented in either an individual session or a group session.

Offensive lyrics can test the therapist's values (see Chapter 1) and it is easy to be unsettled, even angry at the message portrayed in offensive songs, particularly if the lyrics advocate violence to another person. It is essential to control any reaction to the lyrics and to listen to the client's explanation in a manner that tries to understand his or her point of view. Violent songs can be discussed in light of an expression of anger, and a typical intervention might be, 'The lyrics of the song seem to be very angry, is this the way you feel?'

If an aggressive/violent song has been presented in a group situation and other members of the group have become upset during the playing of the song, the therapist needs to address this. Once the client has spoken about his or her feelings about the song, the therapist might open the discussion to the group, saying, 'How do others in the group feel about the song?' This open question allows the opportunity for supportive comments, as well as non-supportive comments.

Sometimes the therapist has to make a choice between allowing a client free expression of an aggressive song, versus the good of the group. It may be necessary to fade out a song that is clearly causing distress for group members. This might occur if, for example, the song advocates violence toward women and the women in the group become distressed. It is also worthwhile reflecting back to the client that the content of the song has impacted on others. This highlights that the group process is, in essence, a vehicle for interpersonal learning (Yalom 1970).

It may be useful for the therapist to know ahead of time what song a client is bringing to the group. This can provide the opportunity to forewarn the group members that the lyrics contain aggressive themes. Alternatively the therapist might talk with the client and suggest he or she brings another song to the group.

Responding to depressed clients / depressive song material

A similar situation might occur if a client shares with the group a song that has depressive or suicidal themes. When the group is operating at the re-constructive level and group cohesion is high, then there can be an open discussion of suicide within the group. However if the group is operating at an activities-based level, it is probably inappropriate to have a depth discussion of suicide as the group may not have established a milieu of support and mutual respect.

The therapist may facilitate the processing of the song by asking the client what feelings the song raises, and then, taking the cues from the client's answer, either guide the discussion away from suicide (if the group will not be able to support the person by discussing the issue in a meaningful way), or encourage further discussion (if the group has a strong cohesion).

Talking about suicide is emotionally highly charged, and a therapist should only engage in facilitating the discussion if he or she is experienced, or if there is a co-therapist to assist. Essentially any discussion of suicide needs to be contained, so that at the end of the discussion the therapist brings the group into the here-and-now, reminding the group members of the support they have, and how far they have come in therapy.

Length and frequency of sessions

The length of the session depends on many factors – whether song lyric discussion is the only method for the session (in which case it may take a full hour), or whether it is part of a music therapy session (in which case only 20–30 minutes might be assigned to SLD).

Within a one-hour session only four to five songs can be presented and discussed (variability in the length of a session also depends on whether this is an individual or a group session, and the duration of the song(s) presented). If there are more songs than can be managed within the session time, the discussion of each can be shortened, but this means the level of discussion may be superficial. Occasionally a song will be presented that has relevance to all members of the group, and it is possible that the entire hour will be devoted to one song only (e.g. this occurred with the song 'Father and son' by Cat Stevens, which prompted a 50-minute discussion). In this situation the therapist needs to make a comment to those who missed out on playing their song by explaining 'We have spent a lot of time on Jo's song today because it was very relevant to a lot of people in the group. Unfortunately we cannot hear everyone's song today, but at the next session we will start with those who missed out this time.' Inevitably by the time the next session is scheduled some people may not be able to attend, or may bring a very different song to the group than previously.

Applications of SLD

John Hedigan is a registered music therapist who works at Odyssey House, a facility for residential drug rehabilitation. The weekly music therapy session comprises two components – improvisation and SLD. The SLD component lasts 45 minutes, however, only one person presents a song, and there is lengthy discussion. In addition Hedigan asks the client in advance what song will be played, and a copy of the lyrics of the song are available for the group members. This means that while the song is playing the group members can reflect on the words, while listening to the emotion expressed in the song. The group at Odyssey House is an example of a closed group, and the clients are experienced in the group process. Therefore it is expected that residents address the issues that the lyrics describe. Over the past few years, the following songs have been presented by members of the group, and the issue that the person chose to discuss is listed in the far right column.

Table 6.3 Songs presented at Odyssey House		
Title of song	**Recording artist**	**The song's meaning for the client**
Not my kind of scene	Powderfinger	Feeling lonely and lost
These days	Powderfinger	Loss of control over one's life
Creep	Radiohead	Feeling different and unliked
Still haven't found what I'm looking for	U2	Feeling lost and searching for meaning
I want to know what love is	Foreigner	Heartache and pain in life, feeling unloved
Imagine	John Lennon	Funeral song
Nothing man	Pearl Jam	Loneliness, sadness, loss
Rescue	Echo and the Bunnymen	Reaching out for help
Family portrait	Pink	Family breakdown from the child's point of view
What I am	Edie Brickell	Wanting acceptance
The boxer	Simon and Garfunkel	Fighting to have a good life
How do I live without you?	Leanne Rimes	Dependence, unwillingness to let go of the past
Always	Bon Jovi	Undying love
Because of you	Kelly Clarkson	Fear as a result of mistreatment, anger and blame

Continued on next page

Table 6.3 continued

Title of song	Recording artist	The song's meaning for the client
Amazing grace	(Traditional)	Funeral song, strength and solidarity in faith
Changes	David Bowie	Acceptance of the unpredictability of life
Cats in the cradle	Ugly Kid Joe	Relationship between father and son
Dyer's eve	Metallica	Anger at mother and father
I will survive	Cake	Getting on with life in the face of adversity
The logical song	Supertramp	Uncertainty about identity, fear of life, innocence of youth
Indifference	Pearl Jam	Ambivalence about relationships, substance use
Throw your arms	Hunters and Collectors	Love song
Crash and burn	Savage Garden	Regrets about lifestyle
My home town	Bruce Springsteen	Reminiscence of youth
Sweet child o' mine	Guns 'n' Roses	Reminiscence of a relationship
I'll be missing you	P. Diddy	Funeral song, loss of relationships
He's my brother	The Hollies	Loss of relationships, unpredictability of life
Unsatisfied	The Replacements	Dissatisfaction with life
I can see clearly now	Hothouse Flowers	Hope for the future
Baker St	Foo Fighters	Drug use in city street
Space oddity	David Bowie	Psychedelic, drug use
True faith '94	New Order	Fears of life and living
Fame	Irene Cara	Hope for the future
Staying alive	Bee Gees	Sadness over lifestyle, 'only just' staying alive

Wonderful world	Herman's Hermits	Situational reminiscence of birth of first child
Edge of reality	Elvis	Feeling tormented by life
Semi charmed life	Third Eye Blind	Wanting something else from life
One	Metallica	Loss of control, confusion, wanting to die
Perfect day	Lou Reed	Recollections of euphoria of heroin use
If I can dream	Elvis Presley	Dreams for the future, optimism
Given to fly	Pearl Jam	Hope for the future
A perfect day	Fisher-Z	Reminiscence of good times before drug use
Two less lonely people in the world	Air Supply	A love song (which was interpreted by a client as a threat to kill two people!)
November rain	Guns 'n' Roses	Reminiscence of wedding day
Everybody hurts	REM	Pain in life, universality
Feel	Robbie Williams	Wanting to be loved
A good heart	Feargal Sharkey	Struggling to find the good in others
Fire and rain	James Taylor	Having seen the hard road, regrets
My immortal	Evanescence	Undying love, support
She talks to angels	Black Crowes	Pain of drug use
Comfortably numb	Pink Floyd	Drug use
My happiness	Powderfinger	Hope that problems in life can change
Scar	Missy Higgins	Regrets, learning from mistakes
Angels	Robbie Williams	Love for children

Variations for individual sessions

SLD can also be used in the individual session context and can then be extended into some active music making during or after the listening. Client and therapist might sing with the recording as a means of enhancing the therapeutic relationship. The music therapist might also suggest singing the song together while providing the accompaniment on guitar or piano.

Sometimes SLD is useful in the beginning phases of individual sessions, as a means of building a therapeutic relationship. As the therapist shows an awareness and understanding of the client's preferred music, an element of trust is established and the client may disclose more information, and be encouraged in his or her relationships with music. This may lead to other music therapy methods such as improvisation and song writing.

Song reminiscence in aged care settings

Similar to SLD, song reminiscence is used with clients to reflect on life events, as identified through song associations. Song reminiscence was first described by Bright, in her book *Music in Geriatric Care* (1972). Normally, preferred songs are sung with the client and then there is discussion about the relevance of the song. Depending on the functioning level of the client, verbal processing interventions might be:

What do you like about this song?

What was happening in your life when this song was written?

What does the song mean to you?

Does the song remind you of anything important in your life?

The therapist might also identify key lyrics from the song itself and ask the client about his or her experience. From the repertory of songs used in aged care, the song 'Cruising down the river on a Sunday afternoon' naturally leads to the question 'Have you ever been boating down the river?' The client can then recall memories of boating, or watching others boating down a river, or any experience of 'cruising'.

In selecting songs for elderly clients, research indicates that preferred songs are those from when the clients were in their 20s and 30s. Therefore the repertoire of songs is always increasing, and as clients live to older ages, music therapists will need to be familiar with a very large repertoire. The songs in Table 6.4 are suitable for people who were 20–30 years old in the 1940s and 1950s, and currently have reached 70–90 years old.

Music life review

Similar to song reminiscence, music life review is a method in which the client and therapist trace significant songs from the client's life that outline life's journey. The review might begin with a song from early childhood, school days, adolescence, courtship, marriage, birth

Table 6.4 Song titles and topics for discussion

Song title	Topic for discussion
Pack up your troubles	What troubles would you like to pack up? What would you like to do with them?
I'm forever blowing bubbles	Looking on the bright side of life
Lili Marlene	Reminiscence about the Second World War
If you were the only girl in the world	Romantic song
Beautiful dreamer	Dreaming of good times
Oh what a beautiful morning	From the film *Oklahoma* – did you see the film?
It's a long way to Tipperary	Travelling to a loved one
We'll meet again	Uncertainty of seeing a loved one; often evokes sadness
My bonnie lies over the ocean	Wanting a loved one to return
Daisy, Daisy give me your answer do	Light-hearted song about proposal of marriage
Amazing grace	Security in faith
Abide with me	Sung at funerals; support in facing death
Mine eyes have seen the glory	Battle hymn
Tie a yellow ribbon round the old oak tree	Waiting for a loved one to come home
As time goes by	Reminiscence; the film *Casablanca*

of children, difficulties in life, celebrations from life, and songs representing the point of life that the client is presently experiencing.

O'Callaghan (1984) first wrote about life review in working with people undergoing treatment for cancer. Life review was a method that enabled the client to overview the uniqueness of his or her life and to affirm the significant events. O'Callaghan chose to sing the songs with the client, however Bruscia (1998a) also uses the method by recording the significant songs onto tape or CD, so that the client can listen to the songs at any time to explore 'autobiographical or therapeutic issues' (Bruscia 1998a, p.120).

Vignette: life review in aged care

Rachel Nendick is a registered music therapist who was working with a resident in an aged care facility. The woman, Mary, wanted to write her life story, and with Rachel's help they wrote a music life review together. Nendick comments 'As I observed Mary becoming increasingly frail on the outside, Mary presented with amazing determination, strength and eagerness to share her story with me' (Nendick 2005, p.13). She remembered significant events from her life, such as surviving the depression, floods and childbirth. She associated specific songs with these events, and Rachel sang these songs with Mary as she reminisced about the unique experiences of her life. Mary's story was enhanced each time she sang the songs, and she remembered more and more about each event. Once the review was completed, Rachel typed up the story, including the lyrics of the songs, and presented Mary and the family with the finished *Music Life Review*. Rachel also included her contact details should the family want to be in touch with her again.

Four years went by, and Rachel was unexpectedly contacted by Mary's son, who told Rachel that Mary had died. He commented that the *Music Life Review* was treasured by the family as a living reminder of Mary's life. He also mentioned that Mary had commented that the relationship with Rachel had been a very special one, and Rachel was acknowledged in the funeral programme.

Conclusion

In this chapter the therapeutic value of songs has been explored and described, particularly in relation to the discussion of song lyrics following receptive listening to the song. The use of songs in this way leads into song reminiscence and music life review as extensions of the emotional connections that exist with songs. In all of these methods the words (lyrics) carry meaning, however in listening to songs the emotional connection is made powerfully through the music – the melody, the harmony, the building up in intensity, and the 'home' base provided by the bridge or the chorus of the song. Therefore the lyrics and music combined create an art form that has meaning to people in all walks of life, and for all age groups.

Note

1 It is interesting to conjecture whether Richard Carpenter wrote this song for his sister Karen, who sings the song, and who battled anorexia. Some of the lyrics, 'look into the mirror, nothing there to see', hint at one of the symptoms of anorexia – that of a distorted body image.

Chapter 7

Perceptual Listening and Musical Appreciation

Introduction

In hospitals, institutions, nursing homes, schools and community units, music is 'played to' child, adolescent and adult clients for different reasons. Typically it is played to provide a recreational background sound or 'entertainment', to connect the clients to the community they are in or their socio-cultural group. It may also be played in order to provide stimulation, or for a pacifying or relaxing effect. These reasons are also potential clinical goals, reported by Bruscia in describing the types of receptive experiences clients will have (Bruscia 1998a, p.121). However, it is also evident that radios are turned on to pop music stations, or CDs are put on to provide a general background environment for the pleasure and enjoyment of staff, carers or parents who are looking after people with a disability. Behind this issue, one also has to consider the general over-use of recorded music or 'musak' in the everyday community for reasons that are never clearly understood. It is used in supermarkets, petrol station forecourts, shopping centres, cinemas, restaurants and of course in institutions such as hospitals, social services units, etc. It's fashionable, it's 'piped' (coming from speakers) and quite often it's continuous.

Therefore, it is important to consider the function of the music, the type of music and perhaps more particularly, the volume at which the music should be played to evoke the best responses and gain the attention and interest of the client population. Recorded music used for receptive music therapy experiences has a particular value, and the direction of this chapter is to illustrate how it can be used within a music therapy session as a moment in time to relax, stop expectations of interactive (interpersonal) experiences and to focus the attention and awareness of an individual client or group of clients. The reason to use it with the population of people with learning disabilities might be more concerned with attracting their attention for some unusual or rather special sounds for a specific period of time and then evaluating how they listened, whether they appeared interested and most specifically whether the responses that are observed indicate musical preference or not.

While this chapter is centred round the use of recorded music with people with intellectual disability and older adults, recorded repertoire can be incorporated into therapy sessions for a wide range of clients in both group and individual sessions. Different styles and genres of music ranging from early classical to twentieth century, folk traditional to heavy rock, and opera to musicals, provide such a rich source of experiences in therapy work.

Principles in evaluating the value of recorded music for clients

Certain questions need addressing when undertaking any therapy work using recorded music with clients, particularly people with intellectual disability.

1.   When is a client listening or not listening?

2.   How does the client show that he or she is attending to the music and for how long is the client able to attend?

3.   What type of music holds the client's best attention and why?

4.   Does the volume of the music feature as important in determining perceptual ability and length of attention?

5.   Does the type of disability, intellectual difficulty or impairment influence the ability of a client to listen or to demonstrate that he or she is listening?

6.   How much does the client's familiarity with the pieces that are played influence his or her interest and attention to listen to them?

Suitability and cautions in selecting and playing music

Suitability and cautions are rarely discussed in clinical reports and research studies in music therapy. Using recorded music may seem a 'non-invasive' and harmless 'safe' intervention. Yet the term 'non-invasive', while usually referring to physical interventions, can equally apply to unwanted stimuli that 'invade' the mind, and are a form of psychological intervention. Using recorded music as a background stimulus or relaxant in institutions may seem a good idea but as with most stimuli in one's life, people like to be in control of the intensity and duration in order to enjoy what is being played or what is happening. The same applies to recorded music and when people have no control over how long or how loud they have to listen to something, they will feel a considerable lack of control resulting in the development of apathy and helplessness, which is as bad as the absence of stimulation in the first place.

Therefore two levels of caution need to be applied through an analysis of individual reaction to recorded music in clients. First, their general reaction to the dynamic of the music played needs to be considered, and an evaluation of their tolerance of length, volume and proximity of sound source. Second, the response to the style and characteristics of the music needs consideration. While we may assume clients may respond to the music we think they like (maybe based on our own personal tastes), this should be carefully evaluated based on some indicators including:

- recognisable behavioural markers of positive (pleasure) responses
- recognisable behavioural markers of negative (dislike) responses
- recognisable behavioural markers of agitation or distress
- known characteristics of behaviour that indicate attention
- known characteristics of behaviour that indicate lack of attention
- known characteristics of behaviour that indicate intentional distraction

Protocol for the use of recorded music for listening in individual and group work

The procedure for using recorded music in a session can be defined in five simple stages:

1. define therapeutic function
2. prepare the space
3. introduce the intervention
4. monitoring the intervention
5. ending the intervention.

Define therapeutic function and identify descriptors for observation

Why are you including this therapeutic intervention in a session? Establish the therapeutic goal or therapeutic direction of doing this – for example:

- clients' request
- relaxation
- pressure off – allowing a space
- looking at responses to different styles of music.

Establishing the therapeutic intention first makes it much easier to form therapeutic criteria to evaluate effectiveness.

Being able to observe and interpret when you think a client is really listening to music relies on knowing quite a lot about how that person normally behaves when he or she is attending to things and also what symptoms may impact on the client's ability to listen and could indicate that he or she is not listening. This is a difficult area but needs to be carefully thought through in order to accurately and with a degree of certainty assess a client's attention to and interest in music. Each person who comes for therapy is an individual with a range of behaviours that are unique to him or her. Having said that, there are also some characteristic behaviours that can be closely linked to pathology such as anxiety-driven behaviours including pacing, restlessness, continuous questioning that might emerge in clients with anxiety neurosis or in children with attention deficit hyperactivity disorder (ADHD)

and rocking or self-stimulation that can be seen in clients with more severe intellectual disability, or confusion in people with dementia, or pain in people suffering from cancer, to
name but a few examples. In order to make accurate observations and come to some conclusion about interest and attention, it would be recommended to do the following:

1.   Take a baseline of a range of behaviours when the client is sitting down and not
       being stimulated to do anything else, nor encouraged to engage in some
       interaction.

2.   Talk to the client or carers about any known symptoms or pathology that might
       interfere when listening to music.

3.   Consider the client's general ability to attend to or be interested in his or her
       environment.

4.   Identify behaviours that generally suggest that the client isn't listening and also
       behaviours that generally suggest that he or she is listening.

Observational data can include a number of different parameters:

1.   an observation of the amount of time the client appears to be listening during a
       pre-set period

2.   any reductions or increase in behaviours that are notable

3.   any emotional reactions that may be notable either from facial expression or
       from physical activity (body language)

4.   the after-effects of listening to some music in terms of the client's level of
       arousal or state of relaxation when the music ends.

Prepare for the intervention and areas of observation – prepare the space
Some of the measures for preparing an environment for listening to music and identifying
the things one wants to observe may seem very obvious but they are still necessary to define
to ensure appropriate practice.

1.   Create the right atmosphere for listening by dimming the lights and shutting
       out the noise of any external stimuli.

2.   Ensure that any distractions are moved out of the way.

3.   Move any instruments that have been used in the session well out of the way so
       that there is no potential 'invitation' for the client or clients to join in with the
       music they are going to listen to.

4.   Position the person or the group so that they are able to benefit most from a
       good stereo system that can reproduce music in the best way.

5.   As therapist, seat yourself in a position where you are able to observe an individual, or the clients in the group, but not in a position where he, she or they might feel under observation!

6.   Explain to the clients what you are going to do, in simple language. For non-verbal clients it might be appropriate to use visual cues or gestures, perhaps with picture exchange communication system (PECS) or ETRAN board for those clients who can use such communicative tools.

Introducing the intervention

For the beginning of the period of listening to music, there are certain 'givens' that need to be addressed:

1.   Whatever activity has been going on prior to the listening period of the session, there needs to be a space where the effects of that activity are allowed to dissipate in order to create a calm and receptive atmosphere for listening to recorded music (this is sometimes referred to as a 'wash out period'). This is particularly true where some physical activities or improvisational music making have taken place.

2.   Whether the clients are able to understand verbal language or not, it's always sensible to explain what you are doing. Consequently some simple script should be used, such as:

> We're going to listen to a piece of music.
>
> We'll just sit here while I switch on the CD player and you can relax for a few minutes and enjoy the sounds you're going to hear.
>
> Let's sit down and be quiet while we listen to the music.
>
> Today's music is from a CD called [title] (show them the CD cover) and we're going to hear a piece that lasts about four minutes.

Some simple explanation or visual cue, such as holding up the CD before putting it into the CD player, will draw the attention of the individuals within the group to what's going to happen. It can also be useful to point out where the music is coming from every time. One of the important arguments for improvisational, live music making with people with severe intellectual disability, psychotic illnesses or dementia is that they are better able to understand the source of the sounds when they can actually watch a guitar string being plucked, feel the vibration of the guitar against their body and understand the cause-and-effect process of the sound that they hear being made by the movement of a finger on a guitar string. The weakness of recorded music is that it comes mysteriously out of a 'black' speaker box. For people with more severe disability, they may not even know the location and certainly won't understand how a full symphony orchestra or a heavy metal pop group can be reproduced through a black box. Nevertheless, identifying the source of the sound and pointing to the speakers is another way of focusing the attention.

3.   Introducing the piece, especially if it starts with loud crashing music, might need to be moderated for different groups. Sensitivity to the impact of sudden and unexpected loud sounds will certainly have to be exercised when working with any groups who already have a level of hyperacoustics (hypersensitivity to sound).

4.   Volume can't be controlled completely but if you know the pieces you are presenting well enough, you can be aware if there are any unexpected and perhaps uncomfortably loud moments in the music which some groups or individuals might find difficult to tolerate. Turning the volume up gradually can be a way of doing this, and most systems have remote control to monitor volume. Additionally, it's possible to monitor the volume from a certain point by the use of a sound level meter that will give a decibel range. However, music does tend to go up and down so you would have to describe the range of the intensity rather than a fixed intensity throughout. This is only relevant if one is working with people for whom the intensity of music is a critical factor, such as those who are hearing impaired or clients with hypersensitivity to sound. When working with older clients, please remember that the tolerance to the volume of sound has increased proportionally over the last 30 to 40 years, so that older people may often prefer music played at softer volumes than younger people, whose tolerance has increased through disco levels of sound and personal stereos.

      When working with groups of older people, be careful to check the sensitivity to and awareness of sound. This does need to be considered in the context of likely hearing loss, but with the consideration that in developing hearing impairment in older adults, it is the higher frequencies that are frequently lost as hearing deteriorates. Therefore increasing intensity will only serve to amplify lower frequencies and possibly distort sound. Therefore attention to individual hearing potentials is also necessary for this intervention to be helpful.

The results of an evaluation that was undertaken which will be reported later in this section also showed that when music is played at a softer volume, attention increases whereas when it is played at a louder volume there was more evidence of distraction techniques, stereotypies and avoidance of listening.

Monitoring the intervention

Monitoring the intervention when using recorded music is partly about ensuring that the music is not having a bad effect and partly about recording or evaluating responses. It is important to collect observational material that can simply describe how somebody is responding and particularly in terms of gathering evidence for music preference. However, therapists must be sure that their role during their music listening section is not to engage in an active interaction with the subject but to be a calm, quiet, discreet observer.

Observation can vary from monitoring the overt behaviours that one can observe such as attention, facial expression, respiration, body language, body activity, mannerisms, stereotypies, rocking, twiddling, head shaking, fiddling, picking at clothes, picking at skin or hair and self-injurious behaviour.

The evaluation of these behaviours and the question of whether somebody is still listening when he or she is undertaking some of these habit-forming behaviours need to be addressed in the individual client's profile. Mannerisms and rituals, particularly in the autistic population, are such developed habits and they have to be accepted within the pattern of a client's behaviour.

Ending the intervention

As the music comes to an end, it is important to again allow a period of silence. This moment of reflection, or post-resonance, is very important to allow the ending silence. Music is a combination of sound *and* silence, and the silence is essential to balance the sound.

When the music ends, this is also a moment particularly to notice who is still listening or attending, or gaining something from the experience. It's interesting to note who has noticed that the music has stopped.

Then there is the potential feedback. If there are any verbal clients in the group at this point, they can talk about what they have just heard, and about whether they liked or disliked the music that was played.

Influencing factors

Using recorded music for the purpose of promoting attention, listening, relaxation, imaging etc., there are a number of influencing factors with a population of people with intellectual disability that might make a difference:

1. *The environment:* the ambient noise in the unit, the weather outside, light, heat or other factors might influence listening ability. If it is a particularly bright sunny day, with lots of shadows falling in the room, this could easily be a distraction to somebody whom you are hoping will listen to some music. Other sounds in the building within which one is working could also be a distraction.

2. *The therapist or co-therapist:* however hard one tries to take a neutral position and not influence or distract people when they are listening to music, there may be occasions when one inadvertently disturbs the attention and concentration. Being over-attentive in observation, forgetting to distance oneself and sitting too near to clients so that they start to attempt to interact with you, involuntary movements, coughing etc., can easily disturb and distract in an environment where one is trying to promote attention.

These are two specific examples. There will be many other potentially influencing variables.

Recorded music as part of the music therapy programme for people with intellectual disability

In group work, one is commonly structuring a period of time for people with developmental or intellectual disability with a number of different group activities or therapeutic experiences. Often groups begin with 'Hello' or welcome songs, moving on to instrumental and improvisation experiences, perhaps singing songs and periods of relaxation. Into this experience, the use of interesting and time-limited recorded music for the specific purpose of 'stopping' all other activity and just focusing on listening is a very useful and important element. It's qualitatively different in individual work, when the structure and pace of the session, as well as the events that occur within it, can be specifically geared to the individual, and adapted to the therapeutic needs and goals of that client. Even so, a period of listening, reducing the 'demand' of the therapist (one-on-one) to maintain an interaction, is also of quite worthwhile therapeutic benefit. However in group work, the 'activity' of listening to music either for the purpose of relaxation, gaining attention or determining musical preference and responsiveness can be introduced one or more times at variable moments in the session. In group work with intellectually disabled children and adults, it is a therapeutic decision to consider a moment in time in the session when the group either need a period of calmness or non-functional activity in order to gain a receptive experience. In the method part of this section, the options for introducing listening activity and the environmental issues relating to it will be discussed.

The involvement of utilising a wide range of different styles and genres of recorded music in therapy work in groups of people with learning difficulties is also driven by the need to be more sensitive to their response and reaction to the environment around them and how much ambient and sometimes intrusive sound is present. There is no doubt that we fill our environment with noise these days (Wigram 1983), and particularly with clients who are pre-verbal and for whom one is reliant on a correct interpretation of their body language, facial expression and general activity level, one has to consider carefully their responsivity to different types of recorded music. Assumptions, for example, that when a client starts rocking this may be an indicator of enjoyment of musical stimuli are not necessarily supported, and one should also consider that people with severe intellectual disability begin rocking in order to self-stimulate themselves to avoid the burdensome presence of stimuli that they either find irritating, annoying or even intrusive and unpleasant. A study undertaken in the late 1970s and early 1980s (Wigram 1983) looked specifically at the issue of style of music, and the volume at which it is presented in order to understand better the type of music which gained attention and in what way. This book is a methods book, and the reason for presenting some material from this study is to illustrate both types of music one can use for purely receptive purposes, and also method of presentation.

Choice of music: a clinical/research example

For people with intellectual disability, many different types of music might evoke a wide range of responses and it would be impossible to say that one piece of music would be more effective than another in gaining attention, or particularly in trying to generalise potential reactions to specific pieces. Music preference is very much the issue here and individual clients will have likes and dislikes. To that extent, the importance of incorporating a 'listening to music' section during a group session, or an individual session, is actually to find out what preferences appear to be expressed and to provide advice on this to anybody else who is caring for the client or giving the client any type of environment where music might play a part.

An empirical study carried out between 1979 and 1981 (Wigram 1983) explored responses to quite a wide range of classical, light classical, television themes and film music, as well as traditional songs with children, adolescents and adults with intellectual disability. The music was divided between instrumental music and vocal music, in order to explore whether clients with these specific disabilities and pathologies showed differentiated responses to instruments when compared to the sound of the human voice or voices. Table 7.1 provides a list of the 17 pieces that were used in this study, demonstrating quite a wide variety of styles.

Most of these pieces were selected because they are quite well known (in most cases), have attractive and easy to listen to melodies and offer a wide variety of styles and genres.

Table 7.1 List of recorded music used in the study		
	Name of piece	**Origin/composer**
1	Elizabethan serenade	Ronald Binge
2	The ash grove	Traditional Welsh folk song
3	The hall of the mountain king	From the *Peer Gynt Suite*, Grieg
4	Moto perpetuo	Paganinni (flute)
5	Oh what a beautiful morning	From *Oklahoma*, Rogers and Hammerstein
6	Eidelweiss	Austrian traditional (German singing group)
7	Wedding march	From *The Sound of Music*, Rogers and Hammerstein
8	Oklahoma	From *Oklahoma*, Rogers and Hammerstein
9	Fossils	From *Carnival of the Animals*, Saint Saens

Continued on next page

Table 7.1 continued

10	Tannhauser march	Wagner, arrangement for organ
11	Come into the garden Maud	Michael Balfe/Tennyson
12	Nuns' chorus	From *The Sound of Music*, Rogers and Hammerstein
13	An die Musik	Franz Schubert, Leider
14	Laudate dominum	From the Solemn Vespers of the Confessor, Mozart
15	Big country	Film music
16	The Alamo	Film music

Method

The study involved two differing groups of clients, all resident in a large institution for children, adolescents and adults with moderate, severe and profound intellectual disability. Group 1 comprised 11 young adolescents (12–18 years old) who were all residents with multiple disabilities, primarily cerebral palsy and severe to profound learning disability. There were residents with spastic and athetoid cerebral palsy, as well as hypotonia, and one resident with Sturge Weber syndrome. All of the group were pre-verbal. Group 2 were 17 adolescents who were predominately ambulant, and were quite a mixed group with autism spectrum disorder, Down's syndrome, severe intellectual disability, and two clients with athetoid cerebral palsy.[1] This group contained a number of clients with poor attention, hyperactivity and, sometimes, aggressive behaviour. Four in this group had poorly developed verbal language that was primarily echolalic.

The music selections were presented as part of a group music therapy session, usually in the middle of the session. Two pieces were always presented at a time in order to find out what differences there may be to music presented at louder or softer volumes.[2] The music selections were presented through a stereo system within intensity bands of either 60–70 dB or 80–90 dB. While it is difficult to be precise due to fluctuations in intensity within each music selection, preparation trials established the correct calibration of volume on the amplifier for each piece based on the receiving position of group members who were all positioned in a semi-circle approximately the same distance away from the speakers. The intention was to attempt an evaluation not only of preferred music by observing clients for their attention to the music selections, but also to see (in a somewhat crude way) if there were any differences in attention to music played at louder or softer volumes. This study was undertaken as fields trials incorporated into a therapy session, rather than as a research project in its own right. The method of intervention followed the protocols defined above.

Observation and evaluation

It is a subjective judgement as to whether somebody is really listening or whether they are just hearing the music and thinking about something else or directing their attention to something else, and relies on knowledge of the client and attention indicators. Nevertheless, the most functional and measurable criterion to use is simply to try and evaluate for how much of a period of time somebody appears to be focused and attentive to the piece of music that is being played. This could be by monitoring client's eye gaze on the source of the sound or it could be on noting that they are more still than they usually are and don't appear to be either focusing their attention on other things or distracting themselves. Consequently, time-based evaluation is the most likely option. Observers who were part of the two separate staff teams working together with the author with these groups were instructed to observe two to three clients each and record their observations regarding the clients' attention.

Table 7.2 is a simple monitoring chart with a key which allows an observer to give a crude score as to the amount of time during the presentation of a piece of music a client appeared to be focused.

Table 7.2 Recording chart for client responses to recorded music selections				
Name of client	1st piece listening time	Comment	2nd piece listening time	Comment
1				
2				
3				
4				

Notes:
0 = none of the piece; 1 = ¼ of the piece; 2 = ½ the piece; 3 = ¾ of the piece; 4 = whole of the piece

While using the key to make a quick evaluation, there is also a comments box to add any particularly noticeable features of behaviour that might either support the evaluation that the person is listening or perhaps provide evidence that there could have been distracted behaviour. Each music selection was presented on two separate occasions to both groups and the results were averaged.

Results

The results from this study are presented in the next two tables, and show the differences in attention and apparent listening in both groups, reporting on scores for vocal and instrumental music selections separately, and also the different intensities at which the pieces were played. The scores reported in Tables 7.3 and 7.4 show the percentage of attention calculated from the cumulated scores in both softer and louder conditions to the music selected in the study. The percentages also identify more or less popular pieces as represented by the degree of attention given to them by the clients in Group 1 or Group 2.

Table 7.3 reports the scores from the observers on all the subjects in Group 1, and have been converted into percentages. The pieces are grouped into vocal music and instrumental music.

Table 7.3 Group 1 responses to the music selections by piece and loudness presentation in percentages			
Name of piece	Vocal/instrumental	60–70 dB	80–90 dB
Elizabethan serenade	Vocal	45	57
The ash grove	Vocal	63	60
Oh what a beautiful morning	Vocal	50	22
Eidelweiss	Vocal	25	33
Wedding march	Vocal	40	61
Oklahoma	Vocal	30	58
Come into the garden Maud	Vocal	38	61
Nuns' chorus	Vocal	34	56
An die Musik	Vocal	33	37
Laudate Domunum	Vocal	32	55
Mean percentage of attention for vocal music		**39**	**50**
'The Big Country' theme music	Instrumental	34	45
The 'Alamo' theme music	Instrumental	48	68
Italian symphony	Instrumental	47	51
Hall of the mountain king	Instrumental	58	35
Moto perpetuo	Instrumental	50	55
Fossils	Instrumental	35	56

Tannhauser	Instrumental	35	47
Mean percentage of attention for instrumental music		**44**	**51**
Overall means		**41.5**	**50.5**

Group 1 had a mean score of 39 per cent for the vocal pieces at 60–70 db, and 50 per cent at 80–90 db, indicating that there was greater attention when the same pieces were played at a louder volume. The difference for instrumental pieces was less, at 44 per cent for 60–70 dB and 51 per cent at 80–90 dB. Overall, there was a difference between softer and louder presentations of 9 per cent in attention, demonstrating that this group attended better when the music was louder. A test of proportions found a significant difference between louder and softer presentations for this group of $p=0.0152$ (95% confidence interval: 0.5580441–0.9532704, sample estimates: $p=0.82$).

This group are quite easily distracted, and it may be that music presented needs to be louder to hold their attention. Also, with a range of physical handicaps, there may be additional physical distraction (spasm, pain) diverting attention when the music is not very loud. As can be seen there is also a suggestion of preference in this group for different music selections. While there is almost an equal preference for vocal as for instrumental music, some selections stand out as particularly attractive to the group, such as The ash grove (a traditional Welsh folk song) at both louder and softer volumes. There are many examples of songs and pieces that elicited more attention at softer volumes than louder, and other pieces that elicited more attention at louder volumes than softer. So no firm conclusions can be drawn about the exact style of music in relation to intensity levels. There is evidently variability, and this fact alone needs to be considered when presenting recorded music to any clients, irrespective of pathology, as the response to specific pieces will be variable, even when overall with this group louder presentation was preferred. Considering the degree of multiple disability and handicap of Group 1, one might consider that louder music actually sustain their attention in a way that is different to the way music is used as a 'background sound' in both their living and day activity environments.

Table 7.4 reports the scores from the observers on all the subjects in Group 2. The scores have been converted into percentages. The pieces are grouped into vocal music and instrumental music.

The pieces are grouped into vocal music and instrumental music. Group 2 had a mean score of 52 per cent for the vocal pieces at 60–70 dB, and 46 per cent at 80–90 dB, indicating that there was greater attention when the same pieces were played at a softer volume. The difference for instrumental pieces was greater, at 48 per cent attention to pieces played between 60–70 dB and only 37 per cent attention to the same pieces at 80–90 dB. Overall, there was a difference between louder and softer presentations of nearly 9 per cent in attention, demonstrating the converse to Group 1 that this group attended better when

Table 7.4 Group 2 responses to the music selections by piece and loudness presentation in percentages

Name of piece	Vocal/instrumental	60–70 dB	80–90 dB
Hoere Lied Elizabeth	Vocal	45	38
The ash grove	Vocal	67	58
Oh what a beautiful morning	Vocal	61	53
Eidelweiss	Vocal	53	26
Wedding march	Vocal	50	45
Oklahoma	Vocal	38	60
Nuns' chorus	Vocal	51	45
Mean percentage of attention for vocal music		**52**	**46**
Big Country	Instrumental	57	50
Alamo	Instrumental	36	33
Italian symphony	Instrumental	53	23
Hall of the mountain king	Instrumental	46	56
Moto perpetuo	Instrumental	43	20
Fossils	Instrumental	64	46
Tannhauser	Instrumental	38	30
Mean percentage of attention for instrumental music		**48**	**37**
Overall means		**50**	**41.5**

the music was softer. A test of proportions found a significant difference between louder and softer presentations for this group of p=0.0161 (95% confidence interval: 0.5615066–0.9748606, sample estimates: p=0.85).

This finding was almost the opposite to Group 1, and caused quite a lot of interest in the staff team at the time. The difference for observers was that many of the group (in particular the autism spectrum disorder clients) demonstrated quite a number of self-stimulatory behaviours, including rocking, hand play, wandering and vocal and manual stereotypies when the music was louder, while these behaviours disappeared, and there was more apparent attention when the same music selections were played more softly. A quieter environment seemed to encourage a quieter state of being, and therefore a more relaxed attentive state. Observing the clients in this group in their living environments at the time, a ward in a large long-stay hospital for people with learning disability, there was a noticeable level of physical activity which, as has been speculated previously, was more likely to be evidence of 'switching off' to the endless sound stimuli that were too complex than a positive response. Recently, some discussion has emerged that people with autism spectrum disorder, for example, are overloaded with stimuli, and have difficulty in separating out what they can process and find relevant.

The volume of music should always be taken into consideration, whether recorded music is being utilised as part of a receptive music therapy intervention, or whether it is being used for background sound. The findings from this study have furthered the use of recorded music as part of a group (or individual) music therapy intervention for clients with severe and profound intellectual disability.

Summary

Overall, this chapter set out to provide suggestions and guidelines on using recorded music in music appreciation sessions, and also to consider the perception and attention of people when listening to it. The choices of repertoire listed in the study described above are peculiar to that particular piece of work, and should be considered in that context. Individual preferences will always be the primary goal for repertoire choices when applying receptive methods with these populations. Yet the underlying issue that will also influence choice is the real function of the music as a therapeutic agent. What exactly is it supposed to be doing? We know from discussion and report that ambient environmental music is frequently played to keep a supposedly relaxing and 'interesting' sound in the background. This music is supposed to entertain, distract, amuse. So the choice of specific music as a therapeutic influence needs to be made for more identified needs:

- when in sorrow – console
- when in rage – soothe
- when in fear – reassure
- when in confusion and anxiety – calm.

Playing recorded music might affect any of these emotional states, or perhaps just create a calm, peaceful listening atmosphere. Perhaps this chapter should end with advice on presentation, namely that the impact of playing music is doubled by the anticipated silence before, and the reflecting resonance after. Silence before and after allows the music played to be experienced in its own special context, something we seem to have forgotten how to do in our modern, noisy world.

Notes

1   After starting work in the middle 1970s at this institution, the author was often involved in group music therapy work in situations in the hospital where large groups were already enrolled in a programme. This group were enrolled at a day unit in the hospital for the children and adolescents. It is surprising now to imagine working with such a large group of people, particularly with such varied and challenging diagnoses. The staff at the unit were all involved in the session, so there were usually four additional staff engaged in the 60-minute music therapy sessions as 'co-therapists' or helpers.

2   At the time, the author was involved in an informal survey to look at the ambient use of music from stereo systems in the wards, and what average decibel ranges residents were exposed to during everyday times and mealtimes. Measurements were being taken at fixed times during the day, when in addition to music played through stereo systems and the radio, noise from the television (often left on for lengthy periods), vacuum cleaners and the sounds the residents made were included. A sound level meter was used to obtain averaged levels for a period of time (Wigram 1983).

Chapter 8

Receptive Music Therapy
and Art Media

There are several methods of receptive music therapy that combine music with other creative arts media, to enable clients to express inner feelings non-verbally. In this chapter methods that combine music and art are explored, including music collage with various age groups and a combination of music, drawing and narrative (MDN). Each of these approaches is explained and illustrated.

Music collage

A collage is a picture made by arranging illustrations, photographs, pieces of coloured paper or cloth, and other materials (including words or drawings) on to a piece of paper or cardboard. The collage can be a pictorial representation of what the clients hear in the music that resonates with their mood or their life situation. Appropriate music is chosen by the therapist, to provide a creative and inspiring atmosphere. The music chosen usually has dynamic changes to foster creativity and encourage shifts in the client's imagination. The music must also be chosen carefully to mirror the therapeutic process for an individual client, or group of clients.

In her book *Music Therapy in Palliative/Hospice Care* (1984), Susan Munro describes the collage technique with a terminally ill patient. Munro decided to use collage because the patient had a number of drawings with her in hospital and Munro thought the patient would respond well to the use of art with music. Another reason for introducing collage was to enable the patient to project conflicting feelings and to gain some clarity on each of these feelings. The collage is illustrated in Munro's book, and as the case vignette unfolds it becomes clear that the most sensitive issue relates to the smallest picture in the collage – the small child. Interestingly, Munro had chosen the music of Schubert, the 'Andante con moto' from the *String Quartet in D minor*, entitled 'Death and the maiden'. The patient's fear was that on her death her 12-year-old daughter would be left without a mother, a situation that the patient had endured herself when both parents died when she was very young. Perhaps it was a coincidence that the music brought out the issue, or perhaps there was something in the music, composed by Schubert and inspired by the poem 'Der Tod und das Mädchen' by

Matthias Claudius. Whatever the reason, the choice of music played an integral part in the patient's expression of grief and despair.

There are many client populations for whom collage is an appropriate technique and, among others, the method has been shown to be effective particularly for the following:

- aged care clients (see vignette on page 200)

- adult psychiatry (depending on the functional level of the client)

- palliative care

- hospitalised adult patients

- clients seeking personal growth

- children and adolescents who are bereaved (see vignette: 'improvising to draw out a feeling' on page 208).

Music collage can be used in individual therapy sessions where the client creates his or her own collage on a large piece of paper. Group collages can also be created on a length of paper (e.g. a length of three metres) that resembles a frieze, which can be displayed on a wall. Each of these approaches is explained below, with information about the choice of music that accompanies the creation of a collage.

Client suitability

Collage requires that the client:

- understands the process and is able to choose pictures with some degree of intention

- is able to concentrate and arranging pictures in a meaningful way in the creation of the collage

- is able to gain value and insight from the technique.

Collage may prove difficult or less effective with clients who have disturbed and reactive behaviour, or have limitations in concentrating on a task of this nature. However, the case vignette of a woman diagnosed with dementia presented later in this chapter does exemplify the potential of the method even when a client has periods of confusion.

Materials

A range of artistic materials are needed for collages, including:

- a wide range of magazines and newspapers on various topics that include images of nature, sport, travel, gardens, birds, animals and fashion. Magazines and newspapers should also cater for the different interests of females and males and the interests of the relevant age group. It is also possible to use pictures that have individual relevance, such as photographs. For group work the magazines need to be spread out or scattered so that clients can choose ones to which they are attracted. Each client may leaf through three to four magazines while listening to the music selection, so there should be sufficient magazines to enable choice

- scissors and glue, for when arranging the pictures into the collage. For clients who cannot manage scissors, the therapist can assist in cutting out. Some clients prefer carefully tearing out the pictures from the magazine and prefer rough edges to the pictures

- oil crayons, felt pens, coloured pencils, etc., should clients want to add words or art-work to the collage

- large pieces of paper for the collage. If working at a table, the paper might be A3 size. If they prefer not to use all the space, clients can use part of the paper if they wish, or fold the paper in half

- for the 'frieze' collage, several metres of paper, which can be purchased from an art suppliers shop. A three-metre frieze is long enough for a group of eight to ten people to work on a section of the collage at the same time.

Procedure

The collage can be done best working in a large room with a carpeted floor. This provides enough space and comfort for each person to spread out. However collages can also be created with clients seated at a table, and this can be modified in aged care settings by people sitting in chairs that have a table attached. Younger clients can work on a carpeted floor.

There are three distinct stages to the method, and within each there are smaller steps. Stage 1 relates to selecting the pictures for the collage, Stage 2 relates to creating the collage and Stage 3 relates to the discussion of the collage.

STAGE 1: THE SELECTION OF THE COLLAGE MATERIALS

Step 1 First, the therapist explains the process to the client(s). A suggested script is:

> One of the methods that we use in music therapy is to match images found in pictures and photographs to music that is playing in the background. We can start by listening to the music and trying to match any pictures or images that stand out as interesting or attractive to you. You can cut these out from the magazines, or quietly tear out the page, then cut them out more carefully later.

Step 2 Having explained what will happen, suggest to the clients that when the music begins, they should listen to the music for a few moments first before leafing through the magazines. In group work, remind the clients that if they are tearing out pictures to do this quietly.

Step 3 Start the music. As the music begins to play, the client(s) begin to select images/pictures from the magazines they have chosen. A period of 10–20 minutes can be allowed for this part of the process. During this time, the therapist's role is to be present but not interactive.

The therapist observes how each person is engaged in the process, and notices the types of pictures being selected, to see if a theme is emerging.

Step 4 When the music has finished, the therapist can suggest the clients take a few moments to finish looking through the magazine they have in their hand, and then to stop.

STAGE 2: MAKING THE COLLAGE

Step 1 When the music has finished, and the clients have finished selecting pictures from the magazines, the second stage instruction can be given:

> Now we can put the magazines away, and then listen to the music again. This time you can arrange the pictures on the page in whatever way you like. You can also add words yourself, or you might like to add other drawings or shapes to the picture. When the music has finished the second time, and when you feel the collage is finished, we can then talk about the collage.

Step 2 Remind the clients that working with the pictures and creating a collage is better done without discussion and talking, and that discussion can be saved until the end. Then play the selection of music again.

Step 3 At the end of the repeat, suggest the client(s) take a few moments to complete the collage. Suggest they give the collage a title.

STAGE 3: DISCUSSING THE COLLAGES

Step 1 Invite the client(s) to talk about the collage – which images stand out for them, and what they are about. The therapist might comment on any particular colours or shapes that stand out as interesting or unusual. The therapist might use open-ended interventions such as:

> Can you say more about this particular picture?
>
> Does anything in the collage stand out as particularly important?
>
> Do any of these images represent something happening in your life at the moment?

As each person finishes talking about the collage, the therapist can make a concluding comment such as 'Thanks for telling us more about the collage.'

Step 2 At the end of the session most clients want to keep the collage, but sometimes they don't. It is a good idea for the therapist to retain it for a period of time, as sometimes clients change their minds! If the client *does* want to keep (and take away) the collage, it is helpful for the therapist to make a quick sketch of the collage, and any important words written on the collage, for future reference. Alternatively, with the client's permission, the therapist might take a photo of the collage with a digital camera.

Choice of music for adult clients

The music used for music collage will differ according to the age group of the client, their music preference, and the issue that the client has discussed with you (if this has happened).

The music needs to have dynamic movement. Very slow relaxing music that has little change will not stimulate the choice of images. Music that is conducive to this technique can be characterised as being written in a form that incorporates repetition – e.g. ABA, sonata form, or theme and variations, where there are contrasting moods. Three suitable works from the Western classical tradition are described below, as examples of what to look for in choosing the music. These three examples are suitable for collages with adult clients.

The Andante from Schubert's Death and the maiden, for example, begins very slowly, but has an underlying repetitive rhythmic motif that suggests movement. The middle section of the Andante has much greater variation in dynamics and builds in intensity. It is during this middle section that images are likely to leap out from the pages as the client skims through the magazines. Then there is a return to a repeat of section A. It is much quieter in mood, however, and having traversed through the intensity of the middle section the client can find this repeat a time to integrate what has been experienced.

Pierne's *Concertstücke for Harp and Orchestra* is a work that forms part of the GIM Relationships programme, compiled by Helen Bonny. It is approximately 14–16 minutes in length (depending on the performance and recording). The Concertstücke is in three sections and each section has two themes, therefore it is romantic in style and emotionally stimulating. There is also variation in the texture of this work. The full climax of the orchestra is contrasted with the cadenza for harp, which is very quiet and thin in texture. In the middle section of the work there is a playful section, based on dotted rhythms and pizzicato string passages (Grocke 2002). Overall the work is musically varied and interesting and therefore stimulates imagery. Collages created to this music usually feature scenes from nature and images of movement (dancers and birds in flight).

Vaughan-Williams' music is also effective in stimulating images that can be matched through collage. His music is impressionist in style, but he bases many of his compositions on English folk songs and folk dances. The folk songs are usually simple in structure (ABA form), and therefore they are useful for collage because the first section is repeated, normally after a middle section of contrasting mood. The *Norfolk Rhapsody* is in three sections. The first section is impressionistic and begins with a haunting melody. However the middle section is bright, almost like a sailor's dance, and this is followed by a repeat of the quietness of the opening. It is the contrast in these works that makes them suitable for expressive creations, such as the collage. Other selections of music that are useful for collage include:

Debussy, *Prelude to the Afternoon of a Faun*, 10:00

D'Indy, *Symphony on a French Mountain Air*, 1st movement, 11:52

Grieg, *Peer Gynt Suite*, 'Morning' and 'Anitra's dance', 9:00

Handel, *Concerto for Lute and Harp*, 1st movement, 12:00

Humperdink, *Hansel and Gretel*, 'Overture', 8:42

Rachmaninoff, *Piano Concerto no.2*, 1st movement, 11:00

Rimsky-Korsakoff, *Scherehrezade*, no.3: 'The young prince and princess', 9:36

Vaughan-Williams, *In the Fen Country*, 17:38

Vaughan-Williams, *The Lark Ascending*, 14:42

Vaughan-Williams, *Norfolk Rhapsody*, 11:46.

The *Star Wars* suite and other film music by John Williams, and jazz and big band music, for example Benny Goodman, Glenn Miller or Jaques Louissier (jazzed-up Bach), may also be useful for collage, particularly with elderly clients. However, selections need to have contrasting moods, and a duration of about ten minutes in a continuous and uninterrupted flow.

Individual music collage
FINDING A FOCUS

In the preliminary discussion prior to commencing the collage it is helpful to search for a focus for the session. This might include whatever is uppermost in the client's mind at that moment in time, or may also be an ongoing theme in the therapy process. Hospitalised patients often miss their home, and this is a common theme for a collage. Clients who are under stress or in pain frequently choose pictures or images of travel (to escape from the stress and pain). If the client is attuned to the music, images of movement are also common – e.g. flowing water, dancers and birds in flight.

Working individually with people inevitably means the therapist may be sitting in close proximity (perhaps side by side, or opposite). Clients may wish to talk to you about the pictures to which they are attracted. Try to keep this talking to a minimum as it diverts attention away from the music. Working with clients in hospital will require that the therapist helps with arranging and gluing the pictures on to the paper, and again talking needs to be at a minimum so that the music is allowed to be the foundational supportive stimulus for the client in this process.

When making a collage with people who are in aged care facilities the therapist may be drawn into conversation, for example to reply to questions and comments. Pictures of nature might stimulate a response from the client, such as 'Oh, isn't that lovely,' and an appropriate response might be 'Oh, yes', or 'Oh, lovely'. However, try to refrain from entering into a long conversation, as the attention should be on listening to the music.

Vignette: elderly woman with dementia

Mrs Smith was a resident in an aged care facility, and was diagnosed with dementia. She loved music, so much so that when the music therapist (DG) appeared in the doorway of her room she would immediately start a very rhythmic clapping of her hands in anticipation of singing songs. Mrs Smith had been a keen gardener and took great pride in her home. She missed her home, and when her husband occasionally took her home for a visit she would be 'transformed', smiling and laughing with happiness. Once back at the care home she would lose that sense of joy.

Since Mrs Smith loved all types of music, I often used the music collage technique. She sat in her comfortable chair and together we would leaf through magazines. She would be particularly drawn to pictures of flowers and houses, and so I chose magazines that had many of these images. Mrs Smith would pause over these pictures and I would ask her if she liked a particular one. I would then tear it out carefully. The music I chose was a CD of songs from the 1930s and 1940s, and this would play quietly in the background. When we had collected six or so images, I suggested she arrange them on the page. Curiously she took pride in doing this. I then glued the images to the sheet of paper. The collage was then placed beside her bed. In the mornings the images of flowers and old houses would be the first thing she saw. Nursing staff commented that she enjoyed looking at her collages. (A reconstruction of Mrs Smith's collage is shown in Plate 8.1, and a colour version can be found at the website: www.jkp.com/catalogue/book.php/resources/9781843104131.)

Plate 8.1 Reproduction of collage created by woman in an aged care facility

When working with Mrs Smith, I often wondered whether the music was really necessary. There were several occasions when I tried the collage method without music (when the CD player was not available). On each occasion Mrs Smith was distracted, not able to concentrate on looking at the magazine, turning away and mumbling incoherently. The music therefore was an essential element, as it provided structure and containment for her, and music playing in the background kept her focused and engaged.

Vignette: a contraindication for music collage

Mrs Jones was resident in the same care facility as Mrs Smith. She was also diagnosed with dementia and also loved music and would sing familiar songs maintaining intense eye contact with me. I considered that collage would be something that would be helpful and therapeutic for Mrs Jones. However, in practice, collage was definitely contraindicated. In her confused state Mrs Jones took hold of the magazine and started tearing it into pieces. She was not drawn to any images at all, and the activity only increased her confusion. Therefore collage is not always appropriate with people who are confused, for instance, and each person needs to be assessed as to whether this technique is helpful or not. With Mrs Jones, singing favourite songs continued to be the best form of music therapy intervention to use.

Collage in groups

The difference in working with groups is that group process contributes to the therapeutic effect. The group members need to be able to:

- concentrate for an hour
- talk about their experience
- potentially gain insight from the technique
- be aware of the principles of group therapy behaviour – e.g. taking turns, listening to others respectfully, not interrupting others when they are creating their collage, etc.

FINDING A FOCUS FOR THE GROUP

In order to select the most appropriate music for the group, it is helpful to know what each person is concerned about at the time, and what mood prevails.

For 'closed' groups (groups that have been formed to work on specific therapeutic issues and don't have an 'open door' to new members), finding a focus for the group will be part of what normally happens. The focus can be relative to whatever the group is working on at the time – e.g. trust, relationships, coping, pain, etc.

CHOICE OF MUSIC

The choice of music depends on the age group and music preferences of the group. Adolescents, for example, relate better to new-age music (synthesised sounds) and popular music than to the classical music selections listed above. However, the music needs to have dynamic variability and contrast, e.g. slow–fast–slow, or the opposite, fast–slow–fast. The choice needs to span about ten minutes, and it is appropriate to involve the group members in a discussion of what music they believe is suitable.

To illustrate the use of music collage in groups method, members of the 2005 music therapy class at the University of Melbourne gave consent to have their collages reprinted in this book. These students were participating in a class where receptive methods of music therapy were taught through an experiential process. It was not a therapy group, and while the experiences of the students were the focus, no therapeutic issues pertinent to an individual student were discussed. It was an experiential session in which students could share their art work (collage) with peers. The students have written descriptions about their collages, and these are reproduced with their permission.

The music for this session was Vaughan-Williams' *Norfolk Rhapsody*. This work is in three sections depicting different moods: quiet–bright–quiet. (See the more detailed description on page 199.) In the collages presented in Plates 8.2 to 8.5, there are several features that stand out.

Collage number 1 (Plate 8.2) is entitled 'Reflecting on the beauty of life' (This, along with the other collages pictured in this chapter, can be viewed in colour at the website: www.jkp.com/catalogue/book.php/resources/9781843104131.). The student who created this collage wrote:

> I think the collage gave me a place to reflect and vent my emotions. There were a lot of thoughts bouncing on/off one another, where I argued with myself. I was struggling with issues of identity, where there was conflict of personality between the true self and ideal self. I found difficulty fitting in around people. I needed to understand myself. When faced with difficulties, most times I just want to run and hide under the wings of my loved ones. There was a lot of conflict with being idealistic, the ambitiousness and the reality of the current situation, the lack of confidence and inadequacies of myself. There was also the fear of unfulfilled purpose of my life, which I thought of.
>
> The flow of the music then took a turn, which probably reminded me of the blessings in my life and to think positive. I thought I could have just been paranoid over little things. And I should count my blessings… I should make peace, and find rest to be revived.

After creating the collage, the student spontaneously composed a poem as a further artistic representation of her feelings. The poem is reproduced here with permission.

Reflecting on the beauty of life…

At times I wake up
I look at myself in the mirror:
Plain…bare…naked!
Then I put on my garments,
Sometimes different hats of expressions.
And I wonder…
If I should hide or just enjoy the day.

I miss the refuge of my loved ones.
Where can I hide without fear?
Time just kept ticking,

And I wonder if I'm losing time and life…
And not doing what I'm supposed to.

At times I yearn for freedom.
And want to just fly away to a greater height…
And experience a life-changing moment.
Maybe I'm just overreacting,
Because all of life is before me.
I don't have to lose trust of life…of love.

No…not death that I should seek,
But a duet with people I love;
To play a symphony of life.

Therefore open the eyes to see…
Rest…rest…the comfort in life is finding a resting place.

Plate 8.2 The 'reflecting on the beauty of life' collage

Collage number 2 (Plate 8.3) is entitled 'Journey'. The music therapy student who created this collage made the following comments:

> The music was unfamiliar to me but very beautiful. It immediately brought images to mind of the two things that I find most inspiring to contemplate – the sea and the sky. The music seemed to flow – rising and falling – and sometimes became more intense –

soaring. At some point, the music returned to flowing and floating. Images of flowing water, of nature and of the sky came into my mind.

I can remember becoming very focused looking through the magazines and, despite being sceptical that I would find suitable pictures, I discovered many images of water, the sky, reflections of sky in water, the lushness of nature, rain, sunsets, an eagle soaring and also people in natural environments taking delight in the beauty of nature. I remember cutting corners and sharp edges off the photographs as I felt that they needed to be smooth and flowing to suit the music. I arranged the pictures with the images of water mainly in the bottom half of the collage, someone under water swimming upwards, then images of bright flowers and lush greenery leading to those of the sky at the top of the collage. It is like a journey from the depths to the heights – hence the word 'journey' written on the collage. Perhaps this 'journey' has a parallel with my journey towards a new career which has led me along new paths to inspiring destinations!

Plate 8.3 The 'journey' collage

The pictures in collage number 3 (Plate 8.4), entitled 'On the prowl', have been arranged to overlap. The student commented about her collage:

> Throughout the process of making the collage I didn't really give anything too much thought. I just listened to the music and picked out pictures that stood out for me. At the end I thought that the picture represented exactly where I was and how I was feeling at the time. As a piece of art, I really like what I have done.

Plate 8.4 The 'on the prowl' collage

Collage number 4 (Plate 8.5), entitled 'Lady in red', demonstrates how each picture is isolated, and all pictures are in black, except for the central figure of the woman who is in brilliant red. The student wrote about the collage:

> I don't remember much about the music when doing the collage, but did have the intention of creating an image that had black and white images portraying a colder kind of exterior that we can use as a type of protection, with some warmer images of food, and fire on the interior and then the striking, beautiful woman in the centre. I guess there's an idea of the inner, basic animal kind of drives/needs lurking under the surface which, like it or not, remain as pretty dominant forces.

Group 'frieze' collage

Another form of group collage is to create one very large collage, similar to a frieze or mural. This requires that the group work together in a collaborative way to create one large collage. The paper might be three metres in length, or whatever size is appropriate to the room or table(s). The process is similar to the method for creating a collage in groups: a wide variety of magazines and newspapers needs to be provided together with a space that has sufficient room for the paper to be spread out, preferably on a carpeted floor.

Plate 8.5 The 'lady in red' collage

FINDING A FOCUS

For this group collage it is important to decide on a focus. The most effective focus is one that provides some contrast – e.g. beginnings and endings, or moving forward versus being stuck. The focus will emerge from a discussion with the group, and the therapist might facilitate this by saying:

Is there something that the group would like to work on?

What is uppermost in your minds at the moment?

As each person makes suggestions, the therapist mentally holds the ideas together and senses whether there are emerging themes in what the group members are saying. The therapist can then offer options: 'It sounds like some of you are saying you would like to focus on X, while others are saying they want to focus on Y. Perhaps we can accommodate both these things (or three, or four things). Can we assign parts of the large collage to these different themes?'

The group also has to agree to aspects of 'sharing' the collage, e.g. what happens if a person wants to place his or her picture overlapping another. It sounds a simple matter, however for some people it requires some negotiating. This may be a therapeutic issue, and can be discussed before the collage begins, and/or after the collage is completed, during the processing.

PROCEDURE

The procedure is the same as Stages 1 to 3 (the first 8 steps) outlined on pages 197–198 – each group member works in his or her own space, listening to the music and being drawn to pictures in the magazines that reflect the music. At the end of the music, the group members are invited to place their pictures on the relative section of the collage. The music is played for a second time. When the music ends, allow time for the group members to finish their creation. This may take some time.

PROCESSING

Each group member is asked to describe his or her section of the large collage and to describe something of his or her experience in making the collage with the group. At the end of the processing, it is time to decide what to do with the large collage. Sometimes, if the group members are part of a hospital unit, the collage can be displayed on a wall. If the group is meeting in a one-off situation, one member of the group could keep the collage, or it can be divided up among the members – each taking away a section of the whole.

In one group situation the group decided to destroy the collage. This is an unusual way to end the process. However, the group process had been a very difficult one and members of the group were eager to finish and leave the group. Therefore destroying the collage paralleled their feelings about ending the group process.

Music therapy and collage with bereaved children

Melina Roberts, a registered music therapist, worked at Calvary Health Care, Bethlehem Hospital where she facilitated a home-based music therapy programme for bereaved children. Melina describes a programme using music and art activities.

Description of programme

Although the music therapy activities were the focus of these sessions, several art activities with music seemed to complement the grieving process. At times children seemed to need a break from the music therapy activities in the sessions. The transition from music therapy to art activities and back to the music seemed to be smooth and complementary in nature.

Art activities with music were used to provide a therapeutic space for non-verbal expression, reflection, discussions and reminiscence but did not move too far away from the music therapy objectives. It was regularly observed that children freely initiated the discussion of profound grief issues, thoughts, memories and feelings when they had finished a music therapy activity and began to focus on an art activity.

Vignette: improvising to draw out a feeling

'Eleanor', aged 6 years, had experienced the death of her grandfather and was experiencing confusion and sadness. Whilst participating in music therapy sessions at home Eleanor was asked to try and explain what these feelings felt like in her body. She explained that they felt heavy and sleepy. Eleanor was then asked to look through the various percussion instruments, play each one, and then choose the instruments that matched the feeling of 'sad'. Eleanor carefully selected five instruments and set them to one side. When the music therapist asked what sad may sound like Eleanor stated that sad would be slow and quiet as she felt like being quiet when she was feeling sad. Eleanor then selected a few instruments for the music therapist to play and kept the remaining instrument for herself. The music therapist suggested that they 'make up music to match sad' and they began to freely improvise a sad sound keeping to Eleanor's suggestions of playing quietly and slowly. At the end of the improvisation Eleanor said that she thought the music sounded sad but now she wanted to do something different. The music therapist commented that they had 'heard' what sad sounded like, and perhaps they could draw a picture of what sad may look like. Eleanor smiled and went to her room to get her pencils and felt pens and the drawing activity commenced. Eleanor liked to have Walt Disney music playing in the background while she was drawing, and she was quite particular about what materials she would use to draw with. Pencils for example were 'too scratchy', whereas crayons were 'soft' and therefore better to use to draw 'sad'. Eleanor carefully chose pastel colours of pink and peach, and her drawing of 'sad' emerged in long, sweeping lines, like a landscape.

Vignette: creating a family tree

'Trisha', also 6 years of age, was referred to music therapy after the death of her step-dad. Trisha's family structure was quite complicated, with step-siblings and step-grandparents, and Trisha was not sure how the family members were related. Although Trisha was only 6 years old she enjoyed popular music, and liked listening to 'Pepsi Hits' and the 'Lion King' CD, and she always chose the music she wanted for music therapy sessions.

The family tree illustrated below is a reproduction of a family tree drawn by Trisha. Because of the complicated family structure, the tree took five sessions to construct. The first session identified the immediate family members, then Trisha's mother helped clarify the other members of the family. Trisha's grandmother on her step-father's side of the family had died, as had Trisha's grandfather on her mother's side of the family. For a 6-year-old child the family structure was confusing, the more so because of the step-relationships. Trisha found photographs of some members of the family, and where there were no photographs, she made a sketch of her own to indicate the person. In the final version of the tree Trisha coloured in the leaves with crayons. She enjoyed stroking her hands over the tree, as if to make a closer connection to what it represented to her.

When other children have created a family tree, they also used pressed flowers, stickers and scrunched up paper and these were stuck onto their family trees. Many children adopted the use of a cross through a person's name to indicate that he or she had died.

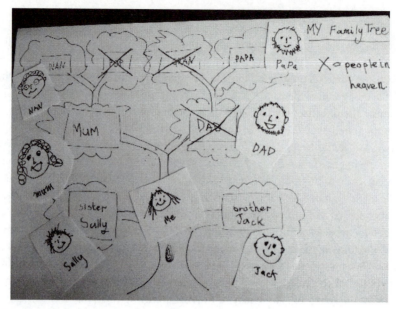

Plate 8.6 'Trisha's' family tree

Other music and art activities that are used for children who are bereaved include:

- listening to the family members' favourite music *or* writing a song for the family member

- drawings of special family memories (e.g. picnics, holiday memories)

- drawings of self; these can be illuminating to the therapist to see how the child perceives him- or herself

- drawings of the funeral while listening to reflective background music, or improvising or writing a song that would have suited the funeral. For example, one child was considered too young to attend the funeral of his father, and the child wanted to know what happened at funerals. In music therapy the child chose music that he thought would suit the funeral, and then drew a picture of what he thought the funeral would look like

- drawings of 'people in heaven' and also making 'music for heaven' for family members who have died.

MUSIC SELECTIONS

Where possible the child should choose the music he or she wants for receptive music therapy sessions. Some of the music selected includes:

Saint-Saens, *Carnival of the Animals*

Prokofiev, *Peter and the Wolf*

Disney movie songs (from *Cinderella*, *Snow White*, etc.) that are slow and gentle with long phrasing and have beautiful melodies.

★ ★ ★

Music, drawing and narrative (MDN)

Music, drawing and narrative (MDN) is a method devised by Joanna Booth, a New Zealand-trained BMGIM therapist. In MDN, the three art media (music, drawing and narrative) are combined to create a vehicle for story making. MDN 'grew out of a desire to extend the application of the BMGIM and generate an even greater flexibility than was previously possible' (Booth 2002, p.44). MND works as an individual therapy process, and can be used by clients for self-therapy. It is suitable for clients who do not wish to recline, or for vulnerable, ill or very tired clients who may be already overburdened with images, and for whom a full BMGIM session is not advisable. It also works effectively in the group context. The role of the client is to listen to the music, to draw and to write a narrative, so the applications of MDN include contexts where the client can concentrate for approximately an hour, and can express him- or herself in the media of drawing and narrative.

In MDN there are two opportunities to hear the music and engage with any imagery that the music evokes, which is then expressed in drawing and also in a narrative.

Materials

Clients should have access to oil pastels, plain A3-sized paper and solid backing (e.g. a board), and writing pen.

Procedure for the group session

Clients are asked to reflect on a topic for their experience, such as a theme or a focus they wish to explore. Participants are invited to find their own space, on the floor or at a table – wherever they feel comfortable (it may be away from others, or close to others in the group). A brief induction is given, with a relaxation component followed by the focus (in a manner that permits choice), and then connecting it with a suitable music programme. Participants are encouraged to align themselves with the music and to stroke colours on their page; to allow themselves to be drawn to a colour and to allow the music to move them. (The initial music on each programme is designed/chosen to encourage movement of colour onto the page.) At the end of the music participants are allowed time to conclude their drawings – as long as needed for each person. It is important that people understand that they can draw as much or as little as they want, and to ensure that they don't feel they have to make an artistic product. However it happens is the right way for each participant.

The music is then played a second time. This time the participants write a narrative/story about the drawing in any order that now suggests itself. This second playing allows recall, keeps participants entrained in their own process, and may suggest new scenes or avenues of exploration, or expand upon the drawing experience. They are encouraged to add a few extra details to the drawings if they desire, as a result of new insights. Again, time is allowed for rounding off the narrative.

The therapist then invites members of the group to be in a circle, and invites each person to share his or her drawings and stories with the therapist, and other members in the group, if that person wishes. The therapist's role is to listen attentively, but not to make any interpretation. The therapist might ask questions to help the client expand the description of the drawing or story – for example, 'Can you say more about what this colour/shape depicts?' Or, 'Is there something more to say about the story? How did it feel when...?' Or the group can form smaller groups for a more extended processing, and then convene in the larger circle for brief group sharing.

The individual session

For dyad sessions, the process is tailored to the individual and his or her current circumstances, as in BMGIM. After the initial discussion, client and therapist generate a focus. A relaxation induction follows and the focus is further developed and connected with an appropriate music programme. The client draws as much as he or she wants until the music concludes. Sometimes it is appropriate for some client–therapist interaction during the drawing phase, but this is minimal, and usually affirming of the client. The narrative of the drawings is written to the second playing of the same music.

The client then reads the narrative aloud to the therapist, and this can be an emotional time. Discussion of the narrative ensues. The therapist makes a full transcript of the session, notes what drawing activity goes with the various musical passages, photographs the drawings and writes the session up afterwards. The client receives a copy and is free to alter, add or delete whatever he or she wants. All this has proved to be very affirming of the client. Both therapist and client have a valuable record of a session series and its evolution.

The music selections

MDN has its own music programmes including 'short, gentle programmes for very vulnerable and fragile clients' (Booth 2002). These programmes are shorter than BMGIM programmes enabling a therapy session to fit within the 50-minute hour. Appropriate music for this technique is music that has changeable dynamics, or different sections that have changes in tempo, rhythm, orchestration, etc. Booth has designed 14 programmes for use in MDN, and four are reproduced here with permission.

TRANQUILLITY PROGRAMME (BOOTH 2002), DURATION: 16:36

Vaughan-Williams, *Romanza for Cello and Orchestra*

Vaughan-Williams, *Serenade to Music*

SUBLIME PROGRAMME (BOOTH 2003), DURATION: 20:39

Vaughan-Williams, *Piano Concerto in C*, 'Romanza'

Koechlin, *Seal Lullaby*

Vaughan-Williams, *Flos Campi*, vi

GOING GENTLY PROGRAMME (BOOTH, PERSONAL COMMUNICATION), DURATION: 17:00

Prokofiev, *Romeo and Juliet Suite* no.1, 'Madrigal'

Brahms, *Symphony no.2*, 3rd movement

Copland, *Rodeo Suite*, 'Corral nocturne'

Debussy, *En Bateau* (arr. flute and harp)

LARKING DANCER (BOOTH, PERSONAL COMMUNICATION), DURATION: 20:24

Vaughan-Williams, *The Lark Ascending*

Vaughan-Wiliams, *Fantasia on Greensleeves*

Processing

As the client(s) tell their story and recount what the story meant to them, the therapist models appropriate listening skills. These include:

- sensing what the story means to the person – how strong the emotion is that is being expressed
- what feeling is being expressed in the story
- reflecting back to the client using his or her own words
- avoiding interpreting the client's story, allowing the client to tell the story as he or she senses it
- affirming the positive and negative feelings the client experiences
- being interested in various key aspects of the drawings
- 'being there' emotionally and responding naturally.

MDN is a suitable method for clients who can engage with drawing and with writing a narrative, and gain therapeutic benefit from the method.

Conclusion

In this chapter a variety of methods have been explained where music interfaces with other creative arts media. These combined approaches allow more variety for the child/client to engage in self-expression. The art productions, such as collages and family tree pictures, can be a lasting memory of the music therapy session and can assist the child or adult client in resolving personal issues.

Chapter 9

Vibroacoustic Therapy in Receptive Music Therapy

Introduction

Vibroacoustic (VA) therapy is a generic term referring to the use of 'vibration' and 'acoustic sound' (music) for therapeutic purposes. It is defined as a method of music therapy where the practitioner carrying out the intervention is a music therapist, and where the intervention involves the use of music as part of the music/sound stimuli as a treatment for specified clinical reasons to achieve therapeutic goals. It is a receptive approach as the client or patient has no active role in creating or participating in music making, and the produced music together with pulsed sinusoidal low frequency sound is intended to be the therapeutic agent.

Many forms of vibroacoustic therapy exist, often administered by clinicians or assistants not qualified as music therapists. In identifying it as a method of receptive music therapy for this book, it is important to emphasise that the intervention still requires a therapeutic approach and therapeutic skills on the part of the music therapist. The procedures described in this chapter rely on a form of vibroacoustic therapy where music is combined with pulsed sinusoidal low frequency tones to achieve therapeutic effect. This combination of low frequency sound vibration used together with different forms of music was seen as a new approach with potential for a wide field of application once efficacy and effectiveness could be demonstrated. Current practice following such research shows that VA therapy is a systematic form of intervention that requires a therapeutic relationship between therapist and patient, and involves musical experiences. It therefore meets criteria defined by Bruscia (1998a) to be categorized as a form of music therapy. Comprehensive reviews describing the equipment to be used, treatment indications and contraindications and collected clinical reports and research studies can be found in reviews, research studies and edited volumes (Hooper 2001; Wigram 1997b; Wigram and Dileo 1997a, 1997b).

Basic theory

Vibroacoustic therapy started to develop in the 1980s, as a consequence of the seminal empirical clinical research of Professor Olav Skille in Norway and the experimental research that was undertaken by Tony Wigram in England, Chesky and Michel in the USA, Lehikoinen in Finland and many others around the world. The concept of using vibration as a form of treatment goes back well before this and has since been applied by various clinicians such as physiotherapists and occupational therapists in treating a variety of conditions (Boakes 1990; Carrington 1980; Darrow and Gohl 1989; Griffin 1983; Hagbarth and Eklund 1968; Madsen, Standley and Gregory 1991; Moller 1984; Pujol 1994; Standley 1991b; Stillman 1970; Wigram 1996,1997a; Wigram, McNaught and Cain 1997; Yamada et al. 1983). The principles and methods of vibroacoustic therapy were first defined by Skille at a congress of the International Society for Music in Medicine (Skille 1982). At that time, the method of using vibroacoustics was described as the use of sinusoidal, low-frequency sound pressure waves between 30–120 Hz, blended with music for use with therapeutic purposes. Skille's experiments in Norway started when he was headteacher of a school for children with handicaps in the very northern part of the country. Some of the children he was working with had physical handicap caused by cerebral damage, resulting in very high muscle tone. They suffered painfully when staff had to move them for the purposes of dressing, eating, washing and other normal everyday functions. The degree of flexor spasm and tight muscles resulted in discomfort to these children. Skille had noticed that they often relaxed to music, and particularly to music which had nice deep, strong-based tones. His early experiments involved putting children on beanbags, against which he pressed large bass woofers (bass speakers). The beanbags were full of polystyrene beads which acted as quite an efficient transmitter of the sound vibration that was produced from the big speakers. These children were noted to significantly relax in this position and also to be affected at a pleasurable level by the different types of music that Skille was trying, including Norwegian folk music, light classical and jazz music (Skille 1986, 1989a, 1989b, 1992).

Skille then took this a stage further and constructed crude, bed-like units. He combined vibroacoustic treatment with a movement approach, placing children on the bed and giving them this comfortable and enjoyable experience of pulsed, low frequency vibration, while at the same time manipulating and moving their limbs to try and maintain their range of movement.

Skille was so encouraged by the results from these early experiments that he built more bed units and loaned them out to colleagues in Norway to try with various conditions ranging from people with neuro-disability from strokes, people with severe learning disability and even women with dysmenorrhoea. He explored its application with clients with autism, with chronic pain disorders from back pain, headaches, migraine, with people who had lung diseases including cystic fibrosis, asthma, pulmonary emphysema and with many other patients he saw who had general physical ailments. Skille was an educator, musician and clinician who was exploring the effectiveness of vibrotactile and vibroacoustic stimulation in real clinical situations.

The consequence of this over time was that a number of other people became drawn into the clinical arena and subsequently began to research the process.

Principles of treatment

In applying vibroacoustic therapy treatment, there are some universal principles of the potential effect of music that should be taken into account:

1. High frequencies commonly induce tension in subjects while low frequencies cause relaxation to occur.

2. Music with strong rhythmic beats potentially induces energy and activity in subjects, while rhythmically neutral music at slower tempos can induce calmness.

3. Loud music (high amplitude) provokes arousal and awareness whereas soft music tends to pacify, calm and relax.

It is too much of a generalisation to define these as universal principles, as there will undoubtedly be exceptions to the general population's response to these principles. However, cross-culturally, and universally, one might work on these general principles in applying vibroacoustic therapy treatment.

The second important feature of vibroacoustic therapy is that it uses frequencies within the hearing range, but also at a pitch where the vibrating effect of the tone can most effectively be felt as a sensed vibration in the body. Any sound vibration works on the principles of sympathetic resonance, where another object has a resonant frequency at which it vibrates in sympathy with the sound. Consequently, the research in vibroacoustics has searched for evidence that frequencies within the range typically used in the treatment (30–80 Hz) can consistently produce the same response in subjects. Wigram (1996) found that the average scores for the sensation of vibration of frequencies in primary sites in the body tended to show that frequencies between 20 Hz and 50 Hz were felt significantly in the lower part of the body from the abdomen, lumbar region and sacrum down through the legs. Particularly, 40 Hz was located in the thighs and lower legs. Frequencies between 40 Hz and 70 Hz were felt in the chest and head. However, while at a very general level these localised sensations of vibration could be identified and located in specific parts of the body, there is considerable variability about where subjects experience simultaneous sensation and vibration in their body on a number of presentations and between subjects. The only conclusion one can reach from the research that has been undertaken is that lower frequency sounds between 30 Hz and 80 Hz in the vibroacoustic range are sensed and experienced as a whole body vibration, with some evidence that there is a localised sensation in specific areas of the body to different frequencies.

Research and theoretical framework

Research into vibroacoustic therapy began after a period of pioneer development when clinicians and other professionals exploring the effects of music vibration and sound vibration reported positive effects on a variety of physical disabilities and psychological problems. Music was already being used effectively in medical procedures (Dileo 1999; Spintge 1982; Spintge and Droh 1982; Standley 1995) and evidence had been presented documenting reductions in pain (Brown, Chen and Dworkin,1991; Chesky 1992; Chesky and Michel

1991; Curtis 1986), stress (Maranto 1994), and to meet emotional needs (Bonny and Savary 1973; Clark 1991; Goldberg 1995). Vibroacoustic therapy as developed in Norway and England is a treatment where a combination of relaxing music and pulsed, sinusoidal low frequency tones ranging from 25 to 75Hz is transmitted through bass speakers built into a bed or chair, upon which a patient sits or lies, usually supine.

The anecdotal evidence from Skille's clinical trials had reported a variety of beneficial effects on muscle-tone, heart rate and general well-being (Skille 1989a). He documented a number of reports on his clinical experiences with a wide variety of mental and physical disabilities or disorders. As well as describing the physically relaxing effects of vibrational sound therapy on children and adolescents with high muscle tone and severe spasticity, he had also explored its effects on people with pulmonary disorders such as asthma, cystic fibrosis, pulmonary emphysema, general physical ailments such as ulcers, poor circulation and post-operative convalescence and even psychological disorders with somatic effects such as insomnia, anxiety, self-injurious behaviour, depression and stress, and pervasive developmental disorders such as autism (Skille 1992; Skille and Wigram 1995).

Clinical applications

Construction of vibroacoustic equipment

Building vibroacoustic equipment is not so difficult, particularly in the form of a bed. Vibroacoustic equipment can be made as either a bed or a chair and the important thing is that low-frequency bass woofer speakers are built in to the chair or bed in a way that somebody can sit or lie on them. Incorporating the treatment system within a bed is quite easy. A strong wooden surface, 4 cm thick, and minimum 80 cm wide by 200 cm long is needed, into which four to six round holes 25 cm in diameter have been hollowed out, a speaker attached underneath (facing upwards) and a flat, smooth wire mesh surface attached on top (to prevent any damage to the membrane of the speaker by someone's body (see Figure 9.1).

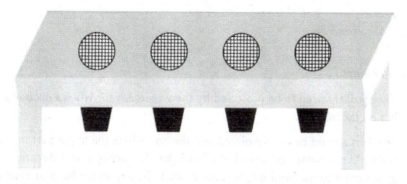

Figure 9.1 Vibroacoustic bed, side view

The best speakers to use are 8" woofers that are capable of effectively reproducing low frequency sound down to 30 Hz. The format for them would be to use four in-line speakers built into a bed (see Figure 9.2a), or six speakers built into a chair with one for the upper and lower back, one for the buttocks and four for the upper and lower legs, two for each leg on an extending recliner section (see Figure 9.2b).

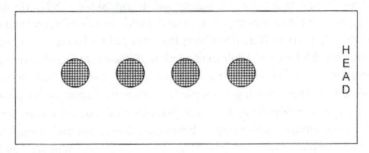

Figure 9.2a Vibroacoustic bed, top view

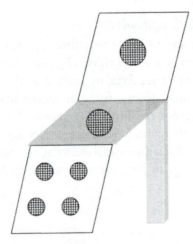

Figure 9.2b Vibroacoustic chair

Construction notes

1. The speakers need to be protected by the wire mesh for when somebody sits or lies on the bed.

2. Speakers should be evenly placed and the one where the upper part of the body is should not come underneath the head (low frequency sound directly generated into the head might cause a 'thick' feeling in the head or even a headache).

3. The speaker holes need to be evenly spaced.

4.   The wooden surface containing the speakers needs to be covered on a bed or a chair by low-density foam, approximately 4 cm to 5 cm thick.

5.   The speakers need to be wired up to connect to an amplifier that can reproduce the pulsed sinusoidal low frequency tone.

6.   A CD player (ghetto blaster) can be used to play different types of music (see the music list at the end of this chapter) which would be complementary to the pulsed low frequency tone.

7.   Pillows filled with polystyrene beads can be used to support a client's legs and other pillows placed for support beside the body in the event of any type of physical disabilities.

8.   A shallow dense foam pillow should be placed under the head to prevent too much vibration being transmitted.

Software

Vibroacoustic therapy was formerly administered through the use of cassette tapes, onto which had been recorded certain types of relaxing and sedative music as well as the pulsed sinusoidal, low frequency tones. This significantly restricted the potential use of different types of music, as the production of this software required the use of two function generators which could generate sinusoidal tones and where tones could be carefully mixed to produce the pulsed sinusoidal effect. This has now changed, as CDs with pulsed sinusoidal low frequency tones are now available and can be used to provide the physical stimulus that has been established to be the significant treatment element in causing change to occur.

It is also possible to create sinusoidal tones quite simply with a computer signal and record them onto a CD Rom in the computer. If one is intending to match the tones to specific notes or keys, Table 9.1 gives the pitch to frequency mappings for some of the notes within the vibroacoustic range used in most of the studies and empirical trials.

It was previously argued (Skille 1986, 1989a, 1989b; Skille and Wigram 1995) that consistency in matching the pulsed sinusoidal tone to the key in which the music was composed to avoid possible dissonance that could be uncomfortable or irritating was necessary. With tones as low as 44 Hz and lower, it is not that noticeable if the underlying sinusoidal tone clashes with the key of the music, and in any event, music does not stay in the same key, unless specially composed for that purpose, and modulates. Trained musicians may notice such dissonance, and above 44 Hz this also becomes more apparent. However, there are no reports of either subjects in research studies, or clients in therapy, reporting this to be a problem.

Table 9.1 Frequencies used in VA therapy	
Note	Frequency (Hz)
B	31
C	33
C#	35
D	37
D#	39
E	41
F	44
F#	46
G	49
G#	52
A	55
A#	58
B	62
C	65
C#	69
D	73
D#	78

Method of intervention and clinical procedures

Current treatment procedures in VA therapy are varied and there are, at present, no specific guidelines governing the application of this form of treatment. As the research to date has been uncoordinated and scattered, there are also limited indicators in terms of which patient populations are not likely to benefit. However, there is some evidence for which pathologies it is likely to be most helpful.

The development of VA therapy within a National Health Service hospital in the United Kingdom has necessitated some defined process or procedure by which people undertake treatment. Initially, these were written up at Harperbury Hospital as an unpublished treatment manual. More recently documents have been formulated of good practice relating to VA therapy referral, assessment and treatment, and guidelines for contraindications (Wigram and Dileo 1997b).

The process by which patients are treated with VA therapy is now more defined, and the subjects who undertook trials for the early experiments in VA therapy were treated using these methods. Guidelines on these procedures currently in use in VA therapy treatment have been documented (Wigram 1995). The protocol for administering a treatment of vibro-acoustic therapy involves all the relevant parameters for good therapeutic practice, requiring adequate preparation of the client, appropriate initiation and application of the treatment and effective closure of a session with post-treatment attention.

The process of the treatment can be defined in six stages:

1.   preparation for the session

2.   introducing the client to the treatment

3.   starting the treatment

4.   monitoring the treatment

5.   ending the treatment

6.   post-treatment work.

Stage 1: preparation for the session

- As part of the preparation for any treatment session with vibroacoustic equipment, the bed or chair needs to be carefully prepared for the patient who is going to be treated.

- The treatment is adversely affected if there are interruptions during the course of the treatment, so preparation is important.

- For physically handicapped patients, appropriate and correct support with pillows or wedges needs to be available and ready. With all clients, there is often a need for side support, to prevent rolling over to one side, and support under the knees (to prevent pressure on the spine when lying supine).

- The room needs to be comfortable and the position in which the patient is going to lie or sit needs to be quiet (without obvious visual stimulation) and well prepared.

- The equipment should be ready, the software prepared at the right point to start, whether one is using a traditional VA tape with low frequency sound combined with music, or a CD of the frequency alone together with music played on a separate system.

- The volume controls should be turned down to zero. This is important, as if a vibroacoustic tape is started with the volume turned up, patients will be subjected to a sudden jolt of sound when the music begins, and perhaps an uncomfortable boost of sound from the low frequency tone.

- The bass tone control hold also be turned down to zero.

- The sound stimulus should be introduced gradually, until at a comfortable volume.

- It is necessary when starting to use VA therapy to self-experience the stimulus and evaluate optimum levels for oneself. This can then be considered when using the equipment with others. Particularly with younger or more fragile clients be sure to set the volume output control at a lower level.

Stage 2: introducing the client to the treatment

- For an initial session of VA therapy, some explanation will need to be given as to what is going to happen.

- Explain the contraindications (see below) and ensure that VA therapy is not contraindicated for the client each time he or she attends (e.g. in case he or she has developed an inflammation since the last session, which would contraindicate the intervention).

- Explain the low frequency sound.

- Music choice procedure: establishing music preference is an important part of the treatment. Guidance on choice of music is found on pages 226–227, with some music selections on pages 232–235.

- Explain your role as the therapist. This will vary from one client to another. For some clients, it is appropriate that the therapist stays in the room, available to the client, but avoiding disturbing the treatment by interacting with them. You should say something like:

This 35-minute rest period is for you to relax and listen to the music you have chosen as your preferred music. I am here just to be with you, but we shouldn't talk during this time. You can listen to the music and relax, and I will read a book.

- The patient may need reassurance that he or she has control over what is happening and that if the stimulus is uncomfortable or irritating, he or she can get off the unit.

- With patients who are severely handicapped or profoundly mentally ill, this reassurance period still needs to happen and the tone of voice and the words used can set the scene and create the environment for a successful session. This is just as much a part of building the patient/therapist relationship as in any other form of therapy. People trust the therapist to treat them and need to be reassured by the way the therapist behaves and interacts.

- Creating the right environment for the beginning of the session is an important part of the process.

- Set the lights low and ensure the patient is happy with the room environment.

Stage 3: starting the treatment

- The stimulus must be started gradually and increased carefully to a point which seems to be the most effective level of intensity for the patient.

- It is important to allow a short period of response only to music, then to gradually increase bass frequencies.

- Experience has shown that some of the non-clinical population trying this equipment have initially wanted the stimulus to be quite strong and they ask for the volume or intensity to be increased.

- After a period of treatment, around ten minutes, it is important to check whether the intensity of the stimulus is too strong.

- At the beginning of a treatment, the low frequency tone can appear gentle and innocuous. However, after some time it is often perceived to be exerting a strong influence. Therefore, until the therapist has established what is the optimum treatment intensity for each patient, a period of evaluation needs to take place. Even then, it cannot be expected that patients would respond the same every time they come for a treatment.

- On some days, the patient may need a greater or a lesser intensity, depending on psychological or physiological state. It is not a precise science and no specific instructions can be given as to what intensity should be experienced by the patient.

Stage 4: monitoring the treatment

- This varies depending on the patient.

- During the course of the treatment, for some patients it is necessary that the therapist stay in the room in an unobtrusive way, to give a feeling of reassurance and comfort.

- For other patients, it can equally be more appropriate that the therapist should leave the room for the patient to have privacy and no distractions during treatment.

- With more handicapped or mentally ill patients, it is necessary to maintain an observation of the patient during the course of the treatment.

- It is important that patients do not feel they are being 'watched', as this is a passive form of treatment.

- It is better if the therapist can sit unobtrusively and appear not to be observing the patient.

- In order to evaluate the responses of people who are not able to verbalise their responses, some observation of facial expression and body movement will be necessary to check whether the patients are experiencing discomfort or a reaction against this treatment.

Stage 5: ending the treatment

- At the end of the treatment the relationship between the patient and the therapist will be important.

- Frequently during VA therapy, patients may go into quite a deep state of relaxation. They may fall asleep and possibly dream, and they may feel vulnerable at the end of the treatment.

- Patients can move into an altered state of consciousness, and will need the therapist for reassurance, guidance and support.

- At the end of the session there will be a need to make some evaluation of the response of the patient.

- With physically handicapped patients this may include some physical manipulation in order to check the significance of any improvement or lack of improvement.

- It may take a little time before patients can be active after a VA therapy session.

- Experience has shown that some people need to rest for two or three minutes after a session.

- When they get up off the unit, sitting or standing, they need to have a good stretch and move around, as they may do after a deep sleep.

- Experience and research has shown that there may be reductions in heart rate and muscle tone during VA therapy, and sometimes also reductions in blood pressure, more than might be expected from 30 minutes lying down, and it might take the patient a little time to come out of such a deeply relaxing state.

- Sometimes a patient can be a little emotional after a session, needing comfort and taking some time on the bed or chair to 'recover' from a deep state he or she may have reached. The therapist needs to pay attention to the needs of the patient at this time, but also to take care not to talk too much or to demand too much of the patient.

Stage 6: post-treatment work

- In some situations, VA therapy is used as a pre-treatment.

- It has been used as an effective pre-treatment for physiotherapy where, after the treatment has finished and a time period has allowed for the patient to become aware again, a relaxed, hypotonic state may have been achieved which is helpful as a preparation for physiotherapy intervention. Verbal psychotherapy may also take place after the treatment.

- If the patient has fallen asleep during the treatment, it may be important for him or her to rest for a period of time before leaving.

- Finally, the equipment needs to be checked after the treatment and it is a good practice to ensure that the controls are reduced to zero.

Frequency and duration of sessions

Treatment procedures will vary depending on the equipment which is being used and the patients who are being treated. The amount of information given in the literature or specification manuals supplied with VA equipment is limited regarding treatment procedures (Wigram 1995).

The period of time for which people are treated using VA therapy varies. Skille (1982) has recommended treatments varying between 10 minutes and 40 minutes. Wigram (1993) has consistently used treatments varying between 30 minutes and 40 minutes, except in the case of patients with disturbed or challenging behaviour, where the period of time may be determined by the tolerance period the patient has to being on a vibroacoustic unit.

There is no research on the effective or optimum length of time for treatment. Many of the original and traditional tapes that have been made with music and low frequency sound recorded on the one tape last for between 25 and 40 minutes. At Harperbury Hospital, treatment tapes and CDs have been included which last for 45 minutes.

Different methods or approaches designed to induce relaxation in subjects have often used 30-minute treatment. Various approaches, including progressive relaxation (PR), progressive relaxation with music (PRM), intermediate relaxation (IR), intermediate relaxation with music (IRM), mental relaxation (MR) and self-relaxation (SR), have proven effective in 30-minute sessions. In the comparison undertaken by Miller and Bornstein (1977) of these various methods, music on its own was not found to have an enhancing effect upon relaxation. All the conditions tested found significant changes in the relaxation from EMG measurements of muscle tone, and also on a state anxiety inventory. They did, however, only use a single trial of a 30-minute session. There were significant decreases in anxiety and muscle tension over the short period of relaxation used. Based on this, and on clinical experience, most of the studies referred to in this chapter involved 30-minute treatment periods, with some by Wigram extending to 40 minutes. It was not intended to investigate effects over different periods of treatment time in the investigations in this chapter.

When treating patients with certain disorders, such as low blood pressure, it has been considered that caution may be necessary to prevent 'overdosing'. For example, in Harperbury Hospital a 65-year-old woman with severe spasticity and dislocated hips, lying supine in a specially adapted wheelchair for most of her life, was given VA therapy in order to reduce her spasm and muscle tone. Over a period of four weeks of treatment, it took an increasingly longer time for her to regain full awareness after a treatment, and she seemed to be very low-toned and drained as the treatments went on. Treating her three times a week appeared to be an 'overdose', and physically affected her, so her treatments were reduced to once a week (see contraindications below).

Choice of music used in vibroacoustic treatment

A wide range of different types of music can be used in vibroacoustic treatment. There are many parameters that can define stimulatory or sedative music. Sedative music might typically have characteristics of softness, gentleness, smoothness, slow basic rhythm and pulse and without high-pitched sounds or accents. Some of the most important characteristics are concerned with identifying the level of predictability of the music. It is clear from the studies that have been undertaken that where the music used is stable, predictable and consistent, it will then be effective in reducing stimulation and promoting a state of calmness and relaxation (Wigram 2004).

The lists below demonstrate the potential for using sedative music as compared with stimulatory music. The elements below are those defined in the potential elements in stimulatory and sedative music (PSSM) (Wigram 2004, p.215).

Potentials in Stimulatory and Sedative Music (PSSM)
POTENTIAL ELEMENTS IN STIMULATING MUSIC

- unpredictable changes in tempo
- unpredictable or sudden changes in: volume, rhythm, timbre, pitch, harmony
- wide variations in texture in the music
- unexpected dissonance
- unexpected accents
- harsh timbres
- lack of structure and form in the music
- sudden accelerandos, ritardandos, crescendos and diminuendos
- unexpected breaks in the music.

POTENTIAL ELEMENTS IN SEDATIVE MUSIC

- stable tempo
- stability or only gradual changes in: volume, rhythm, timbre, pitch, harmony
- consistent texture
- predictable harmonic modulation
- appropriate cadences

- predictable melodic lines
- repetition of material
- structure and form
- gentle timbres
- few accents (list adapted from Wigram 2004)

Many different styles and genres of music can be used in vibroacoustic therapy, and as the intention is to use music that promotes and supports an experience of physical and mental relaxation, providing the above-listed elements are dominant, choice of music can be made to suit individual preference. Popular classical, new-age music, music for relaxation, gentle jazz are all appropriate. Where a client's preference runs to heavy metal, punk or strongly accented rhythmic music, these choices may well not promote relaxation. This does not exclude rhythmic music, as music with a regular and stable underlying pulse and consistent rhythmic patterns can be quite relaxing, as is found in much baroque and classical styles, as well as popular music.

It is relatively easy to find many of the above styles of music, and shops offering a good range of CDs usually stock a variety of relaxation styles. However it is important to note that these have not been compiled in the main by professionally trained and qualified therapists, and the great majority have not been tested for therapeutic effect in experimental studies.

Classical music is often not so easy to categorise as relaxing, as many pieces may contain quite a variety of dynamics and changes in orchestration and style. The music selection 'discography' at the end of this chapter offers a range of suggestions for classical music appropriate for VA therapy.

Contraindications

During the years of its development, a number of contraindications were suggested regarding vibroacoustic therapy. These were based on some theoretical considerations and also empirical experiences where clients identified negative responses when receiving vibroacoustic treatment. In particular, contraindications had been identified previously (Wigram 1995) to include acute inflammatory conditions, psychosis, pregnancy, haemorrhaging and active bleeding, thrombosis, hypotension or patients who use pacemakers. These suggested contraindications were to some extent based on assumptions and more recent research and clinical practice, as well as an increase in theoretical knowledge, suggests that they may have been premature. Certainly, there is no evidence that vibroacoustic therapy increases or causes any damage in haemorrhaging or active bleeding. In fact, vibroacoustic therapy was used in an acute hospital as a pain-reducing relaxant for patients in post-operative cardiac surgery. In this medical situation, the potential for treatment to be contraindicated if it worsened internal haemorrhaging would have been only too evident.

Currently, there is still some evidence that vibroacoustic therapy can cause negative responses to some conditions and also perhaps some natural cautions that would be exercised with others. Therefore it is relevant to consider vibroacoustic therapy to be contra-indicated in the event of the following conditions (or medical advice sought):

1. *Acute inflammatory conditions* This would include conditions where inflammation such as earache, toothache or back pain due to a prolapsed intravertebral disc (a slipped disc) is in an acute phase where the treatment may exacerbate pain. There are also cases where, in the acute phase, rheumatoid arthritis has shown a bad reaction to vibroacoustic and vibrotactile stimulation. In all cases of acute inflammatory conditions, it would be important to seek advice and also to take into consideration treatments that were being administered already.

2. *Pacemakers* Patients who have had pacemakers fitted should not be exposed for any period of time to magnetic fields and it is known that they should avoid going through security systems where strong magnetic fields might influence the functioning of a pacemaker. Therefore, it would be sensible to contraindicate vibroacoustic therapy as a treatment for patients who have pacemakers.

3. *Psychosis* There have been anecdotal reports of psychotic patients who cannot understand the type of stimulus they are receiving, where the experience they undergo provoke paranoid thoughts or insecurity. The sensation of internal vibration, perfectly relaxing, comfortable and mainly enjoyable for any other patients, might be perceived as an internal invasion in their body. This might cause them to react negatively to the experience. Therefore, it would be sensible for vibroacoustic therapy to be administered to psychotic patients only when somebody who knows them well is present and can explain to them what is happening and can also end the treatment if the patient is responding very negatively.

4. *Pregnancy* While there is no apparent evidence from empirical reports that vibroacoustic therapy can do any damage to an unborn foetus, or cause any disturbance to the normal maturation and delivery of the baby, no actual trials have been undertaken to ensure that vibroacoustic therapy is not harmful to pregnant women, especially in the first trimester. Consequently, it would be sensible to contraindicate vibroacoustic therapy as a treatment for pregnant women until more is known about the effects of this stimulus.

5. *Acute physical conditions* Vibroacoustic therapy is not necessarily contraindicated for acute physical conditions. It is necessary to check with a general practitioner or consultant what existing treatments are being administered in order that vibroacoustic therapy would not disturb or affect an existing intervention. In the event of somebody already undergoing an existing treatment for an acute physical condition, it would be necessary to closely and strictly monitor responses to vibroacoustic therapy in the assessment phase before undertaking sustained intervention.

6. *Hypertonia* Vibroacoustic therapy has, in some cases, caused reduction in both systolic and diastolic blood pressure. In patients who suffer from hypertonia, and already have low blood pressure, the effect of VA therapy in further reducing it is to cause inactivity and lethargy and lack of response.

Any further contraindications would be speculative and current literature does not report negative responses to this intervention. It must be emphasised here that vibroacoustic therapy is a non-invasive, relaxing and enjoyable treatment which was never intended to be administered as an aggressive treatment for any condition.

Clinical applications of vibroacoustic therapy

There is a wide variety of populations for whom vibroacoustic therapy has a useful application and some of the research that has been undertaken provides evidence to support its efficacy with some of these populations. The first population on which this intervention can be applied and for which there needs to be a defined procedure are those patients with severe physical disabilities, specifically those with cerebral palsy, a consequence of which is tight muscles and flexor spasm.

During the middle 1980s there was no commercial production of vibroacoustic equipment and much of it was constructed for clinical purposes. Skille reports in his VA therapy manual that 'for ethical reasons it was important and necessary that the therapist and the staff who were experimenting with this equipment tried it on themselves first before they tried it on the patients' (Skille 1986, p.22). The reports that were initially drawn from staff experiences showed Skille that the treatment had effects on several different conditions. In this way, the variety of potential applications of VA therapy began to emerge.

Anecdotal reports have accrued over many years of experimentation and clinical reports from treatment sessions can be looked at as helpful and guiding rather than scientifically significant. There has been a certain amount of objective research into VA therapy, although very few studies that have been undertaken have been replicated. There has been a wide application of VA therapy treatment, and many of these treatments have reported beneficial effects.

Collated reports fall into five main pathological areas:

*   pain disorders
*   muscular conditions
*   pulmonary disorders
*   general physical ailments.

Pain disorders

There have been anecdotal reports of the effective use of VA therapy with colic pains, bowel problems, fibromyalgia, migraine and headache, low back pain, menstrual pain,

dysmenorrhoea, premenstrual tension, neck and shoulder pains, polyarthritis and rheuma-
tism (Skille 1989b 1992).

Some of the treatments undertaken with these conditions have been successful. The use
of frequencies recommended can vary considerably. For example, for polyarthritis, it has
been recommended to use frequencies between 40 Hz and 60 Hz, whereas for migraine and
headaches, the use of frequencies between 70 Hz and 90 Hz were recommended. Low back
pain could be treated by frequencies between 50 Hz and 55 Hz. Over 50 reports have shown
that over 50 per cent of patients treated for fibromyalgia have been successfully helped with
a reduction in pain symptoms (Skille 1989a). There is no objective evidence supporting the
specific use of certain frequencies for specific conditions other than the prescriptive suggestions from Skille (1992) and even less evidence to support short- or long-term effects of VA
therapy. The recommendations above are based on empirical work and anecdotal reports.

There have been a small number of experimental studies, and one study was undertaken
by Chesky and Michel (1991) in an analysis of the effect of music vibration on the sensory
and mechanoreceptors in a study on pain. Their study found a significant effect when given
stimulation within a specific frequency range (60 Hz to 600 Hz) using a music vibration
table (MVT™) on pain receptors resulting in a reduced perception of pain by subjects
(Chesky 1992). Chesky and Michel used equipment which was adjusted to generate greater
activity in the frequency ranges known to produce pain relief (approximately 100 Hz to 250
Hz). This research indicated the effect of music vibration in inducing vasodilatation. The
research studies undertaken on pain relief by Chesky and Michel (1991) indicated that pain
relief associated with music and controlled music vibration is substantial and significantly
greater than music alone or the use of a placebo.

Muscular conditions

VA therapy has been used to aid muscular problems, particularly where those problems can
cause painful conditions. Cerebral palsy has received considerable attention from clinicians
looking at the effect of VA therapy in reducing muscle tone. Cerebral palsy is a condition
which can react with spasm to over-excitement, high stimulation or sudden stimulation, and
therefore relaxing and calming music can be helpful. Some of the treatments that have taken
place using VA therapy have also involved doing active physiotherapy during or immediately after the session.

Other physically handicapping conditions which have shown a positive response to VA
therapy have included multiple sclerosis, Rett syndrome, spasticity and muscular over-use
syndrome (Wigram 1996). Research in the clinic for children and adults with Rett syndrome
at the Harper House Children Service in Hertfordshire, England, has already shown a
positive response to VA therapy from almost all of the patients attending the clinic. In short,
15-minute sessions, using classical and folk music combined with frequencies between 38
Hz and 44 Hz, observational reports have noted increased levels of relaxation, reduced
anxiety, reduced hand plucking, and reduced hyperventilation (Wigram 1997a; Wigram and
Cass 1995).

Anecdotal reports from people who suffer from muscular pain are interesting. One phenomenon is that during treatment for pain in a specific muscle group, patients have reported an experience that, as they relax to the stimulus, they experience the pain focusing on the particular muscle group where the damage has occurred and the effect of vibration has been to relax all other muscle groups or muscle fibres around this area. In this way, the treatment has heightened the sensation of pain and discomfort in the area of primary damage (see contraindications).

Pulmonary disorders

Further anecdotal results have shown some effect on certain pulmonary disorders, including asthma, cystic fibrosis, pulmonary emphysema and metachromatic leucodystrophy. Both metachromatic leucodystrophy and cystic fibrosis have similar symptoms where patients have difficulties in coughing up lung secretions and phlegm in order to keep the lungs clear. VA therapy has a palliative effect here in assisting the patient in coughing up secretions, by generating a vibration in the lungs and shifting mucus on the bed of the lungs causing a cough reflex to occur. Skille reported that up to the end of 1994, four children with this specific disorder in Norway were having VA therapy on a daily basis (Skille and Wigram 1995).

Asthmatic problems have been alleviated by VA therapy, with easier breathing, reduced wheezing and decreased viscosity of the expectorates in the lungs. Because severe asthmatic conditions sometimes cause bronchial spasms, the spasmolytic effect of VA therapy has been helpful in reducing the severity of asthma attacks. The evidence of effect on pulmonary disorders is supported only by anecdotal reports.

General physical ailments

VA therapy treatment has been used to treat decubiditus ulcers, reduced blood circulation, post-operative convalescence and stress-related disorders. VA therapy has been found to be helpful in reducing blood pressure and heart rate, and improving blood circulation (Skille and Wigram 1995). There are anecdotal reports of poor circulation causing a purple colour in legs, which when subjected to a period of treatment of VA therapy turned to a more healthy pink or red colour. There have been several studies on the effect of VA therapy on blood pressure. These studies provide conflicting and inconsistent evidence of effect (Saluveer and Tamm 1989; Skille 1986).

Conclusion

VA therapy influences both psychological and physiological processes. Music is received, processed and interpreted in the brain, and the emotional and associating effect of music stimulates psychological processes. At the same time, physical effects go alongside or are the result of psychological activity and music has an active effect on physical behaviour. Experimental studies in the field of VA therapy have not only identified further evidence of the way music affects us at a psychological level, but have also measured physical response. Because VA therapy is an intervention that presents a physical stimulus in the form of a pulsed sinusoidal low frequency tone, these studies have found some evidence of the effect of sound within this frequency range. The psychological and physiological effect of music and sound is gaining increasing importance in treatment theory surrounding music therapy and music in medicine.

This is undoubtedly an enjoyable form of treatment, with few side effects so far recorded. Therefore, it is easy to propose its application in a variety of clinical conditions. The empirical studies and development by Skille in Norway, and by other people in Europe and America, have explored the application of VA therapy with a wide variety of conditions. However, it is important to clarify that objective research and evaluation of the efficacy of VA therapy when compared with either an alternative relaxation treatment or a control condition has, to date, been limited. The effect of relaxing music can be very influential, and it is known from previous studies that music alone can provide quite a strong influence in reducing anxiety levels, facilitating relaxation and developing altered states of consciousness (Bonny and Savary 1973; Goldberg 1995; Grocke 1999a).

There has been some analysis of the effect of VA therapy in reducing blood pressure, and there is variability in the findings. Chesky and Michel (1991) found significant reductions in blood pressure and heart rate which reinforced anecdotal reports from Skille (1986, 1989a, 1989b), Saluveer and Tamm (1989) and Lehikoinen (1988). Reductions in heart rate have also been noted. Experimental studies have established that the findings in some of these anecdotal reports could not have been attributed purely to a quiet environment, resting mentally, resting physically, the music, or various combinations of these parameters (Chesky and Michel 1991; Wigram 1996). Reductions in arousal level, heart rate and changes in mood state also contribute to the validity of this treatment as physically influential (Wigram 1996). VA therapy is a receptive method which, when used as an intervention by a music therapist, involves a therapeutic approach, a therapeutic relationship and appropriate therapeutic strategies for administration and evaluation of outcomes.

Classical music selections for vibroacoustic therapy: discography

Table 9.2 shows a selection of classical music that can be used appropriately as background music in order to generate a feeling of calmness and relaxation in vibroacoustic therapy. These pieces are all orchestral or chamber music, and while there is variability in some pieces in dyanamics and tempi, overall each piece contains a stable, predictable structure that facilitates the calming and relaxing properties of vibroacoustic treatment. There will be also variability in different performances and recordings. No attempt is made here to identify a preferred recording, as this is a matter of cultural preference and individual taste. When the selected low frequency tone is less than 44 Hz, it usually causes no noticeable clash (as mentioned previously musicians may notice a dissonant effect). Above 44 Hz, the clash of low frequency and key may be more noticeable (i.e. a piece in G major where a 55 Hz (A) tone is used).

Table 9.2 Classical music selections for VA therapy

Composer	Piece	Key
Bach, Johann Sebastian	*Concerto in D Minor*, for 2 violins and orchestra, 2nd movement	F Major
	Prelude no.1	C major
Barber, Samuel	*Adagio* for strings	B flat minor
Beethoven, Ludwig van	*Cello Sonata no.3*, 2nd movement	A minor
	Sonata no.8 for piano ('Pathetique'), 2nd movement	A flat major
	Symphony no.5, 2nd movement	A flat major
	Symphony no.6, 2nd movement	B flat major
	Symphony no.6, 5th movement	F major
	Symphony no.7, 2nd movement	A minor
	Symphony no.9, 3rd movement	B flat major
	Concerto no.5 for piano, 2nd movement	B major
	Romance no.2 for violin and orchestra	F major
Berlioz, Hector	*Harold in Italy*, 2nd movement	E major
Boccherini, Luigi	*Quintet for strings*, 3rd movement	A major
Borodin, Alexander	*Quartet no.2* for strings, 3rd movement	A major
Brahms, Johannes	*Piano Concerto no.2*, 3rd movement	B flat major
	Violin Concerto	F major
	Symphony no.1, 2nd movement	E major
Chopin, Frederic	*Concerto no.1* for piano, 2nd movement	E major
	Concerto No.2 for piano, 2nd movement	A flat major
	Nocturne in B flat minor, op. 9 no.1	B flat minor
	Nocturne in E flat, op. 9 no.2	E flat
	Nocturne, op. 32 no.2	A flat major
	Nocturne, op. 37 no.1	G Minor
	Nocturne, op. 50 no.2	F sharp major
	Nocturne, op. 55 no.1	F minor
Debussy, Claude	*Prelude to the Afternoon of a Faun*	E major
Delius, Frederick	'On hearing the first cuckoo in spring'	A minor
	'A walk to the paradise garden'	E flat major

Continued on next page

Table 9.2 continued

Composer	Piece	Key
Dvořák, Anton	*Serenade for Strings*, 1st movement	E major
	Symphony no.9, 2nd movement	D flat major
Elgar, Edward	*Concerto for Cello*, 3rd movement	B flat major
	Serenade for Strings, 2nd movement	C major
Fauré, Gabriel	*Elegy* for cello and orchestra	C minor
	Sicilienne for cello and piano	G minor
Gluck, Christoph	*Orpheus and Eurydice*, 'Dance of the blessed spirits'	F major
Grieg, Edvard	*Concerto* for piano and orchestra, 2nd movement	D flat major
	Holberg Suite, 2nd movement saraband	G major
	Holberg Suite, 4th movement air	G minor
	Peer Gynt Suite no.1, 2nd movement	B minor
	Peer Gynt Suite no.2, 4th movement	A minor
	Sonata for violin and piano, 2nd movement	E major
Handel, George Frideric	*Messiah*, 'Pastoral symphony'	F major
Haydn, Franz Joseph	*Symphony no.104*, 2nd movement	G major
Ketelbey, Albert	'In a monastery garden'	F major
Listz, Franz	*Liebestraum no.3*	A flat major
Mahler, Gustav	*Symphony no.5*, 'Adagietto'	F major
Mascagni, Pietro	'Intermezzo' from *Cavelleria Rusticana*	F major
Massenet, Jules	'Meditation' from *Thais*	D major
Mendelssohn, Felix	*Violin Concerto*, 2nd movement	C major
	Fingal's Cave, overture	B minor
Mozart, Wolfgang Amadeus	*Clarinet Concerto*, 2nd movement	D major
	Concerto for flute, harp and orchestra, 2nd movement	F major
	Horn Concerto K447, 2nd movement	A flat major
	Quintet in A for clarinet and strings, 2nd movement	D major
	Serenade in G for strings, 2nd movement	C major
	Symphony no.40, 2nd movement	E flat major
	Symphony no.41, 2nd movement	F major

Rachmaninoff, Sergei	*Concerto no.2* for piano, 2nd movement	E major
	Sonata in G minor for cello, 2nd movement	C minor
Ravel, Maurice	*Pavanne for a Dead Infanta*	E minor
Schubert, Franz	*Symphony no.5*, 2nd movement	E flat major
	Symphony no.8, 'unfinished', 2nd movement	E major
Strauss, Johann	*Blue Danube*	D major
	Emperor Waltz	C major
	Tales of the Vienna Woods	F major
	Roses from the South	F major
Tschaikovsky, Peter	*Concerto* for piano, 2nd movement	D flat major
	Concerto for violin, 2nd movement	G minor
	Symphony no.4, 2nd movement	B flat minor
Vaughan-Williams, Ralph	*Fantasia on a Theme of Thomas Tallis*	G minor
	The Lark Ascending for violin and orchestra	G major
Wagner, Richard	*Seigfried Idyll* for orchestra	E major
Warlock, Peter	*Capriol Suite*, 2nd movement	G minor
	Capriol Suite, 5th movement	G major

Chapter 10

Music and Movement

Introduction

Receptive music therapy can also include the use of music to promote movement for clients of different ages and in different contexts. Bruscia refers to this method as 'eurhythmic listening' (1998a, p.123). Here, the music chosen acts as a direct or indirect influence on the facilitation of movement (voluntary or assisted), to achieve therapeutic objectives. There are many instances where teachers or therapists from other disciplines use recorded music as a background to some movement activities. This chapter will illustrate the use of both recorded and live music to encourage, support and facilitate movement in a population of people with severe and profound multiple handicaps. A detailed example of a music and movement protocol designed primarily for use with multi-handicapped children and adults is included to provide a treatment protocol that specifies exact movements and relevant music that can be used.

Clients with physical disabilities

Generally speaking, physical disabilities cause difficulties in mobility, weight-bearing, mobilisation and physical activity. There is a wide variety of physical disabilities, from those caused by cerebral insult due to prenatal anoxia, to people who have suffered strokes which have caused partial paralysis. The value of music and movement for any population with physical disability is in its effect on reducing muscle tone, promoting relaxation and maintaining or increasing range of movement.

Spasticity and spasm

Children, adolescents and adults with cerebral palsy typically experience tight muscles caused by flexor or extensor spasm. Spasms are caused by:

1. physical events: a reaction to movement

2. pain: the feeling of pain in the body can cause a spasm reaction

3. psychological causes that might trigger spasm: general uneasiness, stress, excitement, expectation of what is going to happen or general anxiety about pain.

A spasm is often activated by some external stimuli, for example, as a reaction to people doing something unexpectedly. Common activators of a spasm include people moving suddenly nearby, trying to do something with a person that he or she is not expecting, or trying to do something physical with a person which he or she finds uncomfortable or difficult. For example, when being lifted and moved a person who has a physical disability will commonly go into a spasm reaction of some form, make vocal sound or have other involuntary muscle activity.

People with severe spasticity,who suffer from flexor spasm will commonly experience a deterioration in their range of movement over time and, as a consequence, may ultimately develop fixed contractures in their joints (particularly knees, elbows, wrists and ankles) where they become more physically disabled over time.

Music facilitates movement

Music can effectively facilitate movement. Music is used in a variety of different ways for movement activities whether it be for military marches, ballet, dancing and song on stage, or aerobics, etc. Music is commonly available in gyms and health clubs where people are exercising. People find it very helpful to exercise with a musical stimulus, because music maintains a rhythmic pattern and gives the person something interesting to listen to. The structure of music (particularly rhythm) offers a framework for the movement the person is attempting to do, and it can be a very motivating stimulus for the creation of movement, as is evident from dance traditions ranging from classical ballet to modern creative dance.

Spasm in people with quadriplegic cerebral palsy is an involuntary defensive mechanism in response to some types of external stimuli. The consequence of the spasm is that it may cause pain, and prolonged spasm causes a build up of lactic acid in the muscle group, which also may cause pain. In order to avoid this pain it is advisable to work with the client and move the muscles in order to increase the circulation and relieve the build-up of lactic acid. Another form of cerebral palsy is athetoid disability which is commonly evidenced by fluctuating muscle tone causing involuntary flexor and extensor movements. In either case, movement to a musical stimulus (where the music is a receptive form of intervention for the client) is an effective way of promoting and motivating clients to both allow movements and actively participate in movement. It provides a 'framework' enabling clients to gain control of their involuntary movements.

Music and movement approach

In developing a music and movement procedure, which is applied to a specific group of clients, it is important to remember that the sequence of movements needs to be carefully planned so that they follow a logical process. For example, if the intention is to encourage and promote arm movements that work with the full potential range, first of all we have to take into consideration loosening and relaxing the shoulder joint before expecting to undertake any development of arm range.

The relevance and appropriateness of the music that is going to be used in any music and movement approach is important for the effectiveness and success of the different types of exercises. Style, tempo and the timbre of music in particular have to be carefully selected and applied for each individual movement, and its success very much depends on how well the music fits the shape and timing of the movement. Where the music is being produced live, the effectiveness of the music can also be influenced by how a therapist or musician plays. The receptive process is that the client is hearing and assimilating musical stimuli while carrying out the movement, and therefore the movement must be supported and motivated by the musical structure. The music envelops and supports the client, and the rhythm and form of the music needs to match the rhythm and structure of the movement being undertaken. In many ways, the relationship between the client and the music facilitates the client's physical response and the effort needed to undertake the movement, while the therapist's role is to help the client to respond.

- First, and most important, rhythm and tempo are motivating stimuli for everyone. Tempo and rhythm reach the most primitive parts of our brain and stimulate a *thalamic reflex* causing us unconsciously to beat time, quite often in the tempo of the music we hear. Therefore the music must be at a tempo and contain a rhythm that is primarily connected to the movement one is attempting.

- Second, the melodic and harmonic content of the music must encourage, sustain and develop interest and awareness in the client. The qualities of harmony and melody appeal directly to the temporal lobe, encouraging reminiscence, association and also expectation and anticipation. Where there is a clear melodic structure in the music, the client will feel that he or she can follow the form of the music and that it is predictable. This is very significant in promoting movement responses to music.

- Third, the style and timbre of the music can be adjusted to the aim of the movement, depending on whether it requires relaxation or stimulation. Characteristics of how the music is played or what the music contains (if it's recorded) such as staccato, rhythm and metre, accents, increases and decreases in tempo and increases and decreases in volume will be significant in promoting movement activity.

Badly or inappropriately presented, any one of these elements may have quite the opposite effect to what one might hope or expect, particularly when it relates to the speed at which one is attempting to undertake movements. For example, as any one who is marching will tell you, if the tempo increases beyond a certain point, marching becomes impossible and one develops into either very fast walking or running. Maintaining stability in the movement then becomes increasingly difficult. The most important element for any passive movement is providing a rhythmic or melodic stimulus that has a degree of stability and consistency.

The tempo often has to be slow or slowish, with emphasis on strong beats. If played too fast, with a loosely defined metre and rhythm, it becomes increasingly difficult for the client to match his or her movements to the music and also for the therapist to use the music in passive movement with the client.

Music and movement with clients with cerebral palsy

Cerebral palsy can result in differing characteristics or forms: hypertonic, hypotonic or athetoid. No two people with this disability are ever exactly alike, because in each case the motor dysfunction will depend upon the degree of damage and the site of the lesion. However there are some common characteristics to physical presentation.

- *Hypertonic* clients have an excess of muscle tone in various muscle groups.

- Some clients have *adductor spasm*, which results in scissoring of the legs. This puts the hips at risk of dislocating whilst making it very difficult to cope with dressing, toileting, washing, etc.

- Many people with cerebral palsy have *general extensor muscle spasm*. The main extensor muscle groups have hair-trigger responses and the client suddenly stiffens with straight knees, extended hips, extended spine and head. In extreme cases the neck extends, the mouth opens and the tongue thrusts out. A calm, quiet approach is helpful to minimise these effects of extensor spasm.

- Other people present with the opposite problem: *flexor spasm*. If there is excess tone in the flexor groups of muscles and the clients spend a long time sitting, they can end up chair-shaped. This type of client needs to relax, well supported. If one attempts to extend a flexed muscle it responds by tightening even more, thus increasing the problem.

- *Hypotonic* clients have low tone and 'floppy' muscles. Sometimes they seem uninterested in the world about them. They lack the motivation to move and often cannot stabilise their position if they do try to move. They may well need a brisk, stimulating approach.

- *Athetoid* clients are constantly making involuntary movements. They need help to stabilise their position before attempting a specific movement. They are usually excitable and need a calm approach if they are to succeed with a voluntary movement.

- *Joint deformities* can offer the greatest challenge, both in respect of the current condition and the depressing prognosis. Windswept hips are common. One hip is abducted and externally rotated and the other hip is adducted and internally rotated. They are often associated with fixed flexion deformities of both knees. The abducted hip is stable but the adducted hip is at risk of dislocating and this needs to be borne in mind when working with these clients in movement work. Windswept hips are frequently associated with *pelvic obliquity*, which can in turn lead to *scoliosis*. In this condition, the spine adopts a large C curve to one side. This can become an S curve because clients tend to position their heads 'off centre'. Ribs are crowded on the concave side and respiration is diminished. In severe cases the spine rotates, giving rise to severe deformities.

Lastly there is the problem of increasing stiffness as adolescents become adults and consequently heavier and larger. This means it is not so easy for staff to move them. If they are unable to move themselves very much, it is likely they will develop deformities – mobile deformities at first, which eventually can become fixed deformities. Many clients are wheelchair users. They need to keep mobile, and this scheme of movements helps to fulfil their needs.

Scheme of movements

Two points are important in considering the potential value of music and movement.

1.   Movement is pleasurable. The able-bodied take walks, stretch and move around. The physically handicapped can enjoy being moved or helped to move themselves.

2.   The session is done on the floor on comfortable but firm mats with clients' heads on wedges or pillows. This is for the comfort of client and therapist.

MUSIC INPUT

The music should be played live in order to match the speed of the client's movements, and can be either known repertoire or improvised music. It is also possible, with more experience and with a well-known group of clients who have had many sessions already, to use a recorded version of a live session. But chosen, pre-recorded music from CDs almost always does not contain enough flexibility of rhythm and tempo to work and the client(s) and therapist(s) will typically find they are having to adapt (and compromise) the movement they are making to match the musical structure and, particularly, tempo. With live music, it is much easier for the therapist to adapt tempo and style to the group. It is important that the tempo is set at the speed at which the most 'physically disabled' client is able to manage. It is possible for everyone else to slow down, while it is often impossible or therapeutically counterproductive for some to adapt to a faster speed.

If improvised music is used, it is important to construct it in a musical form that will provide a rhythmic base, a structure in melody and phrases, and predictability. The rhythm and phrasing are fundamental to developing the anticipatory response within the whole movement. Using music from existing vocal and instrumental repertoire is quite appropriate, particularly if in some movements it is valuable to vocalise using appropriate key words. Counteracting or working against the regressing physical disability outlined above requires an encouraging and persuasive element in the musical stimulus. Therefore the quality of the sounds, and the structure and order of the music have to be extremely conducive as a catalyst for the physiological progress one is trying to make. For the clients to be able to participate and engage with the movement experience the musical framework does need to be predictable and motivating.

In each movement of the movement protocol explained below, there will be a section describing style of music, and then a section offering examples of music. In many countries therapists are experienced and skilled in the clinical use of musical improvisation, and the use of improvised music, or the adaptation of songs or composed music, requires the skills and training of a qualified music therapist. Improvised music can be used for music and movement work, and the style of music section provides information about tempo, dynamics and presentation style. However, it is better to use a musical 'framework' that provides a predictable musical structure (Wigram 2004, p.117) in order to help the clients anticipate the movement. In the section on examples of music, therefore, only examples from song or instrumental repertoire will be suggested.

Therapeutic competency and responsibility

The previous section referred to the importance of the musical competency and training which is necessary to undertake the use of music and movement, and how music therapists are trained in applied skills of improvisation. The detailed descriptions of the different movements in this protocol also raise a question as to the level of physiological knowledge and training necessary to carry out this form of intervention.

To undertake most of these movements, a music therapist needs to be guided initially by a physiotherapist specialised in the disabilities associated with cerebral palsy (or any physical handicap arising out of cerebral insult before, during or after birth), traumatic brain injury (incurred through an accident resulting in physical disability), or any spinal injury for which this set of movements (or an appropriate selection) may prove beneficial. When this protocol was initiated in the early 1980s, the combined approach of both music therapist and physiotherapist to achieve a protocol that met the treatment aims of both disciplines resulted in a form of 'co-training' – involving a shared education. Music therapists had to learn a lot about physical handling, and physiotherapists had to learn a lot about musical structure and tempi, as well as metres and part-metres. The helpers involved in the one-to-one treatment in group sessions had to learn both aspects (Wigram and Weekes 1985).

Once this knowledge and skill has been gained, a therapist or helper can safely and appropriately handle a client with physical disabilities. Any new clients that are included in this type of therapy approach will still need to be evaluated as to handling by an appropriate professional, but the more experienced and skilled a music therapist becomes at handling, the more he or she will be able to make relevant and appropriate judgements, with certain limitations. Attention to any available physiotherapy assessments and nursing (or other) reports on the client's physical status should be carefully studied.

Therefore, the competency level to undertake the intervention protocol that follows needs to include a period of interdisciplinary training and knowledge-building, and the movements that are now described should not be undertaken without this period of training.

Music and movement protocol

Opening the session: Good morning song

RATIONALE FOR ACTIVITY

We take for granted our ability to accommodate to the surface we are on, whether it is the floor, a chair or whatever. But many clients with intellectual and physical disabilities cannot do this and, at the start of the session, when clients are put on the floor, they may be feeling uncomfortable, apprehensive or vulnerable to a greater or lesser extent. Some become agitated or disturbed. The 'Good Morning Song' calms and reassures them. It indicates the beginning of the session and promotes trust and confidence between client and therapist.

DESCRIPTION OF MOVEMENT

The 'Good Morning Song' (Figure 10.1) is a short, tonal welcome song that is first sung twice to the whole group. Then the song is sung to each client in the group (also twice) with modulation of dynamics, timbre, and sometimes key to suit the character and also the mood of each person that particular day. It is useful to use the same song consistently for a period of time, to help the client relax to a familiar and known song.

STYLE OF MUSIC

The dynamics and style of the song need to be adjusted to each individual. More vulnerable clients need a gentle, softer approach, while more enthusiastic and extrovert clients can have a louder, more exciting version. The tempo always needs to vary slightly to suit the individual.

EXAMPLE OF MUSIC

The 'hello' song used by Wigram is to be found in Figure 10.1.

> Good morning/afternoon to everyone
> Good morning/afternoon to everyone
> Good morning/afternoon to everyone
> It's music today
>
> Good Morning/afternoon to…Charlie
> Good Morning/afternoon to…Charlie
> Good Morning/afternoon to…Charlie
> It's music today

Figure 10.1 Good morning song

A further example of a 'hello' song can be found in the Nordoff Robbins Play songs.
Typically music therapists often compose their own hello songs. Depending on the cognitive
level and degree of disability of the clients in the group, these need to be carefully tailored to
suit individual and group needs.

In the following sequence of movements, there is a logical order that involves working on the right side and then the left side of the body.

1.   spinal rotation right side

2.   shoulder girdle movement right arm

3.   right arm movement

4.   shoulder girdle movement left arm

5.   left arm movement

6.   spinal rotation left side

7.   rolling from side to side

8.   bouncing legs

9.   flexing and extending right leg

10.   flexing and extending left leg

11.   hip abduction

12.   pelvic tilt

13.   prone lying and hip extension

14.   foot massage

15.   goodbye song

Some of these movements described below where right and left side procedures are the same will be connected together to avoid repetition.

Movements 1 and 6: spinal rotation (a) client lying on right side; (b) client lying on left side

RATIONALE FOR ACTIVITY

Spinal rotation is undertaken to counteract the effects of sitting for long periods in wheelchairs where the client is often slumping to one side or the other. Potential C-curve or scoliosis may result, causing spinal twisting and increasing difficulties with posture and movement. Spinal rotation has the same effect as if a person sitting in a chair, or standing, was turning the top part of the trunk to the left or right, while keeping the bottom half fixed. The movement maintains flexibility of the spine.

DESCRIPTION OF MOVEMENT

This movement is undertaken with the person lying first on his or her left, and then his or her right side. Ensure the client is in a comfortable position, akin to the recovery position with one leg slightly bent and the head/neck extended ensuring a clear airway. Passively rotate the spine by placing one hand on the buttocks and the other hand on the front of the shoulder girdle covering the chest wall. The therapist can apply gentle pressure, pulling gently with his or her hand on the shoulder girdle and chest wall whilst pushing gently with the other hand on the buttocks. This results in a spinal twisting/spinal rotation. The therapist gently tries to increase the range as far as is comfortable for the client.

STYLE OF MUSIC

Music should have a time signature of 2/4 or 4/4, with a medium slow to slow tempo (crotchet = 72). A gentle beginning is necessary. The tempo should remain the same throughout for continuity. Spinal rotation needs a strong rhythm so that the client can anticipate the accents on which the movements are going to take place.

EXAMPLES OF MUSIC THAT COULD BE USED

Songs

'Early one morning'

'Fish goin' to swim' (from *Showboat*)

Instrumental

'Morning' from *Peer Gynt Suite*, Grieg

Melody in F, Rubinstein

Movements 2 and 4: shoulder girdle movement, right arm and left arm

RATIONALE FOR ACTIVITY

Tension and stiffness in the shoulders is very common in clients with physical disability, particularly those with high muscle tone and scoliosis. Loosening and relaxing the shoulder girdle as a main joint is particularly important as a prelude to any work on range of movement in the client's arms.

DESCRIPTION OF MOVEMENT

This movement is in two stages. The client is supine, lying on his or her back in as straight a position as possible, and the therapist's hands are placed on the shoulder joints, one over, one under. One side of the shoulder girdle is then moved rhythmically, depending on the stiffness of the client. Then in the second stage the therapist rotates the shoulder girdle gently, in a circular, slow movement, gradually increasing the range as far as is comfortable for the client.

STYLE OF MUSIC

Music should have a time signature of 4/4 or 12/8 with a medium slow to slow tempo (crotchet = 88).

A very supporting and relaxing style of music is effective. Gently played ragtime or slow syncopated music has proved very successful.

EXAMPLES OF MUSIC THAT COULD BE USED

If using repertoire music, such as ragtime, it is important to play in a calm, slowish and relaxed style for this movement.

The Gladiolus Rag

The Entertainer

Movements 3 and 5: right arm and left arm movements
RATIONALE FOR ACTIVITY

After loosening the major (shoulder girdle) joints, working on each arm, one at a time, is the next stage in the process to maintain range of movement in upper limbs. Proprioceptive neuromuscular facilitation (PNF) requires the movement to utilise complete potential range of the limb. However, with clients with cerebal palsy, expectations must be moderated to potential range.

DESCRIPTION OF MOVEMENT

The client is lying on his or her back, with the head supported and the legs kept as near to midline as possible. Take one arm (the other arm movement will follow the second shoulder girdle movement) and begin by moving the shoulders in a gentle, circular movement, followed by flexion and extension of the elbow, pro- and supination of the forearm. This is either a passive or assisted active movement, according to the ability of the client. The therapist will gradually move the arm in rhythmic, short stages until the hand of the client is reaching over his or her opposite shoulder. This is followed by then moving the arm down until the client's hand is stretching down to his or her side. The possible range that can be achieved depends on the degree of disability of the client. It is recommended to start with the most severely affected arm where there is a difference in the two limbs. Finally, then allow time for the client to perform an active or spontaneous movement, which might take the form of feeling the floor or reaching out for a target.

STYLE OF MUSIC

If this movement was simply limited movements in the mid range of the shoulder, such as elbow or forearm flexion and extension, we would be able to use rhythmic music and make the movement quite rhythmical. However, we are trying to move towards full-range shoulder movements and therefore we have to structure the movement to a phrase of music. The movement can still be done rhythmically but in the context of a phrase rather than to a pulse. Simple words to a song are very helpful for this movement. The music needs to be slow and one tries to achieve a rising and falling style to the phrases, in sympathy with the movement. For the development of spontaneous movement at the end of this movement, the music should lose rhythmic content altogether and become almost atmospheric in quality. Again, rising or falling phrases within the improvisation with crescendo and decrescendo are helpful.

EXAMPLE OF A SONG THAT COULD BE USED
The song that can be used for this movement is sung to the tune of 'I'd Like to Teach the World to Sing (In Perfect Harmony)' (a pop song which originated as an advertising jingle, produced by Billy Davis and sung by The New Seekers, for Coca-Cola, and was featured in 1971 as a TV Commercial). The first four lines of the song are repeatedly used:

> Hold your arms…in the air
> And move them up and down
> Hold your arms in the air
> And move them up and down

Movement 7: rolling from side to side
RATIONALE FOR ACTIVITY
The aim of this movement is to mobilise the spine and encourage spontaneous movement of the head and upper part of the body. There is a similarity with spinal rotation, as the movement facilitates a twisting movement in the spine as if one was turning 90 degrees to the right or left. The difference is that this movement encourages voluntary participation by the client in bringing the upper torso and head over to each side.

DESCRIPTION OF MOVEMENT
All pillows and wedges are removed and the movement starts with the client lying on his or her back. The therapist secures the left leg, bends the right leg and gently moves the right leg over the left, so that the client starts to turn onto his or her left side. If the client finds it difficult to turn, some gentle assistance under the right shoulder will help. Moving the client back to midline, this process is repeated, but this time by flexing and bringing the left leg over the right, to turn the client onto the right side. Special care is needed for clients with a sub-luxed or dislocated hip.

STYLE OF MUSIC
Music should have a time signature of 4/4 (crotchet = 56).

Again this movement needs to feel rhythmic in phrases. A very pronounced first beat provides the target for anticipation. Depending on the size and degree of handicap, the client can roll on to each shoulder at one-bar intervals or two-bar intervals. Whether improvised or playing song or composed repertoire, the piece needs to be broad in style.

EXAMPLES OF SONGS THAT COULD BE USED

'Climb every mountain' (one roll to a phrase)

'My bonnie lies over the ocean' (one roll to a phrase)

The 1976 song 'I am sailing' (sung by Rod Stewart with lyrics by Gavin Sutherland) adapted for this movement is ideal. The first four music lines can be used:

'I am rolling… I am rolling…I am rolling…on the floor
I am rolling… I am rolling…I am rolling…on the floor'

Movement 8: bouncing legs
RATIONALE FOR ACTIVITY

When there is high tone in the legs (or in any part of the body) an option is to gently 'shake out' the tone. With the legs, a pelvic girdle exercise to loosen the main joint is not as easy to achieve as a shoulder girdle exercise[1] so gently bouncing the legs up and down, while also gently flexing and extending them through a small range is an effective way of reducing the tone in preparation for flexing and extending the legs in the next movement.

DESCRIPTION OF MOVEMENT

Client is supine with the head supported. The therapist supports the lower legs behind the knees and ankles and the hips are flexed. The legs are bounced up and down and the effect achieved depends on the way the legs are held. If the legs are fully supported and moved gently up and down, this can induce relaxation in hypertonic clients. The reduction in tone will allow some straightening of the knees in flexed clients. However, in hypotonic clients, if less support is given and the legs are moved up and then allowed to drop a little before they are supported again, this can increase tone. It is important that the therapist ensures they are positioned properly to avoid unnecessary strain on their own back.

STYLE OF MUSIC

Music should have a time signature of 2/4 or 4/4, with a moderate to brisk tempo (crotchet = 112).

This is a very rhythmic movement. The tempo of the music is crucial in this movement. It must not be so fast as to induce spasm but must be fast enough to facilitate involuntary relaxation. Also with hypotonic clients, where the purpose is to increase tone, the music needs to be slow enough to allow them time to work with the rhythm and not so fast that they just become floppy.

EXAMPLES OF INSTRUMENTAL MUSIC THAT COULD BE USED

'Can-Can' from *Orpheus in the Underworld*, Offenbach

'Colonel Bogey march', John Philip Sousa

'Cornish floral dance'

Arrival of the Queen of Sheba, Handel

Movements 9 and 10: right and left leg flexion and extension
RATIONALE FOR ACTIVITY

Having loosened the legs with the bouncy legs movement, this movement is concerned with maintaining maximum range of movement in the legs. Again, proprioceptive neuromuscular facilitation requires the movement to utilise the complete potential range of movement. However, as with the arms, for clients with cerebal palsy (spasticity or athetosis), expectations must be moderated to potential range. Reducing muscle tone and maintaining range of movement in the legs in hemiplegic and quadriplegic disability is also important to prevent the development of fixed contractures. For clients with flexor spasm, as full a range of extension as possible is desirable, while for clients with extensor thrust the aim will be to break the extensor spasm and induce flexor movements.

DESCRIPTION OF MOVEMENT

The client lies supine with his or her head supported, socks and shoes removed. The therapist's hands are placed on the flexor aspects of the client's legs, i.e. behind the knees and on top of the ankles, the dorsal aspect. The legs are then bent, either passively by the therapist or actively by the client (usually one at a time, but sometimes both together depending on the size of the client and the nature and degree of the disability). The therapist's hands are then changed to the extensor aspects, i.e. the soles of the feet, placing the other hand over the kneecaps, gently encouraging the client to push. This can also be done rhythmically, with a series of short pushes, or in a sustained manner with one long push. The therapist attempts to gradually increase the range of extension and flexion as far as is comfortable for the client.

STYLE OF MUSIC

Music should have a time signature of 3/4 or 6/8, with a medium slow tempo (crotchet = 72). There is a need in this movement for a particular emphasis on the first beat, or both beats of a 6/8 rhythm. Also a clearly defined tempo and simple style is needed – either improvised or repertoire (possibly songs with key words for the client, i.e. bend and push). We find two to three pushes to every bend are often necessary with clients who are very flexed and two to three bends with clients with, for example, extensor spasm.

EXAMPLES OF MUSIC

A good song for this exercise is the well known melody, 'Eidelweiss', from the musical *The Sound of Music* (Rogers and Hammerstein). Almost everyone knows it, and the words can be changed (using the music from a verse) to:

> Bend and bend, bend and bend
> Stretch and stretch your le…gs
> Bend and bend, bend and bend,
> Stretch and stretch your le…gs
> Bend and bend and bend and bend
> Stretch and stretch and stretch your legs
> Bend and bend, bend and bend
> Stretch and stretch your le…gs.

The song lyrics can be flexible, in that if someone can bend and stretch more quickly, then the words can be changed to 'bend and bend, stretch and stretch'. If they need more time than in the verse above, the first four lines can all be devoted to bending, while the last four lines to stretching.

Other songs and pieces at the right tempo could include:

'My bonnie lies over the ocean'

'When Irish eyes are smiling'

'Daisy, Daisy'

'Sheep may safely graze'

'Waltz' from *The Merry Widow*, Franz Lehar

Movement 11: hip abduction with gentle rocking
RATIONALE FOR ACTIVITY

It is common in people with cerebral palsy, particularly when wheelchair bound for much of the time, for the adductor muscles to be increasingly tight, causing the legs to lock tightly together. In addition, many are susceptible to a sideways position where the hips are veered to one side, known as 'windswept' hips. Here there is also an increasing danger over time that the hip joint will become sub-luxed or even dislocated. Hip abduction aims to maintain the range in the hips and reduce the risks of increasing physical disability arising from tight adductors.

DESCRIPTION OF MOVEMENT

The clients is placed with his or her trunk as straight as possible, and hips and knees bent. The therapist kneels in front, placing his or her hands on the client's pelvis, one each side of the client's hips. The therapist gently separates the knees as much as possible using the elbows. By introducing a gentle rocking from side to side the therapist maintains a steady but gentle pressure to encourage further relaxation of the adductor muscles and separation of the knees.

STYLE OF MUSIC

Music should have a time signature of 3/4 or 6/8, with a medium slow tempo (crotchet = 80). This movement has a swaying element to it and is effective when using a slow 3/4. Therapists may need to take longer over the abduction with some clients (particularly those prone to dislocated or windswept hips) and therefore a 6/8 rhythm with a one- or two-beat (strong beat) facility is better. This movement needs to be slow because unless it is done carefully it can be uncomfortable for the client. It is important in this movement that the client is able to anticipate the movement rhythmically.

EXAMPLES OF MUSIC

Often waltz music works very well for this movement, as it allows a medium strong emphasis on the strong beat each time to right or left, which helps the client anticipate the movement.

Examples of songs that would be at a gentle tempo are:

'My bonnie lies over the ocean'

'Skye boat song'

'Daisy, Daisy'

Examples of instrumental pieces that could be used

Johann Strauss, Jr., *Waltzes* ('Blue Danube', 'Emperor Waltz') played slowly

'Elizabethan serenade'

'And he shall feed his flock', Handel – from the *Messiah*

'Morning' from *Peer Gynt Suite*, Grieg

Movement 12: pelvic tilt
RATIONALE FOR ACTIVITY

With younger children, this movement is helpful to maintain range of movement in the pelvis, because when spending a lot of time in a wheelchair the pelvis can become fixed in one position.

DESCRIPTION OF MOVEMENT

This is done passively by the therapist with the client lying supine with the head supported. The hips and knees are flexed to take tension off the trunk muscles. The pelvis is then rocked forward and back. The majority of our clients sit on their coccyx and not on their bottoms and they become very stiff in the lumbar region. This movement is not possible with older and larger clients. Holding the pelvic girdle each side with the fingers cradling the lower hips/upper buttocks, the therapist pulls the buttocks up to make a rounded curve in the lower back, and then flattens the hips to reverse the position and flatten the spine.

STYLE OF MUSIC

Music should have a time signature of 2/4 or 4/4, with a slow and rhythmic tempo (crotchet = 60). This is another movement that should be done very rhythmically. It is best in 2- or 4-beat metre and the music must be slow. It is hard work for the therapist and should be done in two sections. An almost staccato style of playing is helpful.

EXAMPLES OF MUSIC

The first and third beat of a faster 4/4 piece can be used.

Examples of pieces that could be used

> *Humouresque*, Dvořák
>
> 'Air on a G string', 3rd Suite, J.S. Bach
>
> 'Mary had a baby' (slowly)
>
> 'Yesterday', The Beatles

Movement 13: prone lying and hip movement
RATIONALE FOR ACTIVITY

To counteract the effects of sitting in a wheelchair, clients are placed lying down on their front in the prone position in order for the therapist to make passive movements of their hips.

DESCRIPTION OF MOVEMENT

The movement begins with the client lying over a wedge on his or her front, with the arms forward. Some clients with hip and knee flexion deformities are put over beanbags or sag bags to accommodate the deformity. The prone position encourages extension of the spine and hips and the therapist facilitates extension where it is most needed – usually the hips. The therapist works with one leg at a time, bending the leg and tucking the client's foot into the therapist's armpit, holding the client's leg under the knee. Placing the other hand on the client's pelvis/buttock, the therapist gently pulls the leg up, whilst maintaining a firm pressure on the pelvis.

STYLE OF MUSIC

Music should have a time signature of 2/4 or 4/4, with a medium slow tempo (crotchet = 76/88). A very supportive and relaxing style of music is important. As with the first movement, gently played ragtime or slow jazz, or improvised music with syncopation is appropriate. It should be somewhat slower than the first movement because the movements are more difficult to do.

EXAMPLES OF MUSIC

Examples of instrumental pieces that could be used

'The entertainer', Scott Joplin

'Wedding day at Troldhaugen', Grieg

'Cornish floral dance'

Examples of songs that could be used

'Go tell it on the mountain'

'Viva Espania'

'Roamin' in the gloamin''

'Kum ba ya'

Movement 14: foot massage work

RATIONALE FOR ACTIVITY

Poor circulation, oedema and sometimes pitting oedema are common with clients with many forms of physical disability. Footwork exercises are essential to stimulate blood flow and circulation in the foot. This movement (as with many in this schedule of movement) is very pleasant and enjoyable for the clients.

DESCRIPTION OF MOVEMENT

Clients lie supine with head supported on a pillow. The therapist works on one foot at a time, taking care to support the leg. The forefoot is placed between the therapist's relaxed hands and firm pressure applied. The underlying structures in the sole and the upper part of the foot are then moved in a circular fashion. This produces a sensation of pleasure which has to be experienced rather than described. The therapist then flexes and extends the toe joints passively and repeats with the other foot.

STYLE OF MUSIC

Music should have a time signature of 2/4 or 4/4, with a slow tempo (crotchet = 60). The music for this movement needs to be slow, steady and quite smooth but with a very strong rhythmic feel to it, particularly in the first half of the movement, when it can be difficult to find the rhythm of the circular movement. With flexion and extension of the toes it is much easier to do the movement rhythmically.

EXAMPLE OF MUSIC

'Air on a G string', J.S. Bach

'Wachet Auf', J.S. Bach

'Nobody knows the trouble I see' (American traditional)

'Michelle', The Beatles

'The little drummer boy'

'Greensleeves'

15: Goodbye song

Ending the session after footwork, or whichever movement in the scheme has been reached, is usually begun with a short period of relaxing quietness. Then a song of ending, or a goodbye song should be sung to say 'goodbye' to each individual, and then the group as a whole.

The goodbye song composed by Wigram for these sessions and also used in other music therapy work with intellectually disabled clients is a tonal song sung first twice to the whole group. Then the song is sung to each client in the group. As with the welcome song, modulation of dynamics, timbre and sometimes key to suit the character and also the mood of each person that particular day is an important therapeutic criterion to individualise and personalise the message of farewell. It is also useful with the goodbye song to consistently use the same song for a period, to help the client relax to a familiar and known song.

Conclusion

This protocol for music and movement relies on a degree of training and knowledge in the therapists undertaking it, whether they are music therapists, physiotherapists, carers, parents or any other person. In developing this model, it became apparent to the original team (Wigram and Weekes 1983) that there needed to be a negotiated collaboration between two disciplines at least. The treatment direction and objectives of physiotherapy need to be moderated, as do the treatment direction and objectives of music therapy in order to develop a truly multidisciplinary approach. This is not a physiotherapy treatment session with background music, nor is it a music therapy session with some movement activities, and it is certainly not an exercise regime such as aerobics. The quality and style of the music the clients hear at a receptive level will have significant influence on their degree of cooperation with, or resistance to movement(s).

Figure 10.2 Goodbye song

It is important to re-emphasise the need for the tempo of the music to be right for these movements to be effective for the client. All the clients are different, although some of their handicaps are very similar. Less handicapped clients can always do the movements more slowly but more handicapped clients cannot do the movements faster, so the tempo should always be judged by the speed which the slowest clients can manage.

The range of different songs, pieces, styles and genres of music provided here again reflect the background of the author. Nevertheless, they have been chosen with care, and are based on experience. Any choices of music, used live or recorded, need to be tried and tested for effect and particularly for relevance to the specific movement for which they have been chosen. While music and movement may seem the least 'receptive model' in this book, the principal issue of an individual's response on hearing and responding to music still remains the bedrock of the approach described above.

Note

1   An exercise to loosen the pelvic girdle which can be undertaken with small children from the age of three to about eight or nine years, depending on degree of disability and size of child, is described in this protocol under 'pelvic tilt'.

References

Achterberg, J. (1985) *Imagery in Healing*. Boston, MA. New Science Library.

Alladin, W. (1999) 'Models of counselling and psychotherapy for a multiethnic society.' In S. Palmer and P. Laungani (eds) *Counselling in a Multicultural Society*. London: Sage.

Altshuler, I.M. (1948) 'A psychiatrist's experience with music as a therapeutic agent.' In D. Schullian and M Schoen (eds) *Music and Medicine*. New York: Henry Schuman.

Alvin, J. (1975) *Music Therapy*. Revised edition. London: John Claire Books.

American Music Therapy Association (2006) www.musictherapy.org/faqs.html (Retrieved 3 March 2006).

Baker, F. and Tamplin, J. (2006) *Music Therapy Methods in Neurorehabilitation: A Clinician's Manual*. London: Jessica Kingsley Publishers.

Baker, F. and Wigram, T. (2005) *Songwriting: Methods, Techniques and Clinical Applications for Music Therapy Clinicians, Educators and Students*. London: Jessica Kingsley Publishers.

Barker, L. (1991) 'The use of music and relaxation techniques to reduce pain of burn patients during daily debridement.' In C. Dileo Maranto (ed.) *Applications of Music in Medicine*. Washington, DC: National Association for Music Therapy.

Baumel, L. (1973) 'Psychiatrist as music therapist.' *Journal of Music Therapy 10*, Summer, 83–85.

Bishop, B., Christenberry, A., Robb, S. and Rundenberg, M. (1996) 'Music therapy and child life interventions with pediatric burn patients.' In M.A. Froehlich (ed.) *Music Therapy with Hospitalised Children*. Cherry Hill, NJ: Jeffrey Books.

Blake, R. (1994) 'Vietnam Veterans with post-traumatic stress disorder: finding from a music and imagery project.' *Journal of the Association for Music and Imagery 3*, 5–17.

Blake, R. and Bishop, S. (1994) 'The Bonny Method of Guided Imagery and Music (GIM) in the treatment of post-traumatic stress disorder (PTSD) with adults in a psychiatric setting.' *Music Therapy Perspectives 12*, 125–129.

Boakes, M. (1990) *Vibrotactile Stimulation*. London: British Association of Occupational Therapists. Unpublished.

Bonde, L., Nygaard Pedersen, I. and Wigram, T. (2001) *Når Ord ikke Slår Til: En Håndbog i Musikterapiens teori og praksis i Danmark (Music Therapy: When words are not enough. A handbook of Music Therapy Theory and Practice in Denmark)*. KLIM: Århus.

Bonny, H. (1983) 'Music listening for intensive coronary care units: a pilot project.' *Music Therapy 3*, 4–16.

Bonny, H. (2002) *Music and Consciousness*. Gilsum, NH: Barcelona Publishers.

Bonny, H. and Savary, L. (1973) *Music and Your Mind*. New York: Harper and Row.

Booth, J. (2002) 'A brief music, drawing and narrative experience.' *Making Connections: Proceedings of the inaugural conference of the Music and Imagery Association of Australia (MIAA)*. Melbourne, pp.44–49.

Booth, J. (2003) 'Music and imagery experiences with the music of Vaughan-Williams.' *Music and Imagery: Sound Connections. Proceedings of the second Australasian conference of the Music and Imagery Association of Australia (MIAA)*. Melbourne, pp.31–41.

Borczon, R. (1997) *Music Therapy Group Vignettes*. Gilsum, NH: Barcelona Publishers.

Bright, R. (1972) *Music in Geriatric Care*. Sydney: Angus & Robertson.

Brown, C.J., Chen, A.C.N. and Dworkin, S.F. (1991) 'Music in the control of human pain.' *Music Therapy 8*, 47–60.

Bruscia, K. (1987) *Improvisational Models of Music Therapy*. Springfield, IL: Charles Thomas Publications.

Bruscia, K. (1998a) *Defining Music Therapy*, 2nd edition. Gilsum, NH: Barcelona Publishers.

Bruscia, K. (1998b) (ed.) *The Dynamics of Music Psychotherapy*. Gilsum, NH: Barcelona Publishers.

Bruscia, K. and Grocke, D. (eds) (2002) *Guided Imagery and Music (GIM): The Bonny Method and Beyond*. Gilsum, NH: Barcelona Publishers.

Bush, C. (1995) *Healing Imagery and Music.* Portland, OR: Rudra Press.

Carpenter, R. and Bettis, J. [1969] (2006) 'Eve', www.lyricsdomain.com/3/carpenters/eve.html (Retrieved 5 June 2006).

Carrington, M.E. (1980) 'Vibration as a training tool for the profoundly multiply handicapped child within the family.' Paper on clinical practice in physiotherapy, Castle Priory College. Personal communication.

Chesky, K.S. (1992) *The effects of music and music vibration using the MVTtm on the relief of rheumatoid arthritis pain.* PhD dissertation, University of North Texas. Unpublished.

Chesky, K.S. and Michel, D.E. (1991) 'The music vibration table (MVTtm): developing a technology and conceptual model for pain relief.' *Music Therapy Perspectives 9*, 32–38.

Clair, A. (1996) *Therapeutic Uses of Music with Older Adults.* Baltimore, MD: Health Professions Press.

Clark, M. (1991) 'Emergence of the adult self in guided imagery and music (GIM) therapy.' In K. Bruscia (ed.) *Case Studies in Music Therapy.* Phoenixville, PA: Barcelona Publishers.

Clark, M., McCorkle, R. and Williams, S. (1981) 'Music therapy-assisted labor and delivery.' *Journal of Music Therapy 18*, pp.88–100.

Colegrove, V. (1995) 'The use of taped music with Validation techniques to support the imagery of a disorientated woman with multi-infarct dementia and glaucoma: a case study.' *Journal of the New Zealand Society for Music Therapy*, 42–45.

Congreve, William (1697) *The Mourning Bride*, Act 1, Scene 1, I.

Crook, R. (1988) *Relaxation for Children.* Katoomba, NSW: Second Back Row Press.

Curtis, S.L. (1986) 'The effect of music on pain relief and relaxation of the terminally ill.' *Journal of Music Therapy 23*, 1, 10–24.

Darrow, A.A. and Gohl, H. (1989) 'The effect of vibrotactile stimuli via the Somatron on the identification of rhythmic concepts by hearing impaired children.' *Journal of Music Therapy 26*, 115–124.

De Backer, J. (1993) 'Containment in music therapy.' In M. Heal and T. Wigram (eds) *Music Therapy in Health and Education.* London: Jessica Kingsley Publishers.

Dileo, C. (ed.) (1999) *Music Therapy and Medicine: Theoretical and Clinical Applications.* Silver Spring, MD: American Music Therapy Association, pp.181–188.

Dileo, C. (1997) 'Reflections on medical music therapy: biopsychosocial perspectives of treatment process.' In J. Loewy (ed.) *Music Therapy and Pediatric Pain.* Cherry Hill, NJ: Jeffrey Books.

Dileo, C. and Bradt, J. (1999) 'Entrainment, resonance and pain-related suffering.' In C. Dileo (ed.) *Music Therapy and Medicine: Theoretical and Clinical Applications.* Silver Spring, MD: American Music Therapy Association.

Egan, G. (1986) *The Skilled Helper*, 3rd edition. Burbank, CA: Brooks-Cole.

Egan, G. (1998) *The Skilled Helper*, 6th edition. Burbank, CA: Brooks-Cole.

Eliot, T.S. (1941) 'The Dry Salvages', in T.S. Eliot *Collected Poems, 1909–1962.* London: Faber and Faber.

Erdonmez, D. (1977) 'Music as a Projective Technique.' *Proceedings of the third national conference of the Australian Music Therapy Association*, Adelaide, Australia. pp.11–16.

Feil, N. (1993) *The Validation Breakthrough.* Baltimore, MD: Health Professionals Press.

Fleming, J. (1990–1992) *Guided Imagery and Music (GIM) training courses.* University of Melbourne: Unpublished.

Frith, S. (1978) *Sound Effects: Youth, Leisure and the Politics of Rock.* London: Constable.

Goldberg, F. (1994) 'The Bonny Method of Guided Imagery and Music (GIM) as individual and group treatment in a short-term acute psychiatric hospital.' *Journal of the Association for Music and Imagery 3*, 18–34.

Goldberg, F. (1995) 'The Bonny method of Guided Imagery and Music.' In T. Wigram, B. Saperston and R. West (eds) *The Art and Science of Music Therapy: A Handbook.* London: Harwood Academic.

Goldberg, F., Hoss, T. and Chesna, T. (1988) 'Music and imagery as psychotherapy with a brain damaged patient: a case study.' *Music Therapy Perspectives 5*, 41–45.

Griffin, M.J. (1983) 'Effects of vibration on humans.' In R. Lawrence (ed.) *Proceedings of Internoise 1.* Edinburgh: Institute of Acoustics, pp.1–14.

Grocke, D.E. (1999a) 'The music which underpins pivotal moment in Guided Imagery and Music.' In T. Wigram and J. de Backer (eds) *Clinical Applications of Music Therapy in Psychiatry.* London: Jessica Kingsley Publishers.

Grocke, D.E. (1999b) *A phenomenological study of pivotal moments in Guided Imagery and Music.* PhD dissertation, University of Melbourne. CD-IV University of Herdecke, Germany.

Grocke, D.E. (2002) 'The Bonny Music Programs.' In K. Bruscia and D. Grocke (eds) (2002) *Guided Imagery and Music (GIM): The Bonny Method and Beyond.* Gilsum, NH: Barcelona Publishers.

Grocke, D.E. (2003) 'Healing an inflamed body: the Bonny Method of GIM in treating rheumatoid arthritis.' In S. Hadley (ed.) *Psychodynamic Music Therapy.* Gilsum, NH: Barcelona Publishers.

Grocke, D.E. (2005a) 'The role of the therapist in the Bonny Method of Guided Imagery and Music.' *Music Therapy Perspectives 23,* 1, 45–52.

Grocke, D. (2005b) 'Case study in Guided Imagery and Music.' In D. Aldridge (ed.) *Case Study Designs in Music Therapy.* London: Jessica Kingsley Publishers.

Hagbarth, K.E. and Eklund, G. (1968) 'The effects of muscle vibration in spasticity, rigidity and cerebellar disorders.' *Journal of Neurology, Neurosurgery and Psychiatry 31,* 207–213.

Hanser, S. (1985) 'Music therapy and stress reduction research.' *Journal of Music Therapy 22,* 4, 193–206.

Hanser, S. (1996) 'Music therapy to reduce anxiety, agitation, and depression.' *Nursing Home Medicine 10,* 20–22.

Hanser, S. (1999a) *The New Music Therapist's Handbook,* 2nd edition. Boston, MA: Berklee Press.

Hanser, S. (1999b) 'Relaxing through pain and anxiety at the extremities of life.' In T. Wigram and J. de Backer (eds) *Clinical Applications of Music Therapy in Psychiatry.* London: Jessica Kingsley Publishers.

Hanser, S. and O'Connell, A. (1983) 'The effect of music on relaxation of expectant mothers during labor.' *Journal of Music Therapy 29,* 50–58.

Holligan, F. (1995) *Clinician's Manual for Music Therapy in Acute Psychiatry.* Melbourne: St John of God.

Holligan, F. (2004a) Unpublished session notes. Wellsprings, June 2004.

Holligan, F. (2004b) Unpublished session notes. Wellsprings. August 2004.

Hooper, J. (2001) 'An introduction to vibroacoustic therapy and an examination of its place in music therapy practice.' *British Journal of Music Therapy 15,* 2, 69–77.

Jacobson, E. (1938) *Progressive Relaxation: A Physiological and Clinical Investigation of Muscular States and Their Significance in Psychology and Medical Practice.* Chicago, IL: University of Chicago Press.

Kabat-Zinn, J. (2003) 'Mindfulness-based interventions in context: past, present, and future.' *Clinical Psychology: Science and Practice 10,* 2.

Kibler, V. and Rider, M. (1983) 'Effects of progressive muscle relaxation and music on stress as measured by finger temperature response.' *Journal of Clinical Psychology 39,* 2, 213–215.

Kildea, C. (1998) Relaxation to Music. Melbourne. Unpublished.

Kobialka, D (2006) Online at www.danialkobialka.com (Retrieved 28 April 2006).

Lathom-Radocy, W. (2002) *Pediatric Music Therapy.* Springfield, IL: Charles Thomas Publications.

Laungani, P. (1999) 'Culture and identity: implications for counselling.' In S. Palmer and P. Laungani (eds) *Counselling in a Multicultural Society.* London: Sage.

Lehikoinen, P. (1988) *The Kansa Project: Report from a Control Study on the Effect of Vibroacoustical Therapy on Stress.* Sibelius Academy, Helsinki. Unpublished paper.

Leuner, H.C. (1969) 'Guided Affective Imagery (GAI).' *American Journal of Psychotherapy 23,* 1, 4–22.

Loewy, J. (1997) (ed.) *Music Therapy and Pediatric Pain.* Cherry Hill, NJ: Jeffrey Books.

Lundin, R.W. (1967) *An Objective Psychology of Music,* 2nd edition. New York: Ronald Press.

McIvor, M. (1998–1999) 'Heroic journeys: experiences of a Maori group with the Bonny Method of Guided Imagery and Music.' *Journal of the Association for Music and Imagery 6,* 105–118.

McKennitt, C. (2006) Online at www.quinlanroad.com (Retrieved 28 April 2006).

Madsen, C.K., Standley, J.M. and Gregory, D. (1991) 'The effect of a vibrotactile device, Somatron, on physiological and psychological responses: musicians versus non-musicians.' *Journal of Music Therapy 28,* 120–134.

Maranto, C.D. (1993) 'Applications of music in medicine.' In M. Heal and T. Wigram (eds) *Music Therapy in Health and Education.* London: Jessica Kingsley Publishers.

Maranto, C.D. (1994) 'Research in music in medicine: the state of the art.' In R. Spintge and R. Droh (eds) *Music and Medicine.* St Louis, MO: Magna Music Baton.

Marek, R. (2002) 'Are we too young? GIM with youth at risk.' *Making Connections. Proceedings of the inaugural conference of the Music and Imagery Association of Australia (MIAA).* Melbourne, pp.36–43.

Marr, J. (1998–1999) 'GIM at the end of life: case studies in palliative care.' *Journal of the Association for Music and Imagery 6*, 37–54.

Marr, J. (2003) 'Sound connections: music, imagery and the faith community.' In *Music and imagery: sound connections. Proceedings of the second Australasian conference of the Music and Imagery Association of Australia (MIAA).* Melbourne, pp.61–71.

Martin, R. (2006) *The effect of a series of Guided Music Imaging sessions on Music Performance Anxiety.* Master's Thesis, Melbourne: The University of Melbourne. Unpublished.

Melbourne Academic Mindfulness Interest Group (2006) 'Mindfulness-based psychotherapies: a review of conceptual foundations, empirical evidence and practical considerations.' *Australian and New Zealand Journal of Psychiatry 40*, 285–294.

Metzler, R. and Berman, T. (1991) 'Selected effects of sedative music on the anxiety of bronchoscopy patients.' In C. Maranto (ed.) *Applications of Music in Medicine.* Washington, DC: National Association for Music Therapy.

Miller, R.K. and Bornstein, P.H. (1977) 'Thirty-minute relaxation: a comparison of some methods.' *Journal of Behavioural Therapy and Experimental Psychology 8*, 291–294.

Moller, H. (1984) 'Physiological and psychological effects of infrasound on humans.' *Journal of Low Frequency Noise and Vibration 3*, 1, 1–17.

Munro, S. (1984) *Music Therapy in Palliative/Hospice Care.* St Louis, MO: Magna Music Baton.

Nelson-Jones, R. (2003) *Basic Counselling Skills.* London: Sage Publications.

Nendick, R. (2005) 'Life Review.' *Bulletin of the Australian Music Therapy Association 28*, 3, 15.

Nolan, P. (1997) 'Music therapy in the pediatric pain experience: theory, practice and research at Allegheny University of Health Sciences.' In J. Loewy (ed.) *Music Therapy and Pediatric Pain.* Cherry Hill, NJ: Jeffrey Books.

Nolan, P. (2005) 'Verbal processing within the music therapy relationship.' *Music Therapy Perspectives 23*, 1, 18–28.

O'Brien, E. (2005) 'Songwriting with adult patients in oncology and clinical haematology wards.' In F. Baker and T. Wigram (eds) *Songwriting: Methods, Techniques and Clinical Applications for Music Therapy Clinicians, Educators and Students.* London: Jessica Kingsley Publishers.

O'Callaghan, C. (1984) 'Musical profiles of dying patients.' *Bulletin,* Australian Music Therapy Association, June, 5–11.

O'Callaghan, C. and Turnbull, G. (1987) 'The application of neuropsychological knowledge base in the use of music therapy with severely brain-damaged multiple sclerosis patients.' *Proceedings of the thirteenth national conference of the Australian Music Therapy Association,* Adelaide, Australia. pp.92–100.

O'Connor, P. (1990) *Understanding Jung.* Port Melbourne: Mandarin.

O'Neill, C. (n/d) *Relax.* London: Child's Play (International).

Pelletier, C. (2004) 'The effect of music on decreasing arousal due to stress: a meta-analysis.' *Journal of Music Therapy 41*, 3, 192–214.

Plach, T. (1996) *The Creative Use of Music in Group Therapy.* Springfield, IL: Charles Thomas Publications.

Plato (1961) *The Republic.* In E. Hamilton and H. Cairns (eds) *The Collected Dialogues of Plato.* New York: Pantheon, Bollingen series 71.

Pujol, K.K. (1994) 'The effect of vibro-tactile stimulation, instrumentation, and precomposed melodies on physiological and behavioural responses of profoundly retarded children and adults.' *Journal of Music Therapy 31*, 3, 186–205.

Radocy, R. and Boyle, J. (1988) *Psychological Foundations of Musical Behavior.* Springfield, IL: Charles Thomas Publications.

Reilly, M. (1996) 'Relaxation, imagery and music as adjunct therapy to narcotic analgesia in the perioperative period.' In R. Rebollo Pratt and R. Spintge (eds) *Music Medicine.* St Louis, MO: Magna Music Baton, pp.206–217.

Rickard, J. (1992) *Relaxation for Children.* Melbourne: Australian Council for Educational Research.

Rider, M. (1985) 'Entrainment mechanisms are involved in pain reduction, muscle relaxation and music-mediated imagery.' *Journal of Music Therapy 22*, 1, 46–58.

Rider, M. and Achterberg, J. (1989) 'Effect of music-assisted imagery on neutrophils and lymphocytes.' *Biofeedback and Self-Regulation 14*, 247–257.

Ritchey-Vaux, D. (1993) 'GIM applied to the 50-minute hour.' *Journal of the Association for Music and Imagery 2*, 29–34.

Robb, S., Nichols, R., Rutan, R., Bishop, B. and Parker, J. (1995) 'The effects of music-assisted relaxation on preoperative anxiety.' *Journal of Music Therapy 32*, 1, 2–22.

Robbins, C. and Robbins, C. (1988) 'Teamwork in clinical improvisation: music therapy and physiotherapy combined.' *Proceedings of the Fourteenth Annual Conference of the Australian Music Therapy Association*. Melbourne, pp.96–102.

Rogers, C. (1980) *A Way of Being*. Boston, MA: Houghton Mifflin.

Ross, C. (2006) *Music for Dreaming*. Online at www.musicfordreaming.com (Retrieved 28 April 2006).

Saluveer, E. and Tamm, S. (1989) 'Vibroacoustic therapy with neurotic clients at the Tallinn Pedagogical Institute.' Paper given to the Second International Symposium in Vibroacoustics. Levanger, Norway: ISVA Publications.

Samuels, M. and Samuels, N. (1975) *Seeing With the Mind's Eye: The History, Techniques, and Uses of Visualisations*. New York: Random Press.

Saperston, B. (1999) 'Music-based individualised relaxation training in medical settings.' In C. Dileo (ed.) *Music Therapy and Medicine: Theoretical and Clinical Applications*. Silver Spring, MD: American Music Therapy Association.

Schultz, J. and Luthe, W. (1959) *Autogenic Training: A Physiological Approach to Psychotherapy*. New York: Grune and Stratton.

Schwartz, F. (2006) *Transitions*. Online at www.transitionsmusic.com (Retrieved 28 April 2006).

Shoemark, H. (2004) *Colour-coded Ranking of Commercially Produced CDs for Use with Hospitalised Newborn Infants and Children* [Guidelines]. Melbourne: Music Therapy Unit, Royal Children's Hospital.

Shoemark, H., Dun, B. and Kildea, C. (2004) *Guidelines for Recorded Music in the Hospital Environment*. Online at www.rch.org.au/emplibrary/ept/RCH_guidelines_RecordedMusic.pdf/ (Retrieved 30 October 2006).

Short, A. (1992) 'Music and imagery with physically disabled elderly residents: a GIM adaptation.' *Music Therapy 11*, 1, 65–98.

Skewes, K. (2000) *The Experience of Group Music Therapy for Six Bereaved Adolescents*. PhD dissertation, University of Melbourne. Unpublished.

Skille, O. (1982) 'Musikkbadet: enn musikk terapeutisk metode.' *Musikk Terapi 6*, 24–27.

Skille, O. (1986) *Manual of Vibroacoustics*. Levanger, Norway: ISVA Publications.

Skille, O. (1989a) 'Vibroacoustic research.' In R. Spintge and R. Droh. (eds) *Music Medicine*. St Louis, MO: Magna Music Baton.

Skille, O. (1989b) 'Vibroacoustic therapy.' *Music Therapy 8*, 61–77. New York: American Association for Music Therapy.

Skille, O. (1992) 'Vibroacoustic research 1980–1991.' In R. Spintge and R. Droh (eds) *Music and Medicine*, St. Louis: Magna Music Baton, pp.249–266.

Skille, O. and Wigram, T. (1995) 'The effects of music, vocalisation and vibration on brain and muscle tissue: studies in vibroacoustic therapy.' In T. Wigram, B. Saperston and R. West (eds) *The Art and Science of Music Therapy: A Handbook*. London: Harwood Academic.

Smith, J. and Joyce, C. (2004) 'Mozart versus new age music: relaxation states, stress and ABC relaxation theory.' *Journal of Music Therapy*, 3, 215–224.

Snyder Cowan, D. (1997) 'Managing sickle cell pain with music therapy.' In J. Loewy (ed.) *Music Therapy and Pediatric Pain*. Cherry Hill, NJ: Jeffrey Books.

Sorrell, N. and Narayan, R. (1980) *Indian Music in Performance: A Practical Introduction*. Manchester: Manchester University Press.

Spintge, R. (1982) 'Psychophysiological surgery preparation with and without anxiolytic music.' In R. Droh and R. Spintge (eds) *Angst, Schmerz, Muzik in der Anasthesie*. Basel: Editiones Roche.

Spintge, R. and Droh, R. (1982) 'The pre-operative condition of 191 patients exposed to anxiolytic music and Rohypnol (Flurazepam) before receiving an epidural anaesthetic.' In R. Droh and R. Spintge (eds) *Angst, Schmerz, Muzik in der Anasthesie*. Basel: Editiones Roche.

Standley, J. (1991a) *Music Techniques in Therapy, Counselling and Special Education*. St Louis, MO: Magna Music Baton.

Standley, J. (1991b) 'The effect of vibrotactile and auditory stimuli on perception of comfort, heart rate and peripheral finger temperature.' *Journal of Music Therapy 28*, 3, 120–34.

Standley, J. (1995) 'Music as a therapeutic intervention in medical and dental treatment: research and clinical applications.' In T. Wigram, B. Saperston and R. West (eds) *The Art and Science of Music Therapy: A Handbook.* London: Harwood Academic.

Stillman, B.C. (1970) 'Vibratory motor stimulation: a preliminary report.' *Australian Journal of Physiotherapy 16,* 118–123.

Summer, L. (1981) 'Guided imagery and music with the elderly.' *Music Therapy 1,* 1, 39–42.

Summer, L. (1988) *GIM in the Institutional Setting.* St Louis, MO: Magna Music Baton.

Summer, L. (1998) 'The pure music transference in Guided Imagery and Music.' In K. Bruscia (ed.) *The Dynamics of Music Psychotherapy.* Gilsum, NH: Barcelona Publishers.

Tsao, C., Gordon, T., Maranto, C., Lerman, C. and Murasko, D. (1991) 'The effects of music and biological imagery on immune response (S-IgA).' In C. Maranto (ed.) *Applications of Music in Medicine.* Washington, DC: National Association for Music Therapy.

Ventre, M. (1990–1992) *Guided Imagery and Music (GIM) training courses.* University of Melbourne. Unpublished.

Weiss, M. (1996–1997) 'Guided imagery and music: group experiences with adolescent girls in a high school setting.' *Journal of the Association for Music and Imagery 5,* 61–73.

Wheeler, B.L. (1983) 'A psychotherapeutic classification of music therapy practices: a continuum of procedures.' *Music Therapy Perspectives 1,* 8–12.

Wheeler, B.L., Shultis, C. and Polen, D. (2005) *Clinical Training Guide for the Student Music Therapist.* Gilsum, NH: Barcelona Publishers.

Wigram, T. (1993) '"The Feeling of Sound": the effect of music and low frequency sound in reducing anxiety in challenging behaviour in clients with learning difficulties.' In H. Payne (ed.) *Handbook of Enquiry in the Arts Therapies: 'One River, Many Currents'.* London: Jessica Kingsley Publishers.

Wigram, T. (1995) 'Psychological and physiological effects of low frequency sound and music.' *Music Therapy Perspectives: International Edition.* NAMT Publications.

Wigram, T. (1996) *The Effect of Vibroacoustic Therapy on Clinical and Non-Clinical Populations.* PhD dissertation, St Georges Medical School, University of London. Unpublished.

Wigram, T. (1997a) 'The effect of vibroacoustic therapy in the treatment of Rett Syndrome.' In T. Wigram and C. Dileo (eds) *Music, Vibration and Health.* Pipersville, PA: Jeffrey Books.

Wigram, T. (1997b) 'Equipment for vibroacoustic therapy.' In T. Wigram and C. Dileo (eds) *Music, Vibration and Health.* Pipersville, PA: Jeffrey Books.

Wigram, T. (2004) *Improvisation: Methods and Techniques for Music Therapy Clinicians, Educators, and Students.* London: Jessica Kingsley Publishers.

Wigram, T. and Cass, H. (1995) 'Music therapy within the assessment process of a therapy clinic for people with Rett syndrome.' 1995 British Society for Music Therapy Conference. London: BSMT Publications.

Wigram, T. and Dileo, C. (1997a) *Music, Vibration and Health.* Pipersville, PA: Jeffrey Books.

Wigram, T. and Dileo, C. (1997b) 'Clinical and ethical considerations.' In T. Wigram and C. Dileo (eds) *Music, Vibration and Health.* Pipersville, PA: Jeffrey Books.

Wigram, T., McNaught, J. and Cain, J. (1997) 'Vibroacoustic therapy with adult patients with profound learning disability.' In T. Wigram and C. Dileo (eds) *Music, Vibration and Health.* Pipersville, PA: Jeffrey Books.

Wigram, T. and Weekes, L. (1983) *The use of music in overcoming motor dysfunction in children and adolescents suffering from severe physical and mental handicap: a specific approach.* Paris: World Congress of Music Therapy. Unpublished.

Wigram, T. and Weekes, L. (1985) 'A specific approach to overcoming motor dysfunction in children and adolescents with severe physical and mental handicaps using music and movement.' *British Journal of Music Therapy 16,* 1, 2–12.

Wikipedia (2006) 'Trance music.' Online at http://en.wikipedia.org/wiki/trance_music (Retrieved 25 April 2006).

Winnicott, D.W. (1971) *Playing and Reality.* New York: Basic Books.

Wordsworth Dictionary of Musical Quotations (1991) compiled by Derek Watson. Ware, Hertsfordshire: Wordsworth Editions.

Yalom, I. (1970) *The Theory and Practice of Group Psychotherapy,* 3rd edition. New York: Basic Books.

Yamada, S., Ikugi, M., Fujikata, S., Watanabe, T. and Kosaka, T. (1983) 'Body sensation of low frequency noise of ordinary persons and profoundly deaf persons.' *Journal of Low Frequency Noise and Vibration 2,* 3, 32–36.

The authors

Denise Grocke is Associate Professor and Head of Music Therapy at the University of Melbourne, Victoria, Australia. She is Director of the National Music Therapy Research Unit (NaMTRU) and is currently Associate Dean (Research). She completed her music therapy qualifications at Michigan State University, and is a Registered Music Therapist (Board Certified) in the US. She holds a Masters degree in Music Therapy, and a PhD in Guided Imagery and Music (Bonny Method), both from the University of Melbourne. She served three terms as Chair of the Commission of Education, Training and Registration of the World Federation of Music Therapy and from 1999 to 2002 was President of the World Federation of Music Therapy. Denise has practised as a music therapist with people who have mental illness, neurological disorders and dementia, and she has a private practice in the Bonny Method of Guided Imagery and Music. She is co-editor of two books, has authored 14 chapters in books and 50 articles on music therapy and Guided Imagery and Music.

Eight principal publications:

Pratt, R.R. and Grocke, D.E (eds)(1999) *Music Medicine 3. Music Medicine and Music Therapy: Expanding Horizons.* Faculty of Music, University of Melbourne.

Bruscia, K.E. and Grocke, D.E. (eds) (2002) *Guided Imagery and Music: The Bonny Method and Beyond.* Gilsum, NH: Barcelona publishers.

Grocke, D.E. (2001) *A phenomenological study of pivotal moments in Guided Imagery and Music (GIM) therapy.* PhD dissertation, University of Melbourne. Available at www.musictherapyworld.de.

Grocke, D. (2002) 'The Bonny music programs.' In K. Bruscia and D. Grocke (eds) *Guided Imagery and Music: The Bonny Method and Beyond.* Gilsum, NH: Barcelona publishers.

Grocke, D. (2002) 'Qualitative research in Guided Imagery and Music.' In K. Bruscia and D. Grocke (2002) *Guided Imagery and Music: The Bonny Method and Beyond.* Gilsum, NH: Barcelona publishers.

Forinash, M. and Grocke, D. (2005) 'Phenomenological Enquiry.' In B. Wheeler (ed.) *Music Therapy Research.* 2nd edition. Gilsum, NH: Barcelona publishers.

Grocke, D. (2005) 'The role of the therapist in the Bonny Method of Guided Imagery and Music.' *Music Therapy Perspectives 23,* 1, 45–52.

Grocke, D. (2005) 'Significant Moments in Music Therapy in Australia.' (Invited paper). *Australian Journal of Music Therapy 16,* 104–118.

Tony Wigram is Professor of Music Therapy and Head of PhD Studies in Music Therapy in the Department for Communication and Psychology, Faculty of Humanities, University of Aalborg, Denmark. He is Head Music Therapist at the Harper House Children's Service, Hertfordshire, UK, Research Advisor to Hertfordshire Partnership NHS Trust, Prinicipal Research Fellow in the Faculty of Music, Melbourne University, and Reader in Music Therapy at Anglia Ruskin University, Cambridge. After reading music at Bristol University, he studied with Juliette Alvin at the Guildhall School of Music, and later qualified with a PhD in Psychology at St Georges Medical School, London University. He has written or edited 13 books on Music Therapy and authored more than 100 articles in peer reviewed journals and chapters in books. His research interests include the physiological effect of sound and music, assessment and diagnosis of autism spectrum disorders and communication disorders, methods of training and advanced level training in music therapy, music therapy research, and advanced improvisation skills. In 2004 he was the first recipient of the European Music Therapy Confederation Award for significant achievements in the development of music therapy in Europe.

Eight principal publications

Wigram, T. and Dileo-Maranto, C. (1997) *Music, Vibration and Health. Jeffrey Books.* Pipersville, Pennsylvania.

Wigram, T. (1999) 'Contact in Music: The analysis of musical behaviour in children with communication disorder and pervasive developmental disability for differential diagnosis.' In: T. Wigram and J. De Backer (eds) *Clinical Applications of Music Therapy in Developmental Disability, Paediatric and Neurology.* London: Jessica Kingsley Publishers.

Wigram, T., Nygaard Pedersen, I. and Bonde, L.O. (2002) *A Comprehensive Guide to Music Therapy: Theory, Clinical Practice, Research and Training.* London: Jessica Kingsley Publishers.

Wigram, T. (2004) *Improvisation: Methods and Techniques for Music Therapy Clinicians, Educators and Student*s. London: Jessica Kingsley Publishers.

Wigram, T. (2005) 'Songwriting methods – Similarities and Differences: Developing a Working Model.' In F. Baker and T. Wigram (eds) *Songwriting: Methods, Techniques and Clinical Applications for Music Therapy Clinicians, Educators and Students.* London: Jessica Kingsley Publishers.

Wigram, T. (2005) 'Survey Research.' In B. Wheeler and K. Bruscia (eds) *Music Therapy Research: Qualitative and Quantitative Methods (2nd edn).* Phoenixville: Barcelona Publishers.

Wigram, T. and Gold, C. (2006) 'Research evidence and clinical applicability of Music Therapy for Autism Spectrum Disorder.' *Child: Care, Health and Development 32,* 5, 535.

Wigram T (2006) Musical Creativity in children with cognitive and social impairments. In Deliege I, Wiggins G (eds.) *Musical Creativity: Current Research in Theory and Practice Psychology Press.* Taylor and Francis

Subject Index

Note: page numbers in *italics* refer to tables and figures

Author Index